SOLDIERS
OF THE LAW

SOLDIERS OF THE LAW

Oklahoma Highway Patrolmen During the Early Years, 1937-1964

DONNA M. STEPHENS

Copyright © 2003 by Donna M. Stephens.

ISBN :   Hardcover   1-4134-3269-7
         Softcover   1-4134-3270-0

All rights reserved. No part of this book may be reproduced or transmitted in any form or by any means, electronic or mechanical, including photocopying, recording, or by any information storage and retrieval system, without permission in writing from the copyright owner.

This book was printed in the United States of America.

To order additional copies of this book, contact:
Xlibris Corporation
1-888-795-4274
www.Xlibris.com
Orders@Xlibris.com

CONTENTS

ILLUSTRATIONS 11
ACKNOWLEDGEMENTS 13
FOREWORD 17

CHAPTER 1. EARLY OKLAHOMA AND
THE ESTABLISHMENT OF THE OKLAHOMA
HIGHWAY PATROL: 1889-1937 23
   The Organic Act 28
   Early Politics in Oklahoma Territory 31
   Law Enforcement in Oklahoma Territory 34
   Natural Resources Create Problems in
      Indian Territory 36
   Politics in Indian Territory 40
   Efforts to Become a State 41
   A New State 49
   Growth Brings New Problems 51
   Steps to Address Problems on the Roads 57
   State Law Enforcement Strengthened 62
   Department of Public Safety Established 67

CHAPTER 2. THE FORMATIVE YEARS OF THE
PATROL: 1937-1946 68
   First Patrol School 71
   The Second Patrol School 77
   First OHP Troopers Go on the Roads 79
   The Second and Third Years of the Patrol 89
   The Third and Fourth Patrol Schools 93
   C.A. Morris Joins the Patrol 97

The Sixth Patrol School and a
  Special School in 1943 100
Auxiliary Patrol Activated 107
Troopers Join U. S. Navy 112
Troopers Return After the War 113

CHAPTER 3. THE POST-WAR YEARS: 1946-1951 118
Experiences in Remote Regions of the State 119
Route 66 121
Troopers Address Diverse Problems 125
The Woodward Tornado 128
Troopers' Varied Responsibilities 130
Politics and the Patrol 135
Special Programs and Plans in 1948 137
Troopers in Communities 142
1949 Legislature Authorizes Many Changes 144
1949 Patrol School 148
Events and Efforts of 1950 155
C.A. Morris Transferred 163

CHAPTER 4. THE THREE-MAN UNIT AT
SHAWNEE: 1951-1955 170
Morris Arrives in Shawnee 172
Patrol Routines 175
Safety Speeches 180
Troopers' Families 184
Korean War Impacts Patrol 187
Dealing With Emergencies and Issues 190
Dangers on the Job 194
Troopers Helped Others 198
Variety of Assignments 201
Unrest Among Shawnee Troopers 206
Morris Stays at Shawnee 209
DPS Leadership Shifts Result in Changes 212
Politics and the Department of Public Safety 219
Morris Promoted to Supervisor 224

CHAPTER 5. MORRIS' FIRST YEAR AS SUPERVISOR:
1955-1956 229
    First Two Months as a Supervisor 230
    Diverse Responsibilities of Supervisor 235
    1955 Holiday Season 242
    Starting a New Year 247
    Safety Education Efforts 254

CHAPTER 6. THE LIFE OF A SUPERVISOR:
1956-1964 261
    Some Highs and Lows of 1956 264
    1957 Legislative Actions 266
    Implementing Plans in the Field 269
    McDaniel Returns to Patrol 271
    New Supervisor Assigned to Enid 273
    1958 Brings Major Changes to OHP 278
    Professional and Personal Issues for Morris 284
    Prohibition Issues in Oklahoma 287
    Supervisor Job Continues As Usual 291
    Personnel Changes and Issues in 1960 298
    Beginning a New Year 1961 303
    Problems Grow in the 1960s 310
    Governor Bellman Institutes Changes 317
    Morris Prepares to Retire 320

POST SCRIPT 327
NOTES 331
REFERENCES 343
APPENDIX A 349
APPENDIX B 335
APPENDIX C 352
INDEX 355

This book is dedicated
to my father, C.A. Morris,
and all of the others who served
as Soldiers of the Law.

ILLUSTRATIONS

Map of Oklahoma

1. Trooper C.A. Morris in the Oklahoma Highway Patrol summer uniform in 1942.
2. Trooper C.A. Morris in the Oklahoma Highway Patrol winter uniform in 1942.
3. Trooper C.A. Morris with his patrol car in 1942.
4. Trooper C.A. Morris with members of Chandler's Safety Junior quiz kids in 1948. His daughter, Donna, is third from left on front row.
5. Troopers Don McDaniel, Nat Taylor, and C.A. Morris in 1953.
6. Trooper Nat Taylor; Pottawatomie Sheriff, LeRoy Flinchum; and Trooper C.A. Morris, January 1, 1954.
7. Trooper C.A. Morris in 1954
8. Trooper C.A. Morris beside his patrol car in 1955.
9. Troopers C.A. Morris and George Moore investigate an accident in 1955.
10. Supervisor C.A. Morris with members of the adult drivers education class in 1957.
11. Supervisor Morris in patrol car passing District 6 Headquarters in Enid in 1961.

ACKNOWLEDGEMENTS

THIS BOOK WOULD not have been possible without the assistance and encouragement of many individuals. The employees of the Jan Eric Cartwright Memorial Library, Archives of the Oklahoma Department of Libraries, Edmond Public Library, Oklahoma State University Library, and Oklahoma Historical Society were very helpful. The work of Bob L. Blackburn, son of a former trooper and Director of the Oklahoma Historical Society, provided an invaluable resource in the areas of the history of Oklahoma law enforcement and the Oklahoma Highway Patrol.

At the Department of Public Safety, Lt. Gerald Davidson and his staff in the Public Information Office and, especially, Mary Haning in the Office of Retirement and Insurance assisted me by providing encouragement and helping me identify information sources. In addition, Patrol Chief Gary Adams was gracious enough to review this manuscript as it was being prepared and grant authorization for its publication.

I give my heartfelt thanks to the retired troopers and their wives, who were patient and cooperative during the process of gathering information and reviewing the draft manuscripts for accuracy. Seven former troopers participated in extensive interviews of two or more hours each, and five of them were involved in follow-up interviews and reviews of the manuscript. Their assistance in maintaining the time-line and providing stories, events, and names was critical to the completion of the book. Nat and Betty Taylor, living in Stillwater, encouraged me to begin this project, which turned into a much longer manuscript than any of us thought it would be. In Durant, Kermit (K.O.) and Gerri Rayburn were extremely helpful at all stages of the project and provided needed moral support to maintain my enthusiasm. Otto and Catherine Rauch, in Enid, assisted by providing important pieces of information and always responding quickly to any request. Don and Bonnie McDaniel, living in Siloam Springs, Arkansas, were most hospitable in giving time and information when Don was already quite ill with Lou Gehrig's Disease. Three of the former troopers were living in Oklahoma City. Eugene Clark cheerfully provided information and reviewed the manuscript through a time of personal change and adjustment for him. Leonard Kelsoe shared information and stories that enriched this manuscript. Dr. Vernon Sisney not only provided information about his experiences during the brief years he served on the patrol but gave an additional point of view about how these experiences enriched his life as he pursued his career in clinical psychology. I met Jack Smith and his wife, Jane, from Tulsa only briefly; however, they willingly shared some of their memories. All of these individuals were cooperative, pleasant, and proud of their experiences with the Oklahoma Highway Patrol.

My family has been most helpful during the course of this project. My mother, Helen Morris, was willing to share her memories and experiences, allow me to go through her photo albums and scrapbooks, accompany me on many of my interview trips, review the manuscript, and respond to numerous questions as they emerged. I thank my brothers, John Morris and Tom Morris, for providing their points of view and important missing bits of information. I also express my appreciation to two of my brothers' friends, Dan Erwin and Joe Sam Vasser, for sharing some of their memories with me. A special thanks goes to my colleague and friend, Joan Butts, for her interest in the project and assistance in the editing process.

I especially thank my husband, E. Robert Stephens, for his patience. His encouragement and expertise during this long process were invaluable. Without his support and assistance, I could not have completed this labor of love.

FOREWORD

THIS EVENING SHIFT began like many others in the early 1950s for Highway Patrol Trooper Don McDaniel in Shawnee, Oklahoma. Nat Taylor, a friend since they met in patrol school two years before and now one of his partners in the three-man unit, had picked him up about 3 p.m. They "shot the bull" as they drove over to Nat's to let him go off duty. Don lit up a cigar as Nat finished his, and they joked that Don would have to put up with C.A.'s griping about the stink they left in the patrol car. C.A. Morris was the third trooper assigned to the unit. He was nearly seventeen years older than they were and had joined the patrol ten years earlier at the age of thirty-five. Since his arrival in Shawnee a year or so before, C.A. had assumed the role of big brother or sometimes, father to the two rookie patrolmen. In spite of his sometimes bossy behavior, each of the younger guys liked him and enjoyed telling one another the different ways C.A. had tried to "straighten him out."

Just before dark, Don swung off of Route 18 into the driveway leading up to C.A.'s acreage home. As usual, C.A. was ready and hopped into the car with a laugh and wave to his family. One of the nice things about their three-man unit was that each of the troopers was a devoted family man. Don and his wife, Jerry, had two little daughters, Donna and Linda; Nat and his wife, Betty, had a daughter and a son, Linda and Johnny; and C.A. and his wife, Helen, had three kids, John, Tom, and Donna. They tried to be considerate of one another and give each man time to be with his family on special occasions. To make the situation even better, their wives really got along well. They were glad that they were working together—even if the younger guys had to put up with C.A.'s advice a little more than they thought was necessary.

Don and C.A. were patrolling the highway north of Shawnee later that evening when they spotted a car that was speeding. A patrolman soon learned how to determine if a car was breaking the speed limit by watching how fast the headlights came toward him. Don pulled to a stop on the shoulder, backed into what they called a bootlegger turn, and was soon close behind the speeding car with their red light flashing. The car stopped, and since it was C.A.'s turn to make the contact, he walked up to the driver's side to ask him to step out of the car. Don also got out and moved behind the patrol car to act as back-up. All of a sudden the door flew open knocking C.A. off balance. Before Don could react, the driver jumped out of the car, shoved a .45 automatic into C.A.'s stomach, and pulled the trigger. The gun misfired. By then Don was running toward his partner to help subdue the driver. But before Don could reach them, C.A. had ripped the gun out of the driver's hand and was using it to hit him over and over. Don came out of his shock, pulled C.A. off of the driver, and then called for an ambulance. While they were waiting, C.A., who was usually cool and collected, went over to the bar ditch and threw up. Later at the hospital they learned that the driver was an escapee from Texas who had been sentenced to life in prison.

As Retired Trooper Don McDaniel related this story to my mother and me in 1997, his voice was strained with emotion. "There wasn't a thing I could do; it happened so fast. Even though I was backing him up, it happened before I could even move. It taught me a lesson that I never forgot. You never knew when something was going to happen, and in one instant your life could be over."

Pottawatomie county authorities decided to try the

escapee for attempted murder, and, according to Don McDaniel, there was a lengthy trial in Shawnee. However, some forty-six years later, this was the first time my mother and I had heard this story about how close my dad, C.A. Morris, had come to being killed that night with Don McDaniel. I surmised that Dad was not proud of the way he had lost his temper and beaten the driver, so he hadn't told us kids about the incident. He also was selective in what he told my mother, Helen, because he didn't want her to worry about him.

My dad loved his job as a peace officer. He enjoyed working night shifts and never dreaded going to work. As a former teacher, he liked working with the public to inform and enlighten them about how they could change their behaviors to keep themselves and their families safer. He always tried to be a good role model, although there were times, like the one cited here, when he showed his weaker human side. C.A. Morris was a faithful husband, a loving father, and a fine man. He was a good highway patrolman, but probably not an extraordinary one. However, I believe his experiences as an Oklahoma Highway Patrolman were very similar to those of many other troopers during the early years of the patrol.

Dad worked for the Oklahoma Highway Patrol from August 24, 1942, until his retirement on February 22, 1964. My entire childhood was spent as the daughter of a highway patrolman. After my retirement from thirty years in public education, most of which was spent in states on the east coast, I began to think about my dad's career on the patrol. I was familiar with how Oklahoma's educational system had evolved, but wondered how the newly organized state had established a state-wide law enforcement unit. Although Dad died in 1985, we still had his scrapbooks and daily journals from his later years as a supervisor on the patrol. I began collecting additional information after attending Nat and Betty Taylor's fiftieth wedding anniversary party in the fall of 1996. Nat loaned me some publications and agreed to help if I wanted to write something about my dad's career in the highway patrol. I began to do research in the state archives, university and public libraries, and in personal scrapbooks and records and also to conduct extensive personal interviews with seven former troopers who worked on the Oklahoma Highway Patrol during the early years. These lengthy interviews that took place between April 1997 and July 1998, were tape recorded, transcribed, and reviewed with each trooper for accuracy.

Using standard ethnographic research methods, my goal was to write an account of the early days of the Oklahoma Highway Patrol that would be of assistance to historians interested in local and state history and yet, be informative and enjoyable to the general public. Factual history from documents about the Department of Public Safety and the highway patrol has been woven together with personal information from my father's scrapbooks and journals as well as recollections and stories from former troopers, their families, and my own family and friends, including my own memories. Some information may seem inconsequential or trivial, but I have incorporated as many personal examples and stories as possible to reflect what the participants thought was important and represented the nature of their lives at that time. Historical information is presented in chronological order as much as possible; however, it is often organized according to the personal experiences cited. I hope the resulting documentation will be useful to those who want to understand how this important Oklahoma law enforcement agency was established and to learn what it was like to be a trooper on the Oklahoma Highway Patrol during my father's time.

The first chapter gives a brief early history of the State of Oklahoma and the establishment of the Oklahoma Highway Patrol. Chapter 2 describes the formative years of the patrol with information from three former troopers who were in the first two patrol schools held in 1937 and four additional troopers who entered the patrol during the early 1940s. The many changes that occurred in Oklahoma during the post-war years of 1946-1951 are presented in Chapter 3 with the additional perspectives of two troopers who attended the 1949 patrol school.

Beginning with Chapter 4, "The Three-Man Unit at Shawnee: 1951-1955," more information is presented about the troopers' personal lives as growth and changes in the Oklahoma Highway Patrol are described. Chapters 5 and 6 continue with a similar format but focus primarily on my dad, C.A. Morris, by including information from his daily journals which he kept from 1955 through 1963. These chapters give the reader a feel for the work of an Oklahoma Highway Patrol supervisor or second lieutenant, which included a wide variety of duties and responsibilities and a pace that may appear to be hectic and fragmented at times. In the Post Script a brief summary is given of the life of each of the interviewed former troopers after they left or retired from the Oklahoma Highway Patrol.

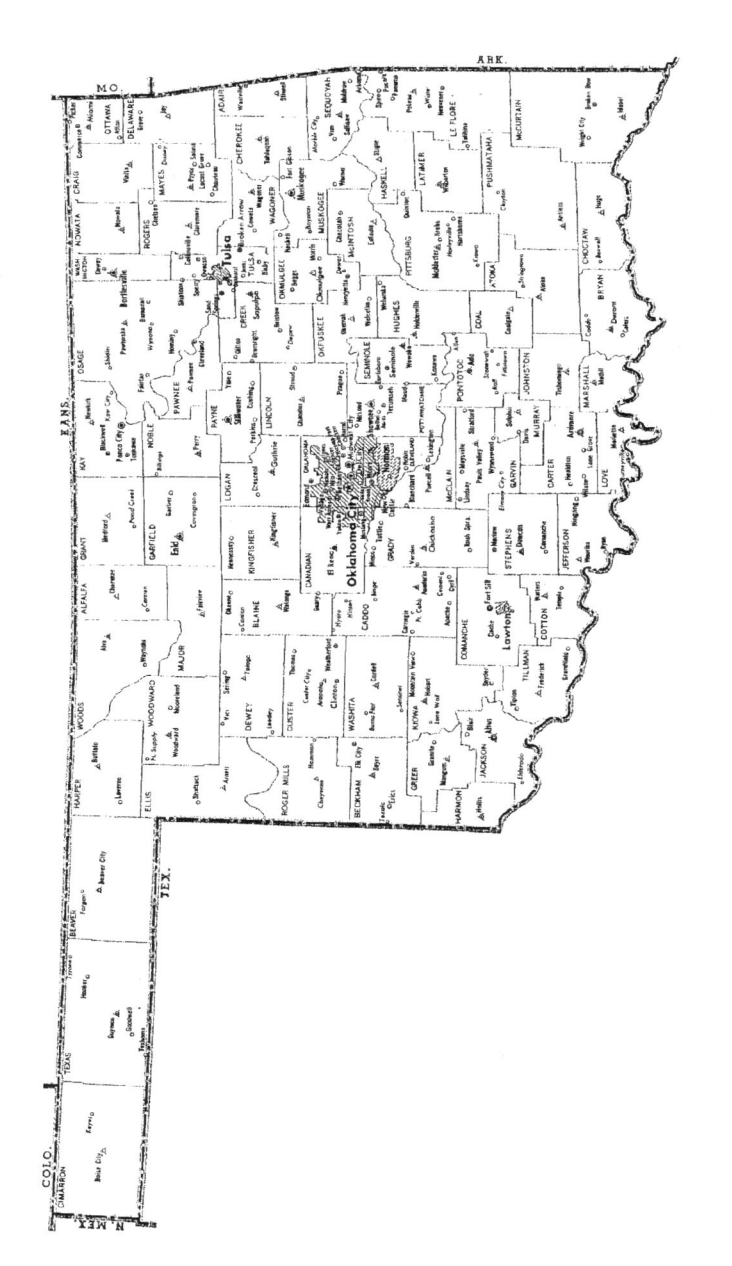

Map. State of Oklahoma with counties, county seats, and major cities and towns circa 1960.

CHAPTER 1

EARLY OKLAHOMA AND THE ESTABLISHMENT OF THE OKLAHOMA HIGHWAY PATROL 1889-1937

THE LAW ESTABLISHING the Oklahoma Highway Patrol, signed by Governor Ernest Whitworth Marland on April 20, 1937, was the culmination of many years of efforts by a number of individuals and groups in the state. This was not just a law to hire men to patrol the roads for safety reasons; it was a major move in the thirty-year-old state's history to establish a state-wide law enforcement arm of the government that would have jurisdiction over local communities. For the citizens of Oklahoma, this was a giant step that many of them were reluctant to take.

To understand some of the political, economic, and philosophical issues leading up to this act by the Sixteenth Legislature of the State of Oklahoma, one needs to know something about the history of the state itself. (1)

Although there have been four other states admitted into the Union since Oklahoma in 1907, no other state has a history quite like that of Oklahoma. It is not the newness of Oklahoma that makes it unique, rather, it is the way in which the state was settled. All other states were created from previous territories that had been settled over a period of time. Over the years, boundaries were defined, trading centers evolved into towns and cities, and governments were established under territorial laws. In Oklahoma this process was condensed into a few short years.

Oklahoma began as a small parcel of land, called the Unassigned Lands. It was surrendered to white settlers because, in apportioning out the forty million acres of Indian lands to various Indian tribes, it had been overlooked and never assigned to any of them. This area which was opened for settlement in 1889 was actually rather insignificant — less than one twenty-second of the Indian lands as its boundaries were finally established by Congress. But by expansion, addition, and absorption it finally grew into the present State of Oklahoma which includes all of the former Indian lands; Greer county, previously a part of Texas; and the Public Land Strip or "No-Man's Land," given this name because it had never been included within the boundaries of any state or territory. (2)

By the late 1800s, much of the best land in the existing states and territories was already occupied. Thousands of homesteaders had built sod houses and dugouts on the plains of western Kansas. In Texas, ranchers and farmers had spread across the Staked Plains. This left the unoccupied lands of the Indian country as a broad peninsula between the two states. Earlier travelers on trails through the region carried stories of millions of acres carpeted with buffalo grass and blue stem that could easily be broken to the plow, which were supporting only sparse herds of cattle and nomadic Indian Tribes. (3) After railroads built lines through the Indian Territories in the 1870s, even more individuals got a first-hand look at these lands.

To many people looking for places to build homes of their own, the lure of this land was irresistible. The opening of these Indian lands for settlement came after many years of disagreements about how the land should become available to whites, or whether the lands should be available to whites at all. Indians and cattlemen wanted to keep white settlers out of the Indian Territories—white settlers wanted in, and both sides had their advocates. They took their cases to Washington and attempted to sway Congress through political pressure.

Up until this time, the U.S. government had followed the British system in dealing with the Indian tribes by treating each tribe independently. Each tribe was self-governing; its people were citizens of the tribe rather than citizens of the United States, and they were subject to tribal law rather than laws passed by Congress. (4) Powerful cattlemen's organizations, the largest known as the Cherokee Strip Live Stock Association, exerted pressure on Congress to keep the grazing land that they leased for Indian tribes closed to settlers who wanted to plow it up for farms. At the same time representatives of the Five Civilized Tribes (Cherokee, Choctaw, Chickasaw, Creek, and Seminole) appealed to Congress to honor their most recent treaties which would allow them to keep the land assigned to them during Reconstruction. (5)

The groups pushing for opening the lands were also varied. From 1870 to 1879, there were thirty-three bills for opening of the Indian lands introduced into Congress. Railroad companies that had constructed lines across Indian Territory (MKT, Frisco, Rock Island, and Santa Fe) wanted the lands opened to settlement so they could benefit from trade that would be generated from farmers and towns that would be established. During this period, railroad companies exerted a great deal of power in Washington.

As strange as it might seem, the Quakers, who claimed to be strong supporters of the Indians, became aligned with the advocates for opening lands to white settlement. In the 1870s while trying to "civilize" the western tribes and convince the Indians to stay on lands assigned to them and become farmers, many Quakers argued that tribalism was one of the great enemies of peace and assimilation of the Indian people. With tribalism came the tradition of Indians owning their lands as groups, not as individuals, and thus, Quakers believed that individual Indians had little incentive or desire to farm their own land like a "civilized" person. A catch phrase of the time was "kill the tribe and save the individual." Two consequences that would result from individual Indian land ownership were that the excess lands could become available for settlement and individual Indians could sell land that they owned. Stating that their desire was to help Indians become assimilated and arguing that "Indians" were not subordinate or domestic nations but individuals, Quakers petitioned Congress to end the authority of the Chiefs and tribes themselves and to refuse further treaty negotiations. Thus the Quakers supported the settlers' cause. (6)

Another advocate for opening Indian lands was equally as unlikely. In February of 1879, Elias C. Boudinot, a Cherokee Indian attorney in Washington, published a letter in the *Chicago Times* claiming that the millions of acres of land taken from the Five Civilized Tribes by Reconstruction treaties were properly a part of the public domain of the United States, so they should be open to settlement under the Homestead Act. He identified specifically the Unassigned Lands located in the middle of the Indian Territories.

Out on the plains, some people were not willing to wait for the slow wheels of government to allow them into the promising farmlands. As early as 1879, Charles C. Carpenter organized the Oklahoma Colony and attempted to lead the group from Kansas into the Indian lands, but the U.S. Army stopped his group. (7) Captain Donald Payne's first Boomers entered the area in 1880 and were chased out again and again by federal troops until Payne's death in 1884. The Boomers continued trying to get the lands opened under the leadership of William L. Couch. (8)

In 1887, the first major official step in opening the Indian lands for white settlement was finally taken when Senator Henry Dawes of Massachusetts persuaded Congress to pass the Severalty Act. This act provided that Indians from each western tribe were to be allotted individual plots of land or homesteads on which to live or farm, and all surplus tribal land would be thrown open to whites for homesteading or purchase. (9) This action cleared the way for the western half of the Indian country to be settled by the white man. The eastern land occupied by the Five Civilized Tribes was to be parceled out separately. (10)

In February of 1889, a provision for opening the Unassigned Lands to settlement with homesteads of 160 acres or town lots was attached as a rider to the Indian appropriations bill in Congress. Notice was served to the opposition that if the rider were stricken, the appropriation bill would be defeated, and the Indians would get no money or services. The Senate was forced to accept the ultimatum, and the ten long years of efforts by Boomers and other backers of the settler movement to get the lands opened finally paid off. (11)

In the April 22, 1909, issue of the *Daily Oklahoman*, Dr. Delos Walker, described the scene at the first opening as settlers waited to be allowed into the Unassigned Lands twenty years before. (12) "No region had been so thoroughly advertised, so favorably advertised . . . The denizens of all civilization came; came from the hills, from the valleys, from the prairie and forest; came from the caves of the earth, from the isles of the sea and, seemingly, from the clouds of the air. They were here in all tongues, in all colors, in all garbs, with all kinds of profanity and every imaginable odor; they were here at high noon." (13) All of the other states had been slowly pioneered as parts of organized territories; the new Oklahoma of 1889 was essentially settled in a day, although it continued to be expanded as tribal lands were opened for settlement.

The Organic Act

The actual settlement of this region had merely begun with the opening of the Unassigned Lands. When the fifty thousand people entered the new Oklahoma on April 22, 1889, they set about establishing homes and bringing order out of the chaos caused by lack of any territorial laws or governing authority. Unfortunately, the Severalty Act and the rider opening the Unassigned Lands had not included any provisions for governing. On May 2, 1890, over a year after the opening, President Harrison signed the Organic Act creating Oklahoma Territory. This new U.S. territory included six new counties with county seats; Greer County, which had been in dispute with the state of Texas; the Public Land Strip, called No-Man's Land; and all other portions of the former Indian lands which would be added as they were opened for settlement. The eastern part of the Indian lands which included the tribal reservations of the Five Civilized Tribes, the seven small reservations of the Quapaw Agency, and the unoccupied portion of the Cherokee Outlet were to be held in a separate Indian Territory, sometimes referred to as "the Nations."

The government established by the Organic Act for Oklahoma Territory was a republican form with the three branches: executive, legislative, and judicial. The governor was appointed by the U.S. President for a four-year term. There was an Upper House or Legislative Council consisting of thirteen members and a Lower House or House of Representatives of twenty-six members. Judges were appointed by the U.S. Supreme Court with three district court judicial districts, and a large portion of the general statutes of Nebraska was adopted for temporary use. Guthrie was designated as the capital of the new Oklahoma Territory.

According to the Organic Act, the law enforcement arm of the government was the United States Marshal's office.

This was not a new arrangement since deputy marshals had been responsible for federal law enforcement in the Indian lands since 1865, when Judge Isaac Charles Parker, who became known as "the hanging judge," had been appointed to the Fort Smith bench. One of Judge Parker's first actions had been to appoint 200 deputy marshals to help United States Marshal James A. Fagan cover the 74,000 miles which made up his jurisdiction. However, with increased populations and the establishment of the Twin Territories, as Oklahoma and Indian Territories came to be known, the responsibilities of the deputy marshals increased. (14) Tribal law enforcement continued to be in effect in Indian Territory. However, at first there was no county government of any kind in Oklahoma Territory and no local law enforcement except here and there where some town decided to extend its jurisdiction to protect the family of an absent homesteader or to bring some renegade in to court. (15)

Settlers in the West had depended on vigilante justice to protect themselves and their holdings for many years. Therefore, citizens in Oklahoma Territory continued to rely on vigilante action for crimes such as horse and stock theft, bank robbery, claim jumping, and vice. They also used their common-law right, which enabled private individuals to make arrests where they had reasonable grounds for believing that the persons arrested had committed felonies. Some of the vigilante groups were stable and remained in effect for a long period of time. For example, a Respective Claims Committee was formed in Beaver City in 1886, to discourage claim jumping and avoid problems among settlers over claims to town lots and homesteads. (16) Another group was the Anti-Horse Thief Association, which began in Missouri before the Civil War and was started in Cleveland county in 1893. By 1900 there were 199 other Anti-Horse Thief Associations with 5,000 members in the territories. The Law and Order League was still another vigilante organization found in the territories. Its goals were to help officers hunt down all criminals, to protect witnesses for the territory, and prosecute any person attempting to intimidate them. From 1882 to 1896, vigilantes lynched seventy-six suspected criminals in Indian and Oklahoma Territories. Of that number thirty-five were horse thieves, while the others were presumed guilty of other crimes from murder and rape to theft and rustling. (17)

Over the next seventeen years after the opening of the Unassigned Lands, other western Indian tribal lands were opened to white settlement and became a part of Oklahoma Territory. On September 22, 1891, surplus land of the Iowa, Sac and Fox, and the Shawnee and Pottawatomie tribes were opened by a run. About 20,000 persons contested for the 7,000 quarter-sections, and the land was occupied in one afternoon. Surplus land of the Cheyenne-Arapaho was opened on April 19, 1892. The eastern half filled promptly, but much of the more arid western part remained unclaimed and continued to be used as grazing land for cattlemen. Approximately 100,000 people poised at the starting lines when the Cherokee Outlet was opened on September 16, 1893. Although there were many skirmishes for the rich lands in the eastern part, many quarter-sections in the western half remained unoccupied for several years. On May 23, 1895, Kickapoo lands in the middle of earlier openings was made available to settlers. The U.S. Supreme Court denied Texas' claim to Greer County, and on March 16, 1896, 4,000 new homesteads were declared open for settlement in that area. Between July 9 and August 6, 1901, the surplus lands of the Kiawa-Comanche and the Wichita-Caddo reservations were opened by lottery. Nearly 170,000 persons registered for the 13,000 quarter-sections. In December 1906, the final parcel of Indian tribal land, called Big Pasture, was opened to whites by sealed bids. Thus, in a span of seventeen years, Oklahoma Territory, which had begun at the first opening in 1889 as a parcel of land with a little less than two million acres which became six counties, had grown to a Territory of over fourteen million acres divided into twenty-seven counties. (18)

Early Politics in Oklahoma Territory

The desire for land was a common characteristic of the thousands of new settlers to Oklahoma Territory; however, that was one of the few things many of this group of people had in common. "Newcomers confronted settled Indian civilizations. The settler with lengthy lineage in another area confronted recent European immigrants. Whites faced blacks. Former Union soldiers resided near former Confederates, and Harrison Republicans collided with Cleveland Democrats. People who favored the gold standard and the predictable economic order it represented argued against proponents of free silver and the reckless experimentation it symbolized." (19) The new citizens of Oklahoma Territory were a diverse lot.

Oklahoma Territory's political parties and attitudes were born in the turbulent times of the land openings. The people who came yearned to be small landholders, and they were desperate to succeed on this last frontier. Many of them had been dissatisfied with the existing establishments in their previous homelands, and they tried to form new communities free from many of the regulations and restrictive attitudes they remembered from the older societies. Quarrels in Oklahoma Territory were usually open and sometimes fierce, and alliances were often fragile. Farmers especially disliked the cattlemen, who, in their view, had profited handsomely from grazing the Indian lands that they wanted to make into family farms. These conflicts between growning numbers of homesteaders and decreasing numbers of cattlemen grew into a broad-based suspicion of big or complex enterprise. This resulted in a bias toward the small farmer which was reflected in the central political attitudes that shaped Oklahoma's future. (20)

The election of the first legislature for Oklahoma Territory came in the midst of the economic depression of 1890, and there were three parties actually contending for the voters' allegiance. By this time, many settlers had become discouraged as they saw their dreams of a new life fading into the familiar patterns they had fled. High local freight rates, a crop-lien system, mortgages, scarce investment funds, and disputed rules of tenancy were becoming all too familiar in the new territory. Frustrated homesteaders soon joined the Populist crusade that was shaking national politics in the turbulent 1890s. The People's party became the dominant voice of agrarian protest in Oklahoma Territory during that decade, and neither older party was secure enough to ignore it. At first Oklahoma Territory was predominately Republican since the first lands opened were closer to Kansas and the upper plains states than to Texas. But as more lands in the south opened, Democratic strength increased. (21)

When the Oklahoma Territorial legislature assembled at Guthrie on August 27, 1890, only two or three of the twenty-six representatives and thirteen councilmen had any prior political experience. There were many vital decisions to make about the territorial government, but none was of more immediate importance to the delegates than the location of county seats, colleges, and other territorial institutions. All of these were up for grabs, and in this process, the political inexperience of the legislators became obvious. (22)

Republicans held a thin plurality in each house, but the mad scramble for the sites of territorial institutions completely obliterated party lines. The small Populist group in the house and council, most from Payne county, bartered its support to gain virtual control of the legislature. They got the agricultural and mechanical college for Stillwater and the dollars guaranteed by the Second Morrill Act.

Edmond got the normal school; Norman the university. After much debate and political struggling among the delegates, Guthrie retained the state capital.

The work of the convention was far from completed. "With little time remaining and not a single enacted statute, they finally began compiling a code of law. Ripping out pages from the statute books of existing states and operating without committee referrals or, for that matter, even printing the bills, the legislature hurried to complete its work. Four-fifths of its acts were adopted in the final two days of the session. More often than not, members lacked any knowledge of what they were voting upon." (23)

A code of laws was adopted; however, some of them were incongruous. For instance, Oklahoma Territory had been range country, and farmers had to fight to compel cattlemen to keep their stock fenced. The new law for this purpose was lifted directly from the Nebraska statutes which addressed a far different situation. Unfortunately, this law proved unworkable for years. (24) One of the most absurd examples of their work—that the legislature would discover only later—was that they had unanimously voted to apply the maritime laws of Michigan, including provisions for the licensing of sea pilots, to the dry, land-locked prairies of Oklahoma. (25)

However, many of the acts of the legislature provided for some basic needs of the territory. A territorial militia was formed following the tenets of the Second Amendment to the U.S. Constitution. Criminals were to be sent to prison in Lansing, Kansas, and the insane to Illinois. (26)

As the elected legislators returned home, citizens across the territory read about their activities in the local newspapers. Newspapers had been given a important role in territory politics. Even the smaller towns usually had at least one newspaper that relegated news to a distant third behind the more important functions of boosting the town and promoting the editor's political party. (27)

Law Enforcement in Oklahoma Territory

Not all of those who came to Oklahoma Territory were motivated to make it a better place to live for families and future citizens. There were those who saw the opportunity to take advantage of the lack of structure and exploit the settlers' weaker human sides. Outlaw gangs swiftly organized outside the towns, where there was not even provisional government and no laws except those generally applicable to federal territory. (28)

Dozens of towns had sprung up along the boundary of Oklahoma Territory to serve as supply centers for the Indians, cowboys, and farm hands who lived across the border in Indian Territory. Many of the towns owed their existence and much of their early development to the fact that liquor was legal in Oklahoma Territory but forbidden a few miles away on Indian lands. That particular situation gave rise to a unique kind of town in Oklahoma, the whiskey town, where saloons lined the streets, bootleggers came to stock up, gambling was widespread, and brothels did a brisk trade in upstairs rooms. In the most notorious of these towns, it was said that outlaws ruled the streets and murder was common. (29)

More than a dozen such towns existed in Oklahoma Territory, and many of the most notorious were in Pottawatomie county. A half-dozen whiskey towns once existed in that county alone which was bordered on the east by the Creek and Seminole nations and on the south by the Chickasaw Nation. The first saloon opened in Keokuk Falls in 1891, and by 1900 there were an estimated sixty-two saloons and three distilleries in the county. The wildest of all of the whiskey towns was Corner, named for its location in the extreme southeastern corner of Pottawatomie county, where the boundaries of the Chickasaw and Seminole nations met. Here the meandering Canadian River cut through many of the square lots created by the township and range survey system, and many small parcels of land remained unsettled. A saloon was built in the briar-filled bottom lands beside the Canadian River that became known as Corner, and it became a haven for outlaws. The Dalton Gang, the Christian Brothers, and Bill Doolin were all outlaws who were believed to be regulars at the Corner Saloon. Corner developed a reputation for violence and lawlessness unsurpassed in the rest of Oklahoma Territory. Elsewhere, towns such as Prague and Stroud in Lincoln county were first developed as railroad towns and cotton marketing centers, but because of their proximity to Indian Territory they also built a thriving whiskey trade. (30)

The land along the border of Indian Territory and Oklahoma Territory came to be known as "Hells Fringe" because persons committing crimes in the territorial counties often fled into Indian Territory or "the Nations" where sheriffs and their deputies had no authority to cross the border in pursuit. To try to address some of these problems, the 1890 Organic Act, establishing the structure for Oklahoma Territory, had given the U.S. Marshal concurrent jurisdiction with sheriffs in criminal matters. This arrangement met only minimal success. (31)

On July 1, 1893, when U.S. Marshal Nix took office, he was assigned some specific tasks to try to address these problems. He was to find and equip proper quarters for and provide protection for the federal courts, curb the destruction of government timber and the operation of whiskey peddlers on Indian reservations, and protect Indian lands from invasion by settlers. Primarily, however, Nix was charged to solve the outlaw problem and restore unmolested transportation and communication to Indian Territory as soon as possible. As one of his first acts, Marshal Nix compiled a list of eligible local officers and made them federal deputies. Of the many deputy marshals who were appointed to work in the twin territories, William "Bill" Tilghman, Chris Madsen, and Heck Thomas, became well known and were sometimes referred to as "The Three Guardsmen" of Oklahoma Territory. (32) Law enforcement in these lands that were being rapidly settled was a complex and difficult job.

A territorial militia had been auathorized by the Organic Act, but it was only a rag-tag bunch of men with no money to fund the units. Volunteers wore whatever old military uniforms they could find and armed themselves with personal weapons. After five years they were reorganized into a national guard to include able-bodied men between the ages of 18 and 45. They were available for service as the governor saw the need. (33)

Natural Resources Create Problems in Indian Territory

As most settlers in Oklahoma Territory were struggling to build homes, establish towns, and form local governments, their neighbors in Indian Territory were dealing with changes of their own. The older towns of Indian Territory with markets and business centers had been joined together by railroads many years before. These railroads had pumped the life-blood for the post-Civil War and Reconstruction economic recovery of the Five Civilized Tribes. Although the land in Indian Territory technically belonged to the tribes as designated by law, there were many non-Indian settlers who had moved into the area over a period of time. Unlike the settlers in Oklahoma Territory who wanted to farm the land, many of these settlers had come seeking resources that were under the land. Despite the absence of gold which was so common in other western territories, Indian Territory did posses valuable minerals. Lead ore, found in lumps above the ground and used for bullets in the frontier era, was common in the northeastern corner. Repeated rich strikes of lead near Miami, along with the discovery of zinc, created boom towns that rivaled the gold camps of Colorado and California. (34)

Lumbering had become a major industry in Indian Territory's eastern forests in 1868. It initially provided wood for building settlers' homes and furniture and was used for fuel. Railroads used the lumber for rail ties and bridge timbers. Excess lumber was shipped by rail to southwest markets for building materials and shingles.

Coal was also abundant in eastern Indian Territory, where it was strip-mined for domestic uses and blacksmithing in the early days. But there had been no market to stimulate commercial coal mining until the coming of railroads in the 1870s. After the Civil War, Arkansas Confederate Colonel J.J. McAlester, of Ft. Smith, had moved to the territory, married a Chickasaw girl, and used her Choctaw/Chickasaw citizenship to get land. He had seen maps of the area with coal and began mining with several others who had also married Indians and received tribal land. McAlester persuaded railroad officials to build lines through the Choctaw coal fields, and commercial coal mining began in earnest. The town of Bucklucksy was renamed McAlester by the MKT railroad in 1872. The Missouri Pacific Railroad and the MKT quickly dominated Indian Territory coal production, opening shafts at Lehigh, Coalgate, Dow, Bache, Hartshorne, and Henryetta. (35)

Finding enough workers to mine the coal was a problem. Indians were reluctant to work underground in mines, but many Choctaw and Chickasaw freedmen, former black slaves, abandoned subsistence farming to dig for coal. In the 1870s unemployment in coal fields of the eastern states caused many miners to accept the railroads' offers of free transportation to Indian Territory. Scores of skilled Irish, Scottish, and Welsh immigrants from the British Isles came to the mines. Other immigrants such as Lithuanians, Slovaks, Poles, Germans, Russians, along with many Italians also came to the mines. They were willing to work long hours for low wages in the hope of ultimately buying farms.

Adding to the mix of ethnic groups, hundreds of Alabama blacks were imported as strike breakers during the long, bitter strikes over union recognition between 1898 and 1903. (36)

In 1859, when the first commercial oil wells had been drilled at Titusville, Pennsylvania, petroleum was accidentally found in the Cherokee Nation. While drilling a water well to boost salt production at Great Saline, Lewis Ross found oil. Petroleum seepages, which Indians called "oil springs" and used for medicinal purposes, were fairly common, but commercial drilling was unknown. Indian Territory was too remote from refining and marketing facilities to result in much more than curiosity or wonder. However, in 1897, Cudahy Oil Company drilled the first commercial well at Bartlesville. There was a great deal of excitement, but because of the distance to market, the well was capped until the Santa Fe Railroad reached the area. Yet the high interest and furor that the brief boom generated spread among the growing number of wildcatters and oil speculators, and they began to zero in on the promising Indian lands. (37)

The growing numbers of non-Indians living in Indian Territory could not own land nor participate in tribal government. Their children could not attend tribal schools. Under Indian tribal laws, they were not allowed to become citizens, so they appealed to the federal government in an attempt to change their situation. After growing pressure from a number of sources, in 1892, Congress passed a law that applied the Dawes Allotment Act to the lands of the Five Civilized Tribes. Since these Indian lands had never been officially surveyed and each tribe functioned as a separate entity, it was a formidable task to identify the plots of land and assign them to individual members of the tribes. This process, assigned to the Dawes Commission, took many years.

The length of time it took to allot land to individual

Indians resulted even more appeals to Congress. For example, oil exploration in Indian Territory had declined in the late 1890s, as oil men waited for the Dawes Commission to complete allotments and to establish a more favorable leasing policy for Indian lands. To encourage limited oil exploration Congress passed the Curtis Act of 1898, which did away with the Indian tribal courts and tribal laws and required that mineral lands be leased for the benefit of each tribe. However, many Cherokees and Creeks continued to negotiate individual leases with outside investors and drillers. On June 25, 1901, when the message "Oil is spouting over the derrick" crackled along the telegraph wires from Red Fork, the surge of oilmen could not be held back. Promoters from Kansas and Texas crossed over the border and others from New York, Chicago, and Pennsylvania scrambled for leases in the area. The Interior Department delayed another year before approving individual lease contracts for citizens of the Five Civilized Tribes, but, by this time, wildcat drilling and speculative madness were in full swing.

Almost overnight, as in the land runs, but with a different atmosphere, new boom towns were born. As had happened with the zinc and lead strikes earlier, towns of cheap wooden buildings or cloth tents appeared. Some structures bore labels such as "hotel," "restaurant," "opera house," but all were designed for one purpose, to separate men from their money as quickly as possible. Congestion, prostitution, and violence soon became hallmarks of oil towns. And although liquor was not legal in Indian Territory, open saloons were abundant until accidents, absenteeism, and violence in the oil fields forced the operators to dry up liquor sources. Most oil towns vanished as quickly as they had come; but if their pool of oil was substantial, like Cushing, Wewoka, and Sapulpa, they prospered. (38)

The increasing southern view of whites who had moved into towns in Indian Territory and the blacks who lived there resulted in many problems. In 1901 whites in Sapulpa actually drove blacks from the town. There were reports of whippings and lynchings of blacks in both territories, although in the final analysis, many more whites were lynched than blacks. (39)

Politics in Indian Territory

Politics in Indian Territory was quite different from that found in Oklahoma Territory. Though administered from Republican-dominated Washington, Indian Territory had a Southern and Democratic tone. Among the Five Civilized Tribes, political attitudes that had been shaped during the Civil War remained strong into the twentieth century. The Democratic party was confident of support from the Chickasaws, Choctaws, and Stand Waite Cherokees, who had aligned themselves with the Confederacy. But Republican influence prevailed among Creeks, Seminoles, and Cherokees who had remained loyal to the Union. (40)

Among the influential landholders and leaseholders of the Five Civilized Tribes, politics grew from a different tradition than that in its twin territory. The focus was on tribal matters, rather than on controversial policies designed to develop new laws and a new governmental structures. The tribes had brought their unique and highly developed tribal governments with them in the 1830s on the Trail of Tears as they were forced to move to Indian Territory from their homes in the southeastern states. The Choctaws, for example, had adopted a written constitution in 1826. (41) Prior to the Civil War, the tribes had reestablished their eastern cultures and developed prosperous and complex societies in Indian Territory. Thus they were called "civilized" as compared with the plains Indians who lived in more loosely organized nomadic tribes. Since each of the Five Civilized Tribes, which owned most of the land making up Indian Territory, functioned as separate entities, discussions among the tribes developed a more covert and subdued tone than found in the white-dominated single unit of Oklahoma Territory. The Indian leaders tried to continue on with their tribal ways as though they were insulated from the changes that were going on all around them. However, political differences sharpened at the beginning of the new century, and they were forced to focus on the emerging question of statehood. (42)

Efforts to Become a State

Settlers in Oklahoma Territory had begun to talk about admission to the Union as a state immediately after the run of 1889. Between 1865 and 1900, statehood had become a popular solution to the political and economic problems of territories west of the Mississippi. In those years, nine new states appeared on the national map. In addition to Oklahoma Territory, the territories of Arizona and New Mexico were also beginning to look toward statehood during this same time. (43) However, national leaders of both parties questioned the wisdom of early admission for western territories. Their populations seemed turbulent, their narrowly based economies were judged to be unsound, and they tended to send radical or unusual spokesmen to Congress. To those in older states, the small territorial populations also seemed over-represented in both Congress and presidential contests. (44)

By the 1890s, that skepticism combined with several special circumstances in Oklahoma Territory were enough to make national leaders cautious about supporting statehood. How to finance state and local government in a new territory was an especially troublesome concern. Much of the land in Oklahoma Territory was exempt from taxation because it was being homesteaded or because of the terms governing allotments to western tribes. Until land could be taxed adequately and predictably, public finances seemed insufficient to support a new state.

The territory's geography and its distribution of natural resources also inhibited early efforts at statehood. Oklahoma Territory consisted of only about 40,000 square miles, about half the land of most states west of the Mississippi. There was good farm and range land, but the timber and minerals necessary for a balanced economy were located in Indian Territory. Leaders of the Five Civilized Tribes, however, had no interest in uniting with Oklahoma Territory. Until the turn of the century, they had successfully resisted every effort to interfere with the remaining treaty arrangements; therefore, hoping to preserve Indian Territory and form their own state. (45)

U. S. Republican leaders wanted the two territories to come into the Union as one state because they feared election of four Democratic senators. Democratic leaders had favored having Oklahoma Territory admitted in 1893 with additional Indian lands to be annexed as they were opened and with Indian Territory also to be annexed in due time. However, Indian Territory leaders did not want to be a minority in a new state. (46)

The leaders of the Five Civilized Tribes became convinced that they should take action on their own to establish an Indian State. The Sequoyah Convention, held in August 1905, at Muskogee to prepare the necessary documents to petition for statehood, in reality, was an opportunity for Indian Territory Democrats, particularly Charles Haskell and William (Alfalfa Bill) Murray, to gain party leadership. There were 305 delegates and alternates chosen, but many of them never came. No representatives appeared from seven of the twenty-six districts, and only about a fifth were in regular attendance. (47)

The Sequoyah Constitution, which was written at the convention, reflected many progressive ideas at the time. It was the product of five men: Charles N. Haskell, William H. Murray, W.W. Hastings, John R. Thomas, and Robert L. Owen. Although they were acting for the Indians of the

Five Civilized Tribes, only two of them were of Indian blood, neither more than one-sixteenth. (48) In addition to a Bill of Rights and a three-branch government, the constitution established a strict corporation commission modeled on Virginia's new statute; absolute tax equity; prohibition of food adulteration; prohibition of price discrimination; social justice guarantees for workers, women, and children; teaching of agriculture and domestic science in public schools; and prohibition of alcoholic beverages. Since this was the first referendum in Indian Territory history, the leaders tied it to the issue of naming county seats to get out the vote. The Sequoyah Constitution was ratified by 86 percent of the citizens of Indian Territory on November 7, 1905, and was sent to Congress with the request that the State of Sequoyah be admitted into the Union. (49) Bills were introduced into both houses of Congress to admit Sequoyah as a state, but neither were acted upon before adjournment. The hopes of Indian Territory leaders were dashed. (50)

Although Indian leaders desperately tried to maintain their old ways, their world was changing. As land had been allotted to individual members of the Five Civilized Tribes, there had been a stipulation that no Indian could sell an allotment for twenty-five years. However, under pressure from oil and land speculators, in 1906, Congress passed a law repealing the stipulation and allowing for "competency commissions" that toured Indian areas declaring certain Indians competent to sell their land. (51)

Just as the relentless Boomers agitating for land in Oklahoma Territory had triumphed in 1889, so men's hunger for the new wealth of oil beneath the land hastened the fall of the barriers that had kept Indian Territory a refuge. By the summer of 1905, there were 255 producing wells in Indian Territory. And by the end of 1906, territorial oil wells had produced more that twenty-seven million barrels of oil, worth about fourteen million dollars. These oil men who came to Indian Territory were different from the miners and businessmen who had entered earlier. An aura of recklessness and extravagance also distinguished them from the more sober pioneers who had come in search of land. The oil men spoke in terms of millions of dollars. The gambling and uncertainty and the scope of operations and risk seemed to attract them as much as either money or oil. Tulsa began to change from a tough cow town to the petroleum headquarters of the world. Profits from oil built palatial residences as well as tasteful middle-class homes. A tradition of civic pride, fine arts, and a desire for public decoration developed there unequaled in Oklahoma Territory. These oil men also had a major impact on the politics of the region as the twin territories looked at a single statehood. (52)

The Enabling Act as signed by President Theodore Roosevelt on June 16, 1906, applied to the New Mexico and Arizona Territories as well as to Oklahoma and Indian Territories. This act "enabled" the people of the two sets of territories to write constitutions so they might be admitted into the Union as single states. The settlers of New Mexico and Arizona Territories refused to join together, but those of Oklahoma and Indian Territories began to prepare for a constitutional convention. (53)

The Act also stated that Guthrie would be the capital for at least six years and there would be prohibition in Indian Territory and the Osage Nation for twenty-one years. A special census of Oklahoma and Indian Territories was authorized by President Roosevelt, and it was determined that there were 1,414,177 people living in the two territories as of July 1, 1907. (54) Of the 750,000 living in Indian Territory, there were only 100,000 Indians and freedmen; the other 650,000 were non-citizens of the Five Civilized Tribes. (55) Indeed, Indians had become the minority in their own territory.

Democrats from both territories campaigned hard to

get elected to the constitutional convention and vowed to support public education, free school books, municipal ownership of utilities, direct democracy, and regulation of corporations. These were reform ideas found in the Sequoyah Constitution and went along with the progressive views of William Jennings Bryan, the well-known national Democratic speaker. Many Democratic candidates also pledged to institute racial segregation in transportation and education. Although both territories had previously been dominated by Republicans who had been appointed by national leaders, there were only twelve Republicans elected to attend the convention held in Guthrie beginning on November 20, 1906. Ninety-nine Democrats and one Democrat running as an Independent were also elected. (56) Seven of the Republicans and twenty-seven of the Democrats had previous political experience. Fifty-five of the delegates had been associated with the Sequoyah Convention, and they were able to elect thirty-seven-year-old William (Alfalfa Bill) Murray president. The convention delegates listed the following as their vocations: 38-farmers/ranchers, 29-lawyers, 14-merchants, 8-ministers, as well as physicians, bankers, editors, and teachers. Twelve had bona fide college degrees, and twenty-four had some type of advanced schooling. (57)

The citizens of the twin territories had sent their representatives to craft a new constitution that would reflect their feelings at the time. Across the country there were major issues that were also impacting the settlers of this newest state. The depression of 1890 had dramatized the unequal distribution of wealth, and there was a yearning for older virtues of liberty and individual effort. Urbanization, ethnic tensions, fear of big business with the resulting impersonality of workers fueled reform movements in Oklahoma as well as national politics. Many of the convention delegates wanted to maintain their pioneer heritage which included a spirit of rugged individualism, yet they wanted their new state to be modern and respectable to the rest of the country. (58) For the most part they believed that government should enhance individual freedom and correct imbalances in opportunities to succeed. These were noble ideals to build upon; however, in the end, many believe that they created a system in their new state with authority that proved to be so dispersed that constructive government was difficult and often impossible. Like many reformers, they lived to see their handiwork grow into a system they did not recognize. (59)

Racism played a big part in the framing of the new constitution. Within the territories, white settlers generally believed that blacks were increasing in numbers in the state at a much faster rate than the figures documented, and this idea had an impact on them. The fear that large numbers of blacks could dominate Oklahoma if they were not properly controlled had contributed to the choosing of many delegates who forcefully called for a racial policy akin to that of the Deep South with separation of the races. (60) In addition, since delegates from Indian Territory did not want Indians to be discriminated against, they pushed to define "colored" or "of colored race" as persons of African descent and declared that all others would be "white." Seventy-five delegates wanted "Jim Crow" restrictions written into the constitution, but fearing President Roosevelt and the National Republican party would not approve the constitution, they agreed to let the first legislature enact Jim Crow laws. It is believed that this racism also prevented by a single vote, women's suffrage, because many feared allowing women to vote would lead to the Negro's vote. (61)

On most matters the delegates were committed to placing the majority of power in the hands of the people. Frustrations from years of Republican-appointed leaders resulted in providing for elected rather than appointed officials, giving the legislature the greatest power. The governor was to be elected on non-presidential years and was limited to one four-year term. To give the citizens the power to make decisions that affected them, the delegates also provided for greater voter involvement through a system of initiatives and referendum procedures. (62)

In one area of the new constitution, the delegates seemed to go overboard. Article IX, dealing with corporations, was longer than the entire federal Constitution, and at a total of 50,000 words, the whole document was reported to be the world's longest constitution. Murray would later admit that all but eight of the first forty-five sections were basically statutory in nature and might well have been left to the first legislature. But he feared that the legislature might be dominated by a revived Republican party, and he did not want to leave anything in this area to chance. (63)

They adopted the Sequoyah Constitution's plan requiring agricultural and mechanical courses in public schools. Murray explained that this kind of education "would enable boys and girls to protect themselves in a vocation rather than to burden them with a false education which leads exclusively to professions and office holdings, the breeder of vagabonds of society." This was a strong statement reflecting the agrarian pioneer's desire for the practical over the theoretical. Over the years, the state would develop a truly remarkable system of agricultural education and teacher training, but many believe that the attitude of anti-intellectualism summarized in Murray's remarks also held back the development of excellence in general education. (64)

Since the Enabling Act required a twenty-one-year prohibition clause for Indian Territory and the Osage Nation, there was controversy about what the stand on prohibition should be for the new state. Charles Haskell, who planned to run for governor, persuaded Murray to delay the decision and offer a statewide prohibition amendment on a separate ballot during the voting for ratification of the constitution. (65)

The election of 1907 was hotly contested. The Republicans favored statehood but objected to the constitution as it was framed. On the other hand, most Democrats insisted that it was the best constitution ever written. As the new constitution was reviewed in Washington, D.C., the most controversial parts were those that dealt with economic issues and land tenure. President Roosevelt sent his Secretary of War, William H. Taft, to Oklahoma to oppose some of these ideas which they saw as radical. Roosevelt and Taft also objected to the statutory nature of the constitution which had become a "code of laws," to its definition of race, and to a provision for the popular election of judges. (66)

As a result of these concerns, the delegates returned to Guthrie for seven days in April and again for six days in July to make some modifications in the constitution. (67) However, protecting individual ownership of resources and, especially, preserving the family farm and agrarian ideals were the major motives for economic regulation found in the constitution, and the delegates stood fast and refused to make many changes. The constitution that was submitted to the people for ratification stated that aliens could not own land, nor could corporations buy, sell, or speculate in land as their sole endeavor. It also emphasized that the state could not engage in the business of agriculture. (68)

By the time all of the votes were counted on September 17, 1907, the new constitution had been ratified by the citizens of Oklahoma, the prohibition amendment had also passed, and the Democrats had won an unqualified mandate to govern — they carried sixty-two of the seventy-five counties. Republicans won ten counties, and three divided evenly. Charles Haskell, at forty-five years of age, was elected governor. Four of the five congressmen were Democrats; there were thirty-nine Democrats and five

Republicans in the state senate; and ninety-three Democrats and sixteen Republicans in the house. (69) For the next half-century, Democratic control of the courthouses in Oklahoma was the party's power base in both state and national campaigns. (70)

A New State

The much debated and controversial progressive constitution for the new state was submitted to Congress for approval, and the people awaited the outcome of the vote on statehood for Oklahoma. Congress approved, and on November 16, 1907, called Statehood Day, Governor Haskell was inaugurated in Guthrie. All across the new state, citizens of even the smallest towns greeted their new status with celebrations and parades. As a result of the passage of the prohibition referendum, saloons which had been legal in Oklahoma Territory were required to close for good on November 16 at 10:16 a.m., when President Roosevelt signed the statehood proclamation. However, Governor Haskell arranged for the saloons in Oklahoma City to remain open until 11:50 p.m. that day. Some of the saloon owners gave away draught beer as the evening and an era grew to a close. Others held on until the very last minute. A photograph, copyrighted by the Brunswick Cigar Company in Oklahoma City, showing men dipping buckets into a pool of beer dumped in the gutter by revenue officers, became a well-known post card reflecting the attitudes and the times. Anti-liquor forces were hopeful that the problems associated with alcohol would now be a thing of the past in Oklahoma. (71)

Governor Haskell led the new legislature to establish a procedure for enforcing prohibition. A unique provision of the alcohol enforcement law, called the "Billups Booze Bill," permitted the establishment of a dispensary store in each county where doctors' liquor prescriptions for medicinal purposes would be filled. Although voters repealed this state dispensary system in 1908, the Oklahoma Supreme Court reopened them. There would be no simple solution to the use of alcohol in Oklahoma. (72)

Although formal segregation was not included in the constitution, the first legislature promptly enacted a set of segregation codes for schools, public facilities, and transportation reminiscent of the Deep South. Fearful that Oklahoma would become a Republican state during the progressive era, Democrats quickly disenfranchised blacks. New voting laws required a stringent literacy test based on the state's lengthy constitution. Known as the "grandfather clause" because it exempted the direct descendants of all persons eligible to vote prior to January 1, 1866, the law effectively kept blacks from the polls. (73)

Law enforcement became the responsibility of sheriffs, police departments, and constables. For federal law enforcement purposes, Oklahoma was divided into the Western District at Guthrie and the Eastern District at Muskogee. Where at one time hundreds of deputy marshals roamed the two areas, each district force was reduced to a half-dozen men, and their work dwindled to federal law violations and routine matters. (74)

A major roadblock to effective law enforcement in the new state was the desire of the citizens for local control. Rich or poor, farmer or businessman, rancher or lawyer, these citizens wanted a stake in Oklahoma because they believed it represented their last chance to achieve success solely on individual initiative. This outlook inspired a fierce determination to keep all institutions local in nature. As a result, every community had its own school system, its own method of levying taxes, and its own law enforcement officers. (75) This spirit of rugged individualism had been vital during the time pioneers first settled the land; however, it began to get in the way as communities and counties needed to work together to coordinate law enforcement efforts for the new state.

As they had done before statehood, citizens of Oklahoma continued to depend upon vigilante organizations for enforcing legal and social issues such as liquor consumption, gambling, and prostitution, which were often overlooked by local lawmen. In 1908, a vigilante group called the Oklahoma City Law Enforcement League was established, and in 1911, another which was a unit of the Law and Order League was formed in Watonga. Other communities relied on their own vigilante groups and social pressures to try to maintain local law and order. (76)

The legislature of the new state had many problems and issues to deal with. However, organization of the state including recognition of counties and county seats continued to occupy the efforts of many lawmakers. One of the most hotly debated issues was the location of the state capital. From before statehood there had been intense legal and political maneuvering to claim the location of the state capital which had originally been placed in Guthrie by national Republicans. By 1910, Oklahoma City had built enough political power to mount a successful challenge for the much coveted capital. An election was held on June 11, 1910, that finally decided the issue as Oklahoma City won over Guthrie and Shawnee. (77) A new capitol building was started in 1914, and was completed in 1917 at the cost of $5,000,000. Although there was supporting structure for a dome, high costs and scarcity of materials during World War I prevented it from being built. (78)

Growth Brings New Problems

After World War I there were at least three major changes that complicated the lives of Oklahomans and led to the request for increased law enforcement measures. One was the development of the automobile, another was the oil boom, and the third was the coming of National Prohibition.

As it was doing in other parts of the country, the development of the automobile was changing the lives of most Oklahoma citizens. The settlers in remote parts of the state were no longer isolated, and travel time from one town to another was cut drastically. Oklahoma's constitution had been drafted before the automobile had made its way into the state in significant numbers, and at first, vehicle law enforcement within the limits of a given community was marginal at best. However, outside of the towns on the state's lonely rural roads, it was "No man's land." (79)

Although there were only 6,500 automobiles in the state of Oklahoma in 1912, pressure for new highway construction began to build. The Highway Department was enlarged, creating the Highway Commission. The Federal Aid Road Act of 1916 was passed which allotted $75 million to help states build highways. This act encouraged more cooperation between local and state authorities when it came to choosing routes and building roads. In Oklahoma under the close scrutiny of Governor Robert Williams, the legislature appropriated one million dollars for new roads in 1917. (80) By the end of World War I, the improved roads movement in America was gaining momentum. However, in 1920, of the almost 3 million miles of highways in America, the majority were fit only for travel by horse and buggy. Only about 36,000 miles had all-weather surfaces that would accommodate automobile traffic. Congress modified the Federal Highway Act in 1921, calling for construction of a system of interconnected highways. States were warned that if they wanted to keep getting federal funds, they would have to designate up to seven percent of their roads as national highways. (81)

Rapid urbanization was another major factor of change in Oklahoma. Between 1910 and 1920 the nation's urban population increased some 29 percent; in Oklahoma, the growth was almost 69 percent. The state's population was still predominately rural, but the growth of cities and towns was accelerating at a staggering rate. Urban growth meant urban problems, based on movement away from the norms that had earlier defined Oklahomans' lives. Oil was often identified as the catalyst for many of the new urban troubles. Discoveries of enormous gas and oil deposits transformed Cushing, Seminole, Okmulgee, Oklahoma City, and especially Tulsa. Farmers left their land, rootless people converged on the strike areas, and the resulting new boom towns were caricatures of everything wrong with American life. Many believed the towns fairly celebrated disorder, greed, violence, and indifference to the earth itself. (82)

Although oil was blamed for creating many problems for the new state, it was also creating revenue desperately needed for growth. On the other hand, problems spawned by on-going liquor consumption brought no redeeming features. When National Prohibition went into effect in 1920, the dry forces in Oklahoma welcomed federal enforcement, hoping this would help curb the flow of liquor into the state. But, instead, they were shocked at the effects of the Eighteenth Amendment. Stills appeared all over Oklahoma, drawing customers from every social level. The new oil fields of the 1920s raised another series of boom towns where illicit and often dangerous liquor fueled crime and violence. No part of the state was immune from the effects of illegal alcohol. Scores of upstanding citizens died from drinking bathtub gin, and for the first time since territorial days, drunkenness was a problem among high school age students and young adults. While many dedicated law enforcement officers were willing to put their lives on the line to uphold prohibition, there was also widespread corruption. Ambivalent public attitudes toward enforcement penalties also undermined the efforts of even the most dedicated officials. (83)

Crime rapidly became the most sensational and widely noted aspect of life in the oil boom towns. Concern became intense as brutal, random attacks on the general public increased, and crimes of passion out paced the usual crimes against property. With increased automobile use, no community seemed secure. These widely reported stories inevitably made citizens of every town feel unsafe and fearful of a spreading change they hoped to stop at their city's limits. The automobile, picture show, and public dance hall seemed suddenly to replace the church, schoolhouse, and fairgrounds in families' lives. Bootleg whiskey flowed freely, and flouting the law gained a certain respect in many circles. Law enforcement agencies seemed corrupt, and politicians could no longer slow down, let alone control, social change. By 1921, many Oklahomans turned, as did citizens in other states, to a revived Ku Klux Klan to enforce both laws and moral behavior. (84)

From the first, the combination of Oklahoma's unwieldy constitution and an exploitive political system rooted in the frontier ethic of grab-and-run had shaped the nature of state party politics and state government. The basic constitutional provision forbidding the governor and other elected officials from succeeding themselves had been designed to prevent the "courthouse gangs" so familiar in American political history. In practice, however, it promoted a spoils system. Ambitious men learned to exchange offices and support each other's campaigns. "Swapping keys," as the practice was called, gave the state some honest and experienced administrators, but it also left a number of corrupt or incompetent officials undisturbed for many years.

The large number of candidates this system generated also thwarted the progressive idea that elected rather than appointed officials best represented the voters' wishes. Confronted with a lengthy ballot, many people voted "by guess or by golly," ignorant of the candidates' abilities. The cynical began to believe that anyone who ran for office was probably a scoundrel anyway; voting him in and then driving him out of office seemed a good plan. Incessant bickering over patronage within state government and pressures from without prevented many conscientious officials from doing their jobs. (85)

There were many other indications that the idealistic dreams for a "new" state, held by the framers of the constitution and the early pioneers, were dimming. The hope for land ownership, which was the initial common denominator of many Oklahoma settlers, had begun to fade soon after statehood. The federal Homestead Act did not apply to Indian Territory, so much of the available land was purchased by landlords who employed tenant farmers. By 1910, at least 70 percent of all farm units in twenty-five eastern counties were operated by landless tenants. In the western counties where most of the ownership of the land had been granted to farmers after they had lived on it and improved it for a period of three years, many of the farmers had taken mortgage loans as high as 20 percent interest in order to operate their farms. It was said that Oklahomans paid higher interest than any farmers in the nation. By 1915, three of every four Oklahoma farmers had been reduced to tenancy or were facing mortgage foreclosure. Many Oklahomans turned to Socialism in the hope of stopping the erosion of their economic power. (86)

Disgruntled citizens began to take to the streets. Draft resistance riots led by Socialists occurred in various sections of Oklahoma, although most were kept quiet through newspaper censorship. Close to McAlester, the Green Corn Rebellion of 1917 was one such riot. A mob, consisting of tenant farmers belonging to the Working Class Union, formed to burn bridges, damage buildings, and create general disturbances. Local police and citizens were finally able to stop the riot by arresting 450 people. There were a number of strikes across the state between 1919 and 1922, which required the presence of the National Guard. (87) A major race riot broke out in Tulsa in 1921. Martial law and the National Guard were required to suppress this disturbance in which eighty persons died and two square miles of the prosperous black business district of Greenwood were destroyed. (88)

However, at the state capital, where Republicans had gained a majority in the House in 1921 for the first time in history, legislators were so busy fighting among themselves, that they seemed oblivious to the underlying causes of the riots. The Republicans hoped to take over the governorship in 1922, and the legislators became so engrossed in their political battles that the sixty-day legislative session expired without the necessary appropriations to run state government. (89)

The post-war prices were low for agriculture, and there was a fierce nationalism and distrust of anyone "different." The Klan became more active, and the focus in many areas of Oklahoma became anti-Catholic. In 1922 and 1923, there were numerous rallies with American flag demonstrations under clouds of hate, prejudice, and fear. The Klan took over Masonic organizations claiming that they were a white man's organization which represented Gentiles, Americans, and Protestants. (90) The Ku Klux Klan became a device for the ruthless dictation of the community-approved morals of sobriety, chastity, and family as a social ideal. The force and intimidation that accompanied this movement did not seem ironic to men accustomed to frontier ways or to their extreme experiences during the recently ended World War I. By 1922, some seventy thousand Oklahomans had joined the Ku Klux Klan with the intent to return society to the old virtues. (91)

By the fall of 1922, many citizens became concerned about the growing strength of the Klan. Anti-Klan forces joined with a league of farmers and workers to elect Democrat John C. Walton governor. However, his administration was a disaster filled with corruption and ineptitude. After angering many factions of the population by appointing friends as officers in the National Guard, granting special state police commissions to hundreds of people of questionable character, commuting all death sentences to life in prison, suspending the privilege of the writ of habeas corpus during martial law in Tulsa county, and tampering with A&M College and the University of Oklahoma, Walton placed the entire state under martial law when a grand jury was formed to investigate him. He ordered machine guns trained on the Oklahoma County Courthouse to prevent the grand jury from assembling. There was so much concern about Walton's ability to govern that in 1923, anti-Klan forces joined with the Klan to impeach him. Walton was convicted and removed from office in November 1923, with more than three years left of his term; he was succeeded by the lieutenant governor, Martin Edwin Trapp. (92)

Steps to Address Problems on the Roads

Governor Trapp tried to bring reason back to the capital. He cleaned up the National Guard and the special law enforcement commissions that Walton had authorized. He attempted to cut state expenditures yet fought for more money for state roads. Trapp wanted a state highway system connecting every section of the state and a reorganization of the Oklahoma Highway Department to a three-man commission to oversee state-financed highway construction. Since this reorganization would take power and money away from the county road commissioners, there was much opposition to his plan. However, by 1925, Trapp was successful in reorganizing the Highway Department and in getting a bill passed that required a title for all motor vehicles and provided $1,800 each year for two clerks in the Highway Commission to record all stolen vehicles. (93) An auto license tax and a gasoline tax of two and one-half cents per gallon were approved to finance state-wide roads. Sixty percent of these new funds went to the state and forty percent to the county, and accelerated highway expansion followed. (94)

In 1925, Governor Trapp also signed a bill establishing the Oklahoma Bureau of Criminal Identification and Investigation. This agency was similar to a state police force, but with limited powers. Although the bureau tried to cooperate with local officers to the fullest extent possible, the very nature of a state force infringed on many duties of local sheriffs and constables. The new mobility of the criminal, which correlated with the development of faster cars and better highways required a different approach in law enforcement. Local peace officers often were confined by county boundaries; however, the bureau's agents could cross county lines while in pursuit of the new breed of outlaw of the 1920s. (95)

There were 3,600 miles of state designated highways in Oklahoma in 1924. By 1926 the number had increased to 5,000 miles, and the first statewide "patrol system" was established for maintenance of these roads. The patrolmen, as they were called, had their own horses and graders with which they would grade and ditch the highways. However, these patrolmen were to focus their attention on the condition of the roads themselves, not on the drivers or the vehicles on the roads. As new roads and bridges were being built and the existing structures maintained, there was an escalation in road building businesses. Along with these great expenditures of money came corruption. (96)

Henry Simpson Johnston, an acknowledged leader of the Masons, a respected proponent of prohibition, and an active member of the Klan, was elected governor in 1926. His inaugural address promised to make education his number one priority, end the abuse of the pardon and parole system, and to move forward in building highways. He was soon in trouble as he appointed a former Klan worker as his confidential secretary. She was seen by many as his shield from legislators and the general public. Governor Johnston kept her in his office even after the legislature asked to have her removed. In addition, opposition to Johnston grew because of his liberal use of pardon and parole powers, his placing of incompetent people in office, as well as his criticism of the state highway department. In this atmosphere, Johnston showed very poor judgment as he selected his controversial secretary's uncle, who represented a number of firms that used asphalt rather than concrete for road building, as one of his chief advisors. (97)

In 1927, recognizing the need to regulate traffic on the increasingly busy and dangerous state road system, the legislature passed a bill amending the 1921 traffic laws. This act set out ten basic rules of the road, established a speed limit of 45 miles per hour, and set fines from $5.00 to $25.00. (Appendix A) However, there were no provisions to enforce these measures included in the law. (98)

Problems between the legislature and the governor continued to emerge. Johnston attempted to lead fellow Oklahoma Democrats to elect Al Smith in the 1928 presidential election; however, Herbert Hoover carried all but eight of the seventy-seven counties. This led to Governor Johnston's downfall, and in March of 1929, he was impeached and removed for incompetency by a newly elected Republican House. (99)

In a period of only 21 years of statehood, the second Oklahoma governor had been successfully impeached. Lieutenant Governor William Judson Halloway took over after Johnston's removal from office. In an effort to stem corruption, Halloway persuaded the legislature to pass a highway bill which cut the number of commissioners from the five Johnston had appointed to three. As in the rest of the nation, Oklahoma highway maintenance and construction had become a major governmental service and a growing responsibility. Between 1924 and 1929, Oklahoma's highway system had increased from 4,523 miles to 6,289 miles, with approximately three-fourths of it unpaved.

By this time, the number of motor vehicles had increased to 602,000. The Highway Department had more than 2,500 employees and a budget in excess of $16 million. (100)

Although improved roads helped the growth of commerce within the state, these improvements also led to problems. Bootleggers, bank robbers, as well as other criminals joined the average citizens on the improving road system, and public concern escalated. To address these concerns, a house bill calling for a state police force was submitted on February 12, 1929, by Raymond Harvey, a Democrat from Kiowa county. It had gained the support of Republican Jerry R. Marker from Oklahoma county by its second reading the next day. Later, Chairman of the Judiciary Committee, R.H. Stanley, a Democrat from Choctaw county, presented a substitute bill with an additional fifteen sections. Clearly there was a bipartisan interest in establishing a state police force of some type, but impeachment procedures against the sitting Supreme Court Justices in April interrupted the session, and no further action was taken on the proposed state police force. (101)

William Henry Murray, one of the crafters of the Sequoyah and Oklahoma constitutions, had left the country in 1924 to establish a utopian agrarian colony in Bolivia. But it failed, and he returned to Oklahoma in 1929, during a time of need for strong leadership. In the gubernatorial election of 1930, "Alfalfa" Bill Murray, as he was called, defeated oilman Frank Buttram of Oklahoma City in a runoff election. E.K. Gaylord, the powerful publisher of the *Daily Oklahoman* and *Oklahoma City Times*, wrote a series of front-page editorials and uncomplimentary articles about Alfalfa Bill, but rather than persuade voters against him, these tactics seemed to help sway public opinion toward Murray. (102) At this point many Oklahoma citizens, who were staunchly anti-establishment, liked the idea of having a "hayseed," as Murray was called by Gaylord, representing them.

Across the country, the Great Depression was underway and by the 1930s, it began taking a foothold in Oklahoma. The first stages of the depression in the state included the predictable steps of falling prices and growing debts. As had happened several times before in difficult economic times, between 1930 and 1933, ten percent of all Oklahoma farms were sold either because of foreclosures or because their owners had gone bankrupt. Retail sales dropped, along with business and factory employment, and some 37,000 Oklahomans left the cities for farms where they believed they could at least feed themselves and their families. However, the weather did not cooperate, and a long period of drought began. (103)

For Governor Murray, emergency relief was a high priority. Although Murray provided leadership in forming the 1931 National Council for Relief, which served as a guide for Congress as it developed a national program of emergency relief, his system of distribution of federal funds in Oklahoma was so controversial that Henry Hopkins of the national administration made all Federal Emergency Relief Administration workers in the state federal employees. Oklahoma was the only state denied the right to administer its own federal relief program during these years. (104)

By January 1933, the calamity of blowing dust and violent weather fluctuations had begun in earnest. With no rain in the state from February to July 1934, eastern Oklahoma's cotton and row crops were ruined, and only three percent of the western wheat crop was harvested. Although blowing dust diminished somewhat in 1934, it returned with full fury in 1935, and a steady stream of people began moving from the region. (105) Four hundred thousand people from Texas, Missouri, Arkansas, and Colorado joined the one hundred thousand Oklahomans in the exodus to California looking for a better life. Contrary to the picture of the farm-owning "Okies" which developed from Steinbeck's *Grapes of Wrath*, those that joined the throng on the road to California were limited mostly to subsistence farmers, farm workers, and tenant cotton farmers of the southeast part of the state; most of the land-owning wheat farmers in northwestern Oklahoma stayed on their land. The truth was, Oklahoma agriculture could no longer support marginal farmers, and their departure helped stabilize the total state agricultural system. (106)

State Law Enforcement Strengthened

Among those who had been elected to the state legislature in 1930 was Nat Taylor Senior, a teacher in Strong City, representing Roger Mills county. He was well educated and had served as a coach and superintendent before going into public office. Two years later Taylor ran for the Senate, where he was elected and served for the next eight years. Taylor, whose own father had been a Texas Ranger, was the father of five daughters and a son. He was an advocate for public education and also a strong supporter of some type of state police force. Senator Taylor was one of the sponsors of a 1933 bill proposing a law enforcement organization to be known as the Oklahoma State Rangers with a colonel, three lieutenants, six sergeants, and thirty rangers. By the bill's third reading that session, the votes were 19 for, 15 against, 6 not voting, 3 absent and 1 excused. The bill failed passage and was stricken from the record. (107) The concern that Bill Murray and other governors after him might use a state police force as their own private army was enough to keep many senators from backing this bill.

Governor Murray had used the National Guard to enforce a moratorium order aimed at stopping bank runs and bank failures. He also had used state troops to halt production from 3,106 Oklahoma oil wells for a period of 618 days, in order to stabilize the price of oil. Murray then began to use the National Guard troops to enforce his wishes or court orders. During his four years in office, from 1930 to 1934, he called out the National Guard twenty-seven times and declared martial law thirty-four times for such diverse reasons as: guarantee the sale of skimmed milk to the poor; close an Oklahoma City park to blacks; protect his friend, Colonel "Zach" Miller of the 101 Ranch from jail for failure to pay alimony; collect tickets at University of Oklahoma football games; and block the Red River Bridge in a dispute with Texas. (108) Many citizens began to be very wary of the governor's use of the state's National Guard troops.

Although the bill calling for the Oklahoma State Rangers was not passed, the first step toward law enforcement on Oklahoma's roads was taken by the same legislature. A bill from the Senate was incorporated with one from the House calling for "enforcement officers" within the State Highway Commission. The resulting bill, which was signed into law on April 26, 1933, provided for six officers to be assigned to the Highway Commission and another six to the Tax Commission "for the Enforcement of the Laws, Rules and Regulations relating to the Public Highways of the State of Oklahoma and the Operation of Motor Vehicles thereon . . ." This same bill also created the five-member State Highway Commission that Governor Murray had wanted. (109)

In addition, the state's liquor laws were liberalized after the national repeal of prohibition in 1933. The referendum authorizing the sale of 3.2 beer, arbitrarily defined as nonintoxicating, was overwhelmingly successful in urban centers and in fifty-seven of the seventy-seven counties. Only the most western counties maintained anti-beer majorities. (110) Many believe that the state's citizens wanted to maintain their public position that liquor was bad for people, but in reality, wanted to allow for some personal legal use of alcohol. Regardless of these changes, on the highways and byways of the state, bootleggers and drunk drivers continued to be hazards on the roads.

As Bill Murray's turbulent administration was coming to a close in 1934, E.W. Marland's successful campaign in the governor's race used the slogan, "Elect me and bring the New Deal to Oklahoma." When he lost his oil fortune, Marland had turned to politics and saw in the New Deal an outlet for his humanitarian beliefs. After a term in Congress, 1933-1934, he entered the Democratic gubernatorial primary and won. He viewed his success during hard times as a compelling mandate to carry out the mission of the New Deal. Voters for Roosevelt in 1932 and for Marland in 1934 believed in the New Deal's general ambition of recovering the economy and preventing future depressions. In practice, however, the national program's general philosophy clashed directly with Oklahoma's historical development. Pioneer tradition always allowed for both individual and communal efforts, but individualism was seen as the source of progress. Communal actions were found acceptable in emergencies or to help sustain individual achievement through public schools, free textbooks, or public roads. But to many, the New Deal involved too much regulation and planning and it proposed to curb the individualistic pioneer ethic. It also seemed to threaten states' rights, skirt the dangerous "problem of the Negro," and frighten many with the prospect of good intentions hardened into bureaucracy. (111) As they had done numerous times before, especially on liquor issues, many Oklahomans had voted one way, while harboring deep feelings for another, and so E.W. Marland was elected governor.

Although Marland had won by a majority that was unprecedented up to that time, his own leadership style did not allow him to accomplish the changes he promised during his campaign. He attempted to run the state as he would a corporation, with him providing the vision and leaving department heads and legislators to work out the details that would bring about the changes. He did not have enough political power or a strong enough constituency group to withstand the various forces pulling back toward the focus on individualism that had always shaped Oklahoma politics. (112) However, during his administration Governor Marland was able to accomplish the task of beginning a highway patrol in Oklahoma.

One of Marland's first acts as governor-elect in November 1934, was to allocate $57,000 to call in a group of experts in government from the Brookings Institution of Washington, D.C., to study state problems and to make recommendations for their solution. Late in 1935, the group completed its long and careful study of Oklahoma's governmental structure, and wrote a lengthy report. (113) Among the recommendations were those for the establishment of a state police force, a drivers license law, and training for sheriffs and other police and peace officers in the state. (114)

Officials in Marland's administration began laying the groundwork for a state police force. With the increase in numbers of vehicles on the nation's roads highway safety had become a major issue across the country. Representatives from Oklahoma attended the National Accident Prevention Conference in September 1935, and the twenty-fifth annual National Safety Conference in Atlantic City, New Jersey on October 5-9, 1935, where they found out what other states were doing to address highway safety problems. The state published the *Annual Report :Safety Division of the State Highway Commission: Year Ending October 31, 1936*. Of its many recommendations, the publication called for voluntary reporting of all automobile accidents by local law enforcement persons within a twenty-four hour period. The Safety Division had begun keeping a spot map to identify the locations of accidents on Oklahoma's roads but often had to rely on a clipping service to get information from local newspapers. The report also stated that 648 vehicles had been involved in fatal accidents between October 31, 1935 and October 31, 1936.

An article included with the report stated that after Iowa had converted its motor vehicle inspection force into a Highway Safety Patrol, their traffic deaths had dropped within five months. The article did not mention the six-man enforcement team in Oklahoma that had been authorized by Governor Murray in 1933, but it stated that a Highway Patrol in Oklahoma with six men, had been organized by Gov. Marland in 1935 in conjunction with new Highway Commission appointments. A summary of activity by the small patrol force during the first four months of 1936 indicated that they had arrested and filed charges against 93 drunk drivers, 56 reckless drivers, and 35 drivers for miscellaneous violations. Warning tickets had been issued to 1,250 motorists driving cars without tail lights, 925 with only one head light, 150 trucks without proper clearance lights and 100 cars without adequate brakes. Thirty motorists who were out of gas had been helped. Several hundred motorists had been given assistance by having their disabled cars towed to garages, pulled out of ditches or having help summoned. This information helped make the case that there was a need for a larger highway patrol force—one that had law enforcement powers.

During the Fifteenth Legislature in 1935, there were four House bills and one Senate bill proposing a state-wide police force. Each of the bills called for a comprehensive police force to include the State Fire Marshals office and the State Bureau of Criminal Identification and Investigation. However, none of these bills passed. (115)

Most citizens of the state did not want a strong state arm of the law that would carry too much authority over them, nor did politicians and administrators of other agencies threatened by such a force want to lose their autonomy or power. Nonetheless, legislators continued in earnest to try to find a way to deal with the growing problems on the highways. Senator Taylor traveled to Iowa with other Senators and Oklahoma government officials to look at the model of a highway patrol that had been instituted there. Other state legislators and government officials traveled to other states with similar forces to find out what they were doing in this area.

Department of Public Safety Established

In 1937, during a turbulent session of the legislature, state lawmakers crafted bills that they believed would provide the enforcement needed on the state's increasingly dangerous roads, but would not be seen as a threat by citizens and local leaders throughout the state. A Senate bill calling for a Department of Public Safety was stricken when it was determined that a House bill creating a Department of Motor Vehicles had enough support to pass. Finally, House Bill No. 26 was signed on April 20, 1937, creating the new Department of Public Safety with three divisions: highway patrol, registration, and traffic control. Other related bills that were signed into law at the same time were those dealing with drivers licenses, vehicle licenses and registrations, and motor vehicle excise taxes. (116)

The escalating problems on Oklahoma highways had finally forced state legislators to take action. With a climbing death toll which was approaching 650 per year, unenforced traffic laws and regulations, and the increasing mobility of criminals, the citizens of Oklahoma had reluctantly chosen to allow the state to begin a highway patrol with police powers but with great legislative control and oversight. In early 1937, the new Oklahoma Department of Public Safety with its Registration, Traffic Control, and Highway Patrol Divisions began to take form.

CHAPTER 2
THE FORMATIVE YEARS OF THE PATROL
1937-1946

Newspapers across the state carried information about the new highway patrol that was being planned at the state capital to help prepare the citizens of Oklahoma for the coming changes. Beginning in early April 1937, articles in local papers described the proposed Oklahoma Highway Patrol which was a part of Senate Bill No. 72 and House Bill No. 26 being discussed in the state legislature. According to an article on the front page of the *Enid Daily Eagle* dated April 5, 1937, the basic differences between the views of the two legislative branches were that the House wanted 77 patrolmen with duties limited to highway safety and automobile laws and the Senate wanted 100 patrolmen with broader police powers. Rumors about the new highway patrolmen jobs had spread as legislators worked within their districts to gain support for the bill. Early plans for the patrol included the provision that the troopers would come from all areas of the state; one from each county, resulting in the 77 member force favored by the House. For many young men and their families, who were coming out of the Depression, with millions in the country still out of work, this was good news—the possibility of a job with the state government, one with some security and a regular paycheck.

After much debate and discussion between the House and the Senate, House Bill No. 26, authorizing the new

Department of Public Safety, was tied together with House Bill No. 7, requiring driver licenses and excise tax on motor vehicles. These bills were approved by both the House and Senate and were sent to the governor to be signed on April 20, 1937. (1) Governor Marland had not been waiting for the bills to be passed and signed before he moved forward with his hopes and plans for the new Department of Public Safety. He had appointed J. M. Gentry as State Safety Director in 1935, two years prior to the authorization of the department, and Gentry began making plans for the department long before the matter had been settled in the legislature. A United Press (UP) article appeared in the *Enid Daily Eagle* dated April 19, 1937, describing a trip Commissioner Gentry made with Jack Treadwell, head of the Oklahoma Highway Department. They were in Des Moines, Iowa studying the Iowa highway patrol system which had served as one of the models for the proposed Oklahoma Highway Patrol.

Publicity for the newly-formed highway patrol continued. By April 22, summaries such as the one from the Taloga *Times-Advocate* "State House Chatter" column stated, "Oklahoma is launching a notable experiment in civil service and state police system. The measure authorizes not to exceed 113 highway patrolmen to be appointed as far as possible and practicable from every county of the state. These are temporary appointments, the patrolmen serving one year on probation but they can be dismissed anytime in a year. After they have been on the job a full year and have proved entirely satisfactory to the commissioner then they are NOT REMOVABLE except for cause before a special board consisting of the chairman of the highway commission, the attorney general, and the commissioner of public safety. These hearings must be public so that everyone can know why the patrolman is being dismissed, and what charges are that were against him."

In Carmen, a small town in northwest Oklahoma, 27-

year-old Eugene Clark had been reading about the new highway patrol, and he could hardly wait to get an application. The requirements included being between the ages of 25 to 35 years old, at least 5 feet 10 inches in height, weight of more than 160 pounds, in good health, a high school graduate or its equivalent, and a resident of Oklahoma for more than two years. The salary would be $1,800 per year. Clark knew that he fit the description perfectly. He was living in his home town with his wife and two little boys and was trying to scratch out a living by working in the drugstore and doing odd jobs. His parents had lost their farm during the Depression and were finally making a go of a cafe in Carmen, but it couldn't support two families. Clark completed his application and sent it in well before the deadline.

Jack T. Smith was attending pharmacy school at the University of Oklahoma in Norman. He heard about the new highway patrol and decided that he would try to be one of the first recruits. He had met a young school teacher and hoped to get married. A state job with a regular income and some security seemed to be just what he needed. He sent in his application and waited for a response.

For many people in Oklahoma, news of the activities in the legislature and the newly forming highway patrol was put in the background as world happenings dominated the newspapers. Their attention was drawn away from the diffuculties they faced in their day-to-day lives and allowed to focus for a time on the coronation of a new King of England and the subsequent wedding of Wally Simpson and the Duke of Windsor. These events captured the headlines and the imaginations of many Oklahomans.

The sixteenth legislative session was not a smooth one, and a fistfight on the floor of the house crowded onto page one of the *Enid Daily Eagle* on May 8, 1937. The article stated, "James C. Nance, house floor leader, knocked Rep. F.N. Shoemake, chairman of the appropriations committee, to the floor of the house with his fist today during debate on the $7,000,000 departmental appropriations bill. Fellow members and sergents-at-arms plunged forward and separated the two. Shoemake was bruised about the left eye. Both men apologized to each other and to the house." By May 12, it was announced: "Legislature Ends Hectic Session Amid Charges of 'Rotten Tactics'." These examples are illustrative of the legislative atmosphere in which the highway patrol was begun. (2)

Commissioner Gentry began new efforts to regulate the highways even before his new troopers were ready. On May 13, 1937, Gentry announced the creation of a "baby patrol" made up of patrolmen and investigators formerly with the title division of the highway department. There were twenty men in ten cars working from 5 p.m. until morning. Their job was to patrol principal highways from Oklahoma City outward for a distance of 40 miles. They were to "show no mercy to drunken drivers and keep careful watch over trucks, especially their lights". (3)

First Patrol School

Eugene Clark and Jack Smith were among the more than 500 Oklahoma men who sent in their applications to become highway patrolmen. On Saturday, May 15, 1937, Department of Public Safety Commissioner, J. M. Gentry and his newly appointed chief of the highway patrol, R.J. "Jack" Hitch and assistant chief, Ted Kurtz, began interviewing all of the applicants who qualified. Eugene Clark described the following sequence of events. He received a letter telling him to report to the new headquarters at Northwest 10th and Broadway in Oklahoma City for an interview on June 6, 1937, at 10:00 a.m. He was the first man to be seen that morning, and as he walked out after the session, he met a friend he had played baseball against, H.A. Stafford from Fairview, who was to be next. Clark told him what they had asked him and wished Stafford luck in his interview. By June 10, 123 men, including Clark, Jack Smith, and H.A. Stafford, had been selected for the first patrol school to be held for three weeks at the University of Oklahoma campus in Norman. In keeping with the laws and the customs of the state at the time, a number of cadets were of Indian blood, but none of them were "colored," or of African descent. (4)

The time and effort Commissioner Gentry had spent planning for the new patrol training was apparent as the school prepared to open. On some of the visits to operations in other states, Gentry and other state officials had made contacts that would aid in their efforts to establish this new organization. They brought in two out-of-state instructors for the patrol school. Richard Tubbs from East Lansing, Michigan, a corporal with the Michigan State Police, and David R. Peterson, marksman and military drill instructor for the Maryland State Police, came to Norman for the school. The school followed military-type training procedures, and the recruits formed bonds similar to those formed in boot camps. As happens in many intensive settings, most men left the experience not only with close relationships but also with nick-names that followed them throughout their careers on the Oklahoma Highway Patrol.

Clark described some of his vivid memories of the first patrol school. "I was made 'Master of Arms.' I didn't know any more what a Master of Arms was than a man in the moon. I hadn't been in the service. Norman Holt [another cadet] came in the first night, after I had just stretched out on my bunk. He yelled, 'Attention Cadet Clark!' I just about fell out of bed as I jumped up to try to come to attention. But he was just kidding." Clark quickly learned what he needed to know to be a Master of Arms, with responsibilities similar to a "sergeant at arms" who preserves order and executes commands in an organization, and carried out these responsibilities during the school.

One of the publications used in the school was a newly published 109 page booklet titled, *Oklahoma State Laws and Rules Regulating Use of the Highways*. No new traffic laws had been passed by the sixteenth legislature; rather, the new troopers were to enforce the "Ten Rules of the Road" which had been established in 1927 and served as Oklahoma's traffic laws until 1949. (Appendix A) Another publication used with the cadets was the 147 page *Training Manual* which outlined the following areas of focus for the three-week patrol school:

> The Department of Public Safety
> Close Order Drill and Discipline
> Motor Pool
> The Patrol Car — Driving and Care
> Safety Education and Traffic Engineering
> Accident Investigations
> Investigation and Preparation of Criminal Cases
> Firearms and Marksmanship
> Jui Jitsui and Self-Defense
> Fingerprints
> Photography for Patrolmen
> Court Procedure
> Criminal Law
> Federal Laws
> Public Relations
> Public Speaking
> General Geography of Oklahoma
> Highways of Oklahoma
> 100 Points of Interest in Oklahoma
> Appendix: Suggested List of Readings for Patrolmen

Commissioner Gentry, Chief Hicks, and Assistant Chief Kurtz had been very selective in hand-picking the first Oklahoma highway patrolmen. Their high and virtually impossible expectations are reflected in the following description of the ideal patrolman found in the training manual.

THE ESSENTIALS OF A PATROLMAN

1. He must be a reference library and information bureau.
2. He must be a doctor and nurse, capable of handling everything from attempted suicides to fractured skulls; from severed arteries to epileptic fits.
3. He must be a skilled marksman.
4. He must be a boxer, wrestler and jujitsu expert.
5. He must be a sprinter who only runs towards danger.
6. He must act as male governess, tutor and model to children.
7. He must be a diplomat and a two-fisted go-getter at the same time.
8. He must be a memory expert, a psychologist and criminologist and an authority on a multitude of subjects.
9. Upon occasion he must act as judge and jury, as well as attorney for both defense and prosecution, playing four roles at the same time and, finally, decide whether to make an arrest or suffer the consequences.
10. He must be loyal, versatile and adaptable.
11. He must have the wisdom of Solomon, the Courage of Daniel, the Strength of Samson, the Patience of Job, the leadership of Moses, the kindness of the Samaritan, the strategy of Alexander, the faith of David, the diplomacy of Lincoln, and the tolerance of Confucius.

The description of the ideal patrolman concluded with this citation from the *Holy Bible*:

Get wisdom, get understanding: forget it not; neither

decline from the words of my mouth. Forsake her not, and she shall preserve thee; love her, and she shall keep thee. Wisdom is the principal thing; therefore get wisdom: and with all thy getting get understanding. Take fast hold of instruction; let her not go: keep her; for she is thy life.

> PROVERBS, Chapter 4: 5-7, 13.

In an effort to keep the public informed and ease the arrival of new law enforcement officers into the communities all across the state, the *Daily Oklahoman* newspaper chronicled the training of the new patrolmen and decisions about their duty assignments as they occurred. One article featured photographs of the new recruits in their khaki uniforms and caps in formation on the first day of the school. However, by the second day, June 12, 1937, some of the political controversy that had plagued the formation of the patrol reoccurred, and the headlines on the front page of the *Daily Oklahoman* read, "Road Patrol Meal Expense Draws Blast". The article described a concern that a former state legislator had contracted to feed the new recruits for $2.10 per day, and others had not had an opportunity to bid on the contract. The costs paid per meal were $.50 for breakfast, $.60 for lunch, and $1.00 for dinner. In spite of this controversy, the school continued. Later news publications featured a photograph of new recruits with their instructors and another with them standing beside their patrol cars and motorcycles.

Eugene Clark recalled the motorcycle training he received at the patrol school. "They had sixteen little Indian Chief motorcycles for us to learn on. I had never ridden a motorcycle in my life, but I had ridden bicycles and just wore 'em out. When I got on for my first ride, the instructor, a former Tulsa police officer, said for me to ride around the track one time in low gear. The first time I rode, I did that.

When I got back, he said, 'That's fine.' A day or two later, after circling the track in low gear each time, I thought I knew how to ride—but I didn't. The next time I got on, as soon as I was out of the instructor's sight, I turned the damn thing on high. I just went to beat the band. When I got back, he bawled me out. He said, 'You're not gonna ride anymore! You disobeyed my orders!'" Clark concluded with a chuckle, "Well that was all right with me; I hadn't liked the motorcycle very well anyway."

On July 3, 1937, an article on page three of the *Daily Oklahoman* discussed the issue of patrolmen assignments. Commissioner Gentry had announced that "no patrolman will be assigned to his own community. Each will be stationed as far to the opposite side of the state as possible. This is to eliminate any chance of partiality in dealing with friends and acquaintances who are stopped for violations of the law." The article also reported that the new patrolmen would be sent to temporary assignments until September 1, and would not have the opportunity to see their families until then. After that, each would be placed in a nine month assignment to complete his probationary period. The article continued, "While on the road, patrolmen will have all expenses paid. In addition they will receive $150 per month. Sergeants will receive $200 per month and expenses."

Jack Smith described how he learned of his patrolman's salary raise during the first patrol school's graduation ceremony. "They had told us we would make $125 per month when we started the school. When the commissioner announced that we would actually make $150, we all shouted and threw our hats into the air! That was a good raise to happen so quickly."

By the end of the first school, 86 of the 123 recruits were graduated. Eugene Clark, known as "Chick," commented about his fellow cadets. "A lot of them quit right away. They didn't like the military training. One had to resign because he kept getting drunk." In order to fill all of the allocated positions, another patrol school began within thirty days of the first. Some of the graduates from the first patrol school remained at the Norman campus to help with training in the next school.

The Second Patrol School

Two candidates for the second patrol school were Otis Haltom from Hopeton and Vernon Sisney from Geary. Haltom had gone to school at Northwestern State Teachers' College in Alva, where he played on the football team. He quit school before graduating to teach in a one-room school. After one year, he realized that he didn't like teaching very much, and with a family to support, he needed a regular year-round income. The highway patrol sounded like just what he was looking for. Sisney had attended the University of Oklahoma, where he was a wrestler and had won a national championship in college wrestling. In the late 1930s, they didn't have scholarships as such; the coaches helped students get jobs to pay their way. Sisney explained, "I worked at the cafeteria for my board. I lived in Bennie Owen's basement and did handyman jobs around his place for my room." Sisney was at the university for six years and completed a Master's Degree in Psychology before signing on to attend the patrol school.

Although there were stringent qualifications for selection of candidates for the patrol school, exceptions were made. With a mischievous sparkle in his eye, Sisney recounted his experience in joining the patrol, "I wasn't quite old enough to join the highway patrol, and I wasn't quite tall enough or heavy enough either. I stated that I was the right age, because I soon would be that age, but I couldn't stretch my height enough to meet the requirement. So I challenged them to bring out anyone they chose, whatever his size, and I'd take him." His record as a champion wrestler had made a difference. Sisney laughed as he concluded, "They let me join." The second school was as intensive as the first, and at the end of the three-week session fifty-two men were graduated to join the others in the assignments across the state.

While the second school was in session, some of the graduates from the first school began the process of going out to the communities across the state to work with local law enforcement officers and citizens. An article in the *Daily Oklahoman* on Saturday, July 10,1937, had the headline, "State Patrol To Get First Test On Road." The article stated that thirty-six men would be dispatched to six divisions on Saturday and Sunday on a preliminary tour "to get the feel of the thing and get acquainted with city and county peace officers." The participants were listed in the following way:

Tulsa:	Car #1	Albert Briscoe — Acting Sergeant
		Roy Blankenship
	Car #2	C.B. Powers
		J.W. Boyce
	Motorcycle #1	Charles G. Williams
	Motorcycle #2	F.W. (Doc) Pendleton
Muskogee:	Car #1	Leonard Fox — Acting Sergeant
		Gene Barnes
	Car #2	Harold Stafford
		Ormus Soucek
	Motorcycle #1	Archie Hamilton
	Motorcycle #2	Jackson Webb
McAlester:	Car #1	Howard Cress — Sergeant
		Christopher (Spot) Gentry
	Car #2	John Reading
		Cecil Snapp
	Motorcycle #1	Raymond Reus
	Motorcycle #2	John Boyd
Lawton:	Car #1	Eugene Riggs — Acting Sergeant
		Leo Bellieu
	Car #2	H.B. (Burhead) Lowrey
		Rex O. Presley
	Motorcycle #1	Sylvester Smith
	Motorcycle #2	William (Boots) Acton

Enid:	Car #1	Paul Montgomery — Acting Sergeant
		J.W. Wheeler
	Car #2	Grady Neal
		Archie Merriott
	Motorcycle #1	Johnny Hayes
	Motorcycle #2	O.P. Fagala
Perry:	Car #1	Andrew Jackson Roberts — Acting Sergeant
		Dudley P. Lester — Acting Sergeant
	Car #2	Stratford Duke
		Leedee Hunter
	Motorcycle #1	Jack Cochran
	Motorcycle #2	Carl M. Johnson

First OHP Troopers Go on the Roads

On July 11, 1937, the *Daily Oklahoman* listed the assignment of each new trooper for the remainder of July through September 1. The headline again emphasized that troopers would not patrol their home sectors. Six trailers which were to serve as troop headquarters had been sent out to the locations selected and set up. And on July 12, the first new troopers went to their assignments. Most were in three-man units, with one man working days and two men working at night on a rotating basis. There were sixteen troopers assigned to a motorcycle squad known as the "Flying Squadron." These men were to move across the state for special patrolling purposes. Captain Dale Petty assigned each trooper within the designated area. A week later, Petty would round up the cycle squad leaving for another area where the process would be repeated. (5)

The *Sunday Oklahoman* ran a feature article on July 18, 1937, which had individual photographs of each new trooper, the names of their home towns and their new assignments, and a map of the state showing the locations of the fifty-nine stations or trooper units. Citizens could easily check to be sure that no trooper was assigned to work in an area close to where he lived and could also see what each trooper looked like.

The article said in part, "Here are the men of the highway patrol who are now blanketing the state to promote safety on the roads. It will be their duty to aid motorists in distress, to issue courteous warnings to minor offenders, and to deal with dangerous drivers through the courts, but this is not the limit of their powers, although it is their primary purpose under laws creating the state public safety department. Patrolmen carry commissions giving them the powers of a peace officer. They will enforce laws governing commercial carriers and excises[sic] taxes on gasoline. They will serve warrants and aid in apprehending criminals. They will serve in emergencies as state police, on any assignment the governor directs."

The article further identified the location of the six headquarters each having ten patrol units within its district. The commanding officers of the new Highway Patrol, Commissioner J.M. Gentry, Assistant Commissioner H.E. Bailey, Chief Jack Hitch, and Assistant Chief Ted Kurtz, were also pictured. F.D. (Dale) Petty was listed to work at the Oklahoma City office; his assignment was to be the driver for Governor Marland. Transportation and security for the governor was not mandated by statute but was the prerogative of the governor and, as years passed, became a custom.

Trooper Jack Smith was assigned to Clinton, where Paul Montgomery, from Oklahoma City, was Sergeant. Chick Clark described his first assignment as a trooper. "I went to Muskogee. They made one of the troopers sergeant. The one that was with us was a former boxer that acted kind of punch drunk. We called him 'Punch Drunk' Fox. There were six of us, and we set up our headquarters. We were all working, but we weren't doing much because we didn't have much to do at first."

Clark continued with a smile, "All we had was our

khaki uniform and a cap. I didn't even have a gun, so I borrowed a pistol from a Muskogee motorcycle cop. I guess I thought I needed a gun because I might have to shoot somebody," he laughed. Clark remembered that the people who knew what the new highway patrolmen were there for were cooperative. But he recalled that there were some who disliked them from the beginning. "The sheriff in Okmulgee county couldn't stand us at first. He thought we were there to take his job. Once he figured out that we were there to help, he was just fine."

A July 13, 1937, *Daily Oklahoman* article described one reporter's two-hour cruise with troopers on their first day of patrolling. The reporter wrote that there was much safety work needed with drivers on Oklahoma roads. Running stop signs, lack of headlights, and driving too close were some of the areas highlighted. The article also stated that troopers were using "courteous correction" to help citizens become more safety conscious. The article reminded the public that the highway patrol had responsibility for monitoring all highways with all enforcement powers with the exception of serving civil processes. They were responsible for providing assistance to motorists, making spot checks for vehicle safety, making safety education talks at schools and civic organizations, as well as driving and providing security for the governor.

At the beginning of August 1937, graduates from the second patrol school went out to their assignments. Otis Haltom, who had become an expert motorcycle rider, was assigned to the "Flying Squadron" based in Edmond. Clark laughed as he reported that Haltom was called "Old Square Pants" among some of the troopers, but more often he was called "Oatie."

Vernon Sisney described his first assignment as a trooper. "They sent me over to McAlester on a little Indian '74 motorcycle. It took me eight hours to get over there because about one mile from Dale, I ran out of gas. They had emphasized that we must never leave our equipment, so I walked the motorcycle to a service station at Dale. When I told the attendant that I was out of gas, he asked, 'In both tanks?' Well, I had no idea there were two tanks on it. He showed me how to change the tank over, but to make sure I could make it all the way, I filled the empty tank with gas anyway. By then, the patrol had a call out for troopers to be looking for me. When I finally got to McAlester, they put me in a car. We didn't have our uniforms or a pistol. They had us wear khaki pants and shirts and a cap that looked like a cab driver's. They did give us a shotgun to carry in the car." These were 12 gauge model 97 Winchester shotguns with an open bore but no choke. The shotguns were loaded with 00 buckshot and slugs. (6)

Sisney continued, "One of the first days I drove down the street in McAlester, feeling very proud to be an Oklahoma Highway Patrolman, a man came out and tried to stop me by waving and calling out, 'Taxi! Taxi!' Now, that made me feel kind of bad. But most citizens were in awe of the new highway patrolmen."

As with most new organizations, many adjustments had to be made in the highway patrol as it was being put into place. At first each patrol unit was assigned to specific roads. But, within two months, it became clear that troopers needed more discretion in patrolling where they were needed, and the assignments were changed to the roads of specific counties.

In order to provide needed follow-up, a centralized system to keep track of warnings for vehicles in need of repair was devised by the Department of Public Safety. The patrolman gave a postcard to the citizen who received the warning. This card was to be mailed to the department after the repair was completed and the card signed by the mechanic who had made the repair. This information was compiled and used when it was time to renew the license tag on the vehicle. A new tag was not issued until there was verification that the repairs had been completed. However, troopers charged with keeping unsafe vehicles off of the roads did not always want to wait for this lengthy procedure to pressure citizens into getting needed repairs.

Vernon Sisney gave an example of how he dealt with this problem and how much he had to learn about the law and how to enforce it. "We new troopers enforced the law the best we knew. We had to learn as we went. They gave us a framework about the laws we were to enforce, but we had to go out and learn a lot on our own. One of my first learning experiences had to do with a guy who didn't have tail lights on his car. I wrote him a warning and told him to get them fixed. Later I came upon him, and he still didn't have the tail lights fixed, so I impounded his car."

Sisney continued, "It wasn't long until the constable came and told me I had to let the man have his car because he had a 'replevin.' Now I didn't know what a replevin was, so I got on the phone to Oklahoma City. They said I had to let him have his car." (The replevin was a legal document indicating that the car had been illegally taken.)

He concluded, "But I figured out that the next time I saw him on the road without tail lights, I could arrest him and impound his car again. So I told the man, 'You are on private property now, but as soon as your car is in the street, I'm going to arrest you again.' We had to deal with things as we went along. He got the lights fixed." The new troopers had to quickly learn many legal terms and actions which the public and their attorneys used, and they also learned how to use the law to their own advantage.

Troopers also learned how to circumvent or bend the law a little in some cases. Chick Clark recounted one of his first experiences as a trooper in Muskogee and how he and his partner worked with a law enforcement officer in another state. "Bob Lester and I were working together. We got a call that a blind man had been robbed by some gypsies of $13.10. Our sergeant said, 'Go get 'em,' so we left in our '37 Ford. At every filling station we'd come to, they'd say that the gypsies had just been there, got a gallon of gasoline, and moved on. They told us that they were driving a 1936 Cadillac and were headed to Siloam Springs, Arkansas. Sure enough, we followed them on to Siloam Springs and went to the Chief of Police. He said that he would help us find them, and he took us out to an area under a bridge. There they were, cooking roasting ears on an open fire in one of those old fat rendering kettles. There were two men, two women, two little red-headed boys, and five Bantam chickens."

Clark continued with a smile, "The police chief told them to get into the cars and to come with us. Bob put the two men into the patrol car and took the chief back up to the police station. I was to drive their Cadillac and take the women, kids, and chickens. The chief told us to take them back across the state line and then to arrest them. The back of their car was filled with stuff, and with the live chickens on top, the smell was just awful. Just as we were pulling out, it started to rain, so I had to roll up the window. In all of the commotion, I ran off in a ditch. Bob had to come back, hook on the tow chain, and pull us out. We finally got them back to Muskogee and turned them over to the sheriff [where they could be legally arrested]. What an experience that was!" he concluded with a laugh.

One of the primary functions of the newly authorized Highway Patrol was to help coordinate law enforcement efforts in capturing criminals who were using the state's roads to escape. However, the equipment issued to the new patrolmen did not always measure up to the need. The '37 Ford patrol cars had mechanical brakes, and the new troopers were never sure if they were going to work or not. They had to be ready to pull the emergency brake in case the foot brake didn't work. The cars didn't have heaters or windshield defrosters and certainly no air conditioners. At first there were no radios in their cars, and the troopers had to keep in contact by stopping to use a telephone. In those early years, troopers were pretty much on their own to deal with emergencies and found it difficult and, at times, impossible to communicate with other troopers or agencies.

One of the first coordinated manhunts using local and state law enforcement officers that was documented was to apprehend Pete Traxler, a notorious outlaw who had escaped from prison and was terrorizing southeastern Oklahoma. The media noted that cooperation between the new patrol troopers and sheriffs managed to confine him where he was captured. (7) Contrary to the cut and dried public report of this operation, Vernon Sisney described his view of what may have been the same manhunt soon after he went to McAlester. "Right after I went on the patrol my partner, Arch Merritt, and I were sent to Atoka to help look for an escapee. As we drove about 95 miles per hour in our Ford, with only a shotgun between us, we sure hoped someone else would catch up with him first. Fortunately the sheriff picked him up. That escapee had all kinds of guns, and we only had the one shotgun."

By the fall of 1937, all troopers had been issued a regulation side arm: 38.44 Smith and Wesson Revolver with a five inch barrel that weighed 40 oz. empty. The new Oklahoma Highway Patrol uniforms had also arrived, and troopers were proud to wear the new wool uniforms designed especially for their organization. There were distinctive chocolate brown long sleeved shirts with tan epaulets and shoulder patches worn with black neckties and collar pins with the OHP monogram. They had tan riding pants with a brown stripe worn with knee-high riding boots. Sam Browne belts crossed waists and chests with cross-draw holsters on the left hips. The distinctive tan with black visored caps and badge numbers completed the troopers' uniforms. (Figures 1 and 2) These uniforms gave the men a military presence, one that symbolized an authority behind the badge. (8) Troopers were given an allowance to keep their uniforms cleaned and pressed and were to keep their brass polished and the leather Sam Browne Belts shined. They were also responsible for keeping their own side arms cleaned. The individuals assigned to the three-men units shared responsibility for keeping their vehicle cleaned and serviced and for keeping the shotgun in the patrol car clean and ready to be used if needed.

There were many factors to be considered as the new highway patrol troopers began to work together and to meet the requirements set out by the legislature. Their first priority was safety on the roads. A major responsibility was to investigate wrecks or accidents that occurred in their territory and complete the reports that were sent in to Oklahoma City. For most troopers the memory of their first bad traffic accident was one that stayed with them throughout their careers. Chick Clark shook his head as he recounted a train and car collision that occurred just after he arrived in Sapulpa as a trooper in 1937. "A train hit a car, an old Whippet. In that car was a man, his wife, and two little girls and every thing that they owned. The train hit the car and spread it out over a mile-and-a-half. I got a red checkered tablecloth and went along picking up body parts—bones and flesh. I never did get over that accident. Those innocent little girls . . . . The dad just drove right up in front of that train."

In addition to accident reports, arrest, warning, and patrolling reports were important to document work being done and the impact of new troopers on the roads of the state. Accurate completing of all of these reports was sometimes a problem. Clark recalled, "Gene Barnes was a former police officer from western Oklahoma and was at Muskogee. Our sergeant, Punch Drunk, told us to go down south of town and work an accident. He told Gene to write up the report; he thought Gene knew more than I did. After we worked it, I made out the report and turned it in. Well,

Punch Drunk just tore it up and threw it in the trash. He said that he had told Gene to make it out. Well, Gene was up at the hotel with one of his girlfriends. So I made it out again and had Gene sign it. It was fine with Punch Drunk this time, because Gene had signed it." Through the years, the completion of reports was one aspect of the job most troopers did not enjoy.

By September 1, 1937, the new troopers were reassigned for completion of their probationary periods. Vernon Sisney was sent to Atoka, and Chick Clark was sent to Sapulpa. Most of the married troopers moved their families with them and lived in rented houses or apartments. However, the families of the troopers were not considered when work assignments were made, and any expenses for the move of the family had to be covered by the troopers themselves. To further complicate matters, troopers were transferred frequently, many times with only a few days notice. Otis Haltom, still one of the motorcycle "Flying Squadron" members, moved all around the state, rooming with friends, relatives, or with other trooper's families.

September 1, 1937, had also been the date established for all Oklahomans who qualified, to get a driver license. Drivers of trucks and buses had been required to get their licenses by August 1. Prior to this time anyone who could start a vehicle could drive it on Oklahoma roads. There were eleven license examiners who had been trained in the first patrol school and had gone out into the field in July. These examiners had to type and give their tests in any place the community provided. To get one of Oklahoma's new driver licenses, a person had to be 16 years old, be fingerprinted, and pay the cost of $.50. (9) For many Oklahomans this new licensing procedure marked a direct invasion of the state government into the lives of citizens throughout the state. It would take many years for people who had driven without regulation to accept these new requirements and their enforcement.

During their training, the new troopers had been reminded repeatedly that they must assert their authority without creating undue negative reaction from the public. Their patrol school training manual had stated that "the three major phases of traffic control: engineering, education, and enforcement will (1) reduce accidents, (2) cut down property loses; and (3) increase the pleasure of driving which is rightfully due every motorist under adequate, properly enforced laws." The manual continued, "the chief trouble with present enforcement machinery is that it was designed to deal with criminals. Most traffic violators are not criminals and should not be treated as such."

Reducing traffic fatalities from the 648 in 1936, was one of the patrol's main objectives. Educating the public about traffic laws was one way to bring about change, and removing unsafe vehicles from the highways was another. During the first nine months of the new highway patrol, troopers issued 288,277 warnings compared to 5,518 arrests. During that same period troopers assisted more than 250,000 motorists who were stranded on the highways. (10) Since a large number of Oklahoma's citizens were still struggling from the Great Depression, troopers were well aware that many of the motorists didn't have much money. These people were barely scraping by and didn't have extra money to put into their vehicles. Most troopers and their families were in the same situation, so they were sympathetic toward the average person who was having car trouble. One of the former troopers described the prevailing attitude of most patrolmen at that time. "We would never pass by a car that was stopped along the road. It could have been me or a member of my family who needed help. The tires were poor in those days and many of the vehicles were held together by baling wire. We always tried to make sure anyone who needed help got it." (11) By acting as a friend in need, troopers hoped to foster a positive understanding of the patrol.

To build further good relations with the public, Commissioner Gentry encouraged every trooper to give at least one safety talk each month to school or civic groups. By educating community members about the purpose of the patrol, it was hoped that they would build a more cooperative relationship with the public. During these talks troopers also tried to emphasize the importance of safe driving habits and the need to obey the law.

To remove unsafe vehicles from the roads, troopers not only carried out formal vehicle inspections with roadblocks, but also remained vigilant as they patrolled the roads to identify vehicles that did not have proper lights or brakes. At the end of 1937 the number of fatalities on Oklahoma highways decreased from 648 the previous year to 639. This was not a great improvement, but at least the number was decreasing instead of increasing. Commissioner Gentry was forced to disband the Driver License Examining Corps at the end of 1937 due to lack of adequate funding by the legislature, and this responsibility was added to the highway patrol. Patrolmen had schedule times to give driver's tests in the larger towns in their areas. In addition to meeting their other responsibilities related to cars and drivers, during 1938, troopers inspected 1,823 school buses across the state. There were 269 buses that were removed from the roads because they were unsafe and another 476 that were found to be in only fair condition requiring major repairs. Although there was a separate division in the Department of Public Safety for vehicle safety, it was the highway patrol that had to provide the manpower to accomplish checks needed to remove unsafe vehicles from the state's roads. (12)

The Second and Third Years of the Patrol

By the time the new troopers had completed their probationary first year and were placed on permanent duty, most had been transferred several times. Chick Clark had worked in Muskogee, Sapulpa, and Edmond, before being assigned to Norman. Vernon Sisney had worked in McAlester, Atoka, back to McAlester, and Edmond, before being assigned to Chickasha. By late 1938, the motorcycles from the "Flying Squadron" were dispersed and assigned to individual districts across the state. Otis Haltom, who had been part of this group, was assigned to work in Oklahoma City. In Norman, Chick Clark and his partners, Norman Holt and Arch Hamilton, were all assigned motorcycles in addition to their car. Clark had a Harley Davidson, and Holt and Hamilton had Indians.

Chick Clark described one accident he and his partner investigated while on motorcycles. "One time the bridge on the North Canadian River washed out. Arch and I got a call about an accident in Newcastle in which two people had been killed. A car had hit a watermelon truck. Arch went around on the road, but I decided to ride my cycle across the creek bed. Arch couldn't believe that I was already there when he arrived. We always had some kind of contest or bet going on between us." He concluded shaking his head, "The two girls had been drunk when they hit the watermelon truck parked at Newcastle. They were really torn up bad."

At statehood, Oklahoma law set the limit of its governor to one four-year term. The governor had appointive powers over top officials in the Department of Public Safety: the commissioner and the chief of the patrol. Since these officials controlled the internal organization of the patrol, new policies instituted by incoming governors and commissioners every four years greatly influenced the personnel of the patrol. "For example, if a governor wanted fewer arrests made for political purposes, he could manipulate the patrol leadership through his commissioner and attain the goal. Any captain or lieutenant opposing that new policy could be thrust aside, either demoted, or transferred." (13)

In 1938, Leon Phillips, a former Oklahoma legislator, was elected governor of Oklahoma on a platform of economy and efficiency in state government. He appointed Walter B. Johnson commissioner of public safety. After Phillips took office in 1939, he reminded the legislature that not only was illegal liquor draining money from the state, but drunk drivers were becoming an increasing danger to its citizens. Although sale of 3.2 beer was legal after the repeal of National Prohibition in 1933, illegal liquor was still being brought into Oklahoma from the surrounding states that were wet. Newly appointed Commissioner Johnson directed the patrol to begin what was to become a twenty-year ebb and flow of efforts to enforce Oklahoma prohibition laws, in addition to their primary responsibility of enforcing the state's traffic laws. The Oklahoma Highway Patrol first became involved in enforcing state liquor laws during 1939 and 1940, when they conducted 325 raids arresting 421 men, confiscating 49,000 pints of whiskey, and seizing thirteen automobiles used for hauling the liquor. (14) Over the next two decades, the patrol's involvement in liquor raids vacillated with the leadership of the patrol and the priorities of the governors of the state. Unless they were specifically told to do so, most former troopers interviewed said that they usually hadn't gone looking for illegal whiskey, but if they happened onto it, they had not ignored it.

     The Department of Public Safety's responsibilities were broadened in March of 1939, when Governor Phillips signed a bill abolishing the Bureau of Criminal Identification and Investigation, transferring its duties, records, equipment, and property to the Department of Public Safety. The department began to assume state-wide responsibilities for criminal investigations, and consequently troopers had more responsibility for investigations and follow-up. (15) Fortunately, Commissioner Johnson managed to acquire funds to once more assign eleven driver license examiners to deal with this responsibility full time. Giving tests to drivers was taking up too much of the troopers' time, and there continued to be a large number of Oklahomans who had not yet obtained the required licenses.

During these early years, communication with troopers across the state was a challenge. The patrol cars had radio receivers but no transmitters, so troopers could receive calls, but they had to use the telephone to call back in to let someone know where they were and what they were doing. The local sheriff's radio system was sometimes used by troopers who had established good relationships with those officers. By 1939, the patrol had established a transmitting station in Oklahoma City, KOSO, an experimental one-way AM station, broadcasting on Frequency 1626. This station carried messages to district base stations for the next year, and the radio dispatcher became a key person in each headquarters. Beginning in 1940, the radio operator and radio dispatcher jobs were listed in the Department of Public Safety budget with salaries the same as the troopers, $1800 per year. The support division called the Communication System had begun in 1939, along with another support division termed Transportation. The patrol's fleet of more than 50 cars needed constant service as the three-man patrol units stayed on the roads 18 to 20 hours a day, so mechanics were hired to work on patrol cars full-time.

In 1940, the first two-way radio units were installed in patrol cars, and fifteen-foot wire-wrapped bamboo antennas were attached to the bumpers. The troopers laughed about the "fishing poles" on the backs of their cars. Actually, they did use cane fishing poles to replace the ones issued to them when theirs broke. This antenna system proved inconsistent, with inclement weather often preventing a distant unit from receiving signals from its district base. However, strangely enough, contact was sometimes made with the West Virginia State Police, which was on the same frequency. Some patrol radiomen even received letters indicating Oklahoma Highway Patrol signals had been received as far away as India and China. (16) Although the communications system was a major step toward modernization, the AM network was inefficient and left many troopers out on the roads with no way to ask for help or to coordinate their actions with other law enforcement personnel.

With general attrition from the ranks and the events in Europe that marked the beginnings of World War II, the patrol needed more men. Economic times were still very hard; there were reports that as many as 10 million people nationally were still out of work and children were starving. Under the strong legislative over-sight provisions setting up the Department of Public Safety, the Oklahoma State Legislature had to approve budgetary appropriations every two years, as well as approve the number of troopers that would be allowed. It was up to the governor and the commissioner to request the necessary appropriations from the legislature. (17) Through this political process, funds were made available in 1940, and a new patrol school, the third, was scheduled.

The Third and Fourth Patrol Schools

Otto Rauch, from Oklahoma City, went to the school held in 1940. He recounted the events leading to his becoming a member of the Oklahoma Highway Patrol. "I was working for Carroll, Broughs & Robinson Oklahoma City Wholesale Grocery at 3 East Main. I got tired of unloading freight cars and transporting groceries into a warehouse. I had been reading in the newspaper about the patrol activities and had come to admire the organization. I had broken my big toe, so I couldn't work for a few days. On July 29, 1939, I went out to the highway patrol headquarters on N.E. 23rd at the Oklahoma Emergency Relief Administration building and asked when they were going to have the next school. The lady at the desk said to inquire again about November. I went back in November, and she said, 'Not yet.' She said to come back in the spring. I went back the next spring and filled out an application. Finally on June 9, 1940, I got a letter saying I had been tentatively approved to attend the next patrol school, providing I could pass a number of tests of certain types, not specified. Later I had a physical exam, interviews, and written examinations. I had to go there three times before I got the next letter saying that I had been accepted." He had wanted the job very badly and was willing to stay with the long, drawn-out process until he had the opportunity to attend a patrol school.

The third patrol school was held at Central State Teacher's College in Edmond, beginning on July 20, 1940. Otto Rauch was one of the seventy-six graduates from that scaled back two-week school. At the conclusion of the school, Rauch described how he began his new career. "The Chief, John Reading, thought every trooper should have the experience of giving the driver's license examinations. So I was assigned to give them in Tulsa. I was there for four or five weeks, August 16 through September 19. Then I was assigned to the highway patrol unit in Miami. I actually went on the payroll on September 16, 1940. Hitler had just conquered 5 countries in Europe starting in April and finished up with France in June. President Roosevelt federalized the National Guard beginning on September 16, 1940. Several troopers were in the Oklahoma National Guard, so they left their patrol assignments. One of the men was Cecil Pevy—he wore badge #115. Well, I wore that badge number for many years. I inherited his badge and all of his uniforms, but the only part of his uniform that fit were the neckties," he said with a smile.

Rauch continued, "I started to work on September 21, with W.L. (Hot Ditty) Abbot, and A.E. (Doc) Eaton, who transferred out in December. Then 'Shock' Wilkinson came to Miami. Wilkinson had been in my school. Those of us who made better grades in the academy went to work ahead of those who ranked lower."

The first death of a patrolman killed in the line of duty occurred on May 7, 1941, near Lawton. Trooper Sam R. Henderson, who had joined in 1937, was killed by a hit-and-run driver while he was making a contact with the driver of a vehicle he had stopped for defective lights. This incident had a sobering effect on the remaining troopers.

In 1941, the legislature approved thirty additional patrolmen for the following two years. It established the salary of beginning troopers at $130 a month for the first year, $140 for the second, and $150 for the third and succeeding years. (18) This meant the original troopers did not get a raise, but at least their salaries were maintained. A fourth school was held in Stringtown in 1941, and thirty-eight new troopers were graduated.

These new troopers went on the roads just as a new guide, called *Manual of Uniform Traffic Control Devices for Streets and Highways*, (June 1941) was made available for regulating the use of streets and highways in Oklahoma. Without a state law mandating the types of signs and traffic control devices to be used across the state, each jurisdiction could use whatever it chose. This new guide published by the Oklahoma State Highway Commission and the Oklahoma Department of Public Safety was patterned after the Uniform Act Regulating Traffic on Highways developed on the national level. It was hoped that communities throughout Oklahoma would follow these guidelines, but there was no law requiring it.

The United States was getting ready to enter the war, and the highway patrol was having difficulty keeping troopers. Although Governor Leon Phillips exempted troopers from the draft for one year, many voluntarily enlisted in the armed forces, and others went to work in defense plants. In addition to the manpower shortage, the legislature had passed a budget-balancing amendment, and the budget for the Department of Public Safety was reduced from the $704,897.95 in 1940 to $624,852 in 1941. (19) Costs had gone up, responsibilities had increased, but allocations had gone down. This pattern was to be a problem for the department for years to come.

As men reported to duty in one of the United States armed forces, they were often transported across the country by train or bus. Troop trains became a familiar sight along the rails of Oklahoma. And although they were not romanticized as much, troop buses transporting servicemen where there were no railroads, were common also. Chick Clark described an incident involving one of these buses. "I was working in Enid with Bill Large and Elwood Lee. We had a train hit a bus-load of soldiers. It took Bill and me three report forms to write up all of the details of that accident." Saddened by the thought, Clark did not elaborate on how many were killed in this accident.

When the Japanese attacked Pearl Harbor on December 7, 1941, most of the remaining troopers knew that it was only a matter of time until they would be called on to participate more directly in the war effort. From 1940 until 1943 there were four patrol schools graduating a total of 177 new troopers; however, the number of troopers on duty in the state declined from 140 to 47 during the same time period due to the impact of World War II. (20) The fifth patrol school was held at Central State College in the summer of 1942, and thirty-two new patrolmen were graduated.

The highway patrol attempted to stretch its manpower as much as possible. During 1942, Otto Rauch, who was still single, had nine different assignments, Muskogee, Bartlesville, Oklahoma City, Chandler, Wewoka, McAlester, Sallisaw. McAlester, and Lawton. With the war on, the number of troopers kept declining. Rauch described the excessive work-load some troopers had at this time. "One of the troopers assigned to Snyder said he was responsible for five counties where he investigated eighteen fatality accidents during just one war year."

On July 12, 1942, Oklahoma Highway Patrolman James A. Long, who had joined the patrol only months earlier, was shot and killed in Oklahoma City while trying to assist an eighteen year-old girl who was being beaten. The murderer was never apprehended. Although there was a war on and servicemen were being killed every day, the new patrol recruits as well as the troopers on the roads were forced to realize that they could be shot and killed right there in Oklahoma.

C.A. Morris Joins the Patrol

There were several patrol schools of short duration held from 1942 through 1944, to meet emergency manpower needs. The stringent requirements of height, weight, and age had been relaxed a bit to allow for men who would not have previously qualified as a patrolman. The state was in dire need of new troopers.

C.A. Morris, my dad, was teaching U.S. Government and History and coaching at the High School in Piedmont, where he and my mother owned a home and had added two more children to their family. (21) Although he was a popular teacher who also performed in school plays and coached boys basketball and track, he was not really happy being tied down in a classroom. He was also concerned about making a living for his wife and three small children. Teachers only got paid for nine months and then had to figure out how to make some money for the remaining three months of the year. Dad often said, "You know, my kids eat all twelve months."

Although he had grown up in Kansas, Dad had graduated from Northwestern State Teacher's College in Alva, where he played football with Otis Haltom, who had gone on the patrol in 1937. Often Trooper Haltom and his partner, Guilford "Cactus Face" Duggan, a well-known Oklahoma athlete, had ridden their motorcycles out to Piedmont to see Dad where they would talk about their jobs and how much they thought he would enjoy being a patrolman. They knew that he had not always been used to the quiet, small-town life. Before he was out of high school, Dad had hitch-hiked around the country with a friend. Over several years they had traveled from coast to coast sometimes riding the rails, and on one occasion, they had been arrested for vagrancy and briefly jailed. As a former athlete and coach, Dad enjoyed the camaraderie that went along with sports and saw the highway patrol as an opportunity to join a group of men who were having a good time while involved in a noble effort which also was a job with a regular paycheck.

Encouraged by Haltom and Duggan, Dad completed an application for the highway patrol. Within a short time he was contacted and told to come for an interview at 7:30 a.m. Dad, who was a night owl, couldn't imagine that they would start so early in the morning, so he assumed the information was a mistake. He reported at 7:30 p.m. When he got there that evening, the patrol officials laughed at his error and told him to come back the next morning. Dad had always been a bit of a joker, so he laughed along with them as he made fun of himself. But he was concerned that he had made a terrible mistake, and he didn't want to risk missing this opportunity to join the highway patrol. He knew that the patrol had relaxed their requirements somewhat in order to get enough men to be on the force, but he also knew that he was almost thirty-six years old, husky, balding, and just under the height requirement. So the night before the interview, he cut pieces of cotton batting to fit into the soles of his shoes to boost his height a little, and this time he made sure he was there bright and early in the morning. Within a few weeks Dad was notified that he had been selected for training in one of the special patrol schools. Although C.A. Morris was listed with the cadet class of the fifth patrol school, Mother remembered that he did not go to Edmond, nor did he stay away from home at night during his training. He reported to patrol headquarters every day over a two-week period for individual instruction, and then was put out on the road.

Dad was sent to Cushing on August 24, 1942, for his preliminary assignment with Trooper "Mose" Adams. I was only eighteen months old, but my older brother, John who was five, has some memories of these times. Our family stayed at home in Piedmont, and on Dad's days off, we would meet him at Bradbury's Corner, a filling station located at the intersection of Route 66 and Route 77 just east of Edmond. The patrol cars were not supposed to be taken across county lines, so families arranged to shuttle the men back and forth to spend time together until more permanent assignments were made. After the first few months, Dad was assigned to Edmond. He was able to stay with us in Piedmont, although he did receive mail addressed to 420 E. Main in Edmond during that time. While Dad was still in training, his photograph appeared in the *Daily Oklahoman*. He was pictured with Trooper Joe Lenochan and a suspect in a hit-and-run accident. The troopers had traced the driver, a mechanic at Tinker Field and city musician, by some parts which fell from his station wagon when he struck a pedestrian. (22)

Later, Dad's actions were the subject of another newspaper article titled, "Safety Chief Nabbed By Alert Patrolman." The article said, "Rating as a state official doesn't warrant any exceptions to the rules when C.A. Morris, Edmond, state trooper for the highway patrol, is on duty. Wednesday night he hailed a car with only one light at the intersection of Eastern avenue and Twenty-third street and ordered it to the nearest filling station to obtain repairs—the customary procedure in such cases. Occupants of the car were J.M. Gentry, state safety commissioner, and Freeman Scarlett, superintendent of transportation for the patrol." (23) The new governor, Robert S. Kerr, elected in 1943, had appointed Gentry back to the commissioner position. Henry B. Lowrey, an original trooper, was appointed assistant commissioner, and J.M. Thaxton was the new chief of the patrol. Dad's reputation as a no-nonsense trooper had begun.

Troopers were not immune to the dangers from which they were attempting to protect the public. Otto Rauch described an incident that occurred on March 11, 1943, near Lawton. "The trooper who was driving the car was a rookie. He had less than a year of service. I should have said, 'Phil, slow this thing down. We are going too fast, and we can't see where we are going.' We were chasing a car on the highway, and he took off on a dirt road. He was giving us the dirt. The bridge was at an angle on the road. By the time we saw it, it was too late, and we hit it. We didn't have seat belts then. He held onto the steering wheel, so he wasn't hurt, but the bridge got me pretty badly. I broke my left hip and crushed my finger joint. I spent 18 days in Southwestern Hospital."

The Sixth Patrol School and a Special School in 1943

The need for additional troopers continued. Kermit O. (K.O.) Rayburn, who grew up on a farm between Lindsay and Bradley, described the events that led to his joining the Oklahoma Highway Patrol. When Rayburn's dad had asked him what he wanted to do after high school, he replied, "I don't want to cut broom corn or pick cotton." In 1933, he was graduated from high school at Bradley on one Friday night and enrolled at Central State Teacher's College in Edmond on the following Monday morning. While attending college he heard from a friend who had a one-room rural school in Grady County. There were some large girls in the school, and the teacher was small. One day the girls whipped the teacher, and she quit. She called Rayburn and asked if he would be interested in the job. At that time a person could get a one-year teaching certificate by taking an examination. Her call came on Friday, saying they needed a teacher by Monday. Over the weekend he went down to Grady County and talked to the clerk. "He said there was no need to talk to the other School Board Members, because, he said, 'You're all we've got.' I did meet the others and finished the school year there," Rayburn recalled.

The next year Rayburn moved to a three-room school in Garvin County where he was teacher and principal. He worked there nine years. "While teaching, I took classes at Chickasha and Lindsay. I did my practice teaching at the old North Tower at Central State in Edmond and got my Bachelor's Degree there."

"In 1942 the county superintendent came to the school board and told them not to rehire me for the next year. The County Draft Board had given him a list of three teachers in the county who would be drafted, and I was one of them. While waiting to be drafted, I went to work for the Welfare Board, and they sent me to school in Oklahoma City. The first day at noon, I was out walking and passed by the highway patrol headquarters in the Armory near the State Capitol. A lieutenant was standing beside his car, and we started talking. He asked me to come over and attend the school that they were just starting, and I did."

In that summer of 1943, the sixth patrol school was held at Ponca City at a Boy Scout Camp. The accommodations consisted of small stone huts with no windows. Rayburn remembered that he and many of the other cadets took their cots outside where there was a little cool air and they could get some sleep. At the end of the academy there were thirty-one new troopers ready to go on the road.

During the time after Rayburn had completed the

academy but before he was assigned to a unit, he rode one shift with Trooper Vernon Sisney, who had been transferred to El Reno. Sisney stopped a truck driver for drunk driving. Sisney asked Cadet Rayburn if he could drive the truck which had a trailer with a fifth wheel arrangement. Since Rayburn had grown up on a farm, he thought he should be able to drive any kind of truck. But when he got into the cab, he saw two levers where the floor gear shift should be. He started the truck and pulled one lever. Since that didn't put it into gear, he quickly pulled the other one. With relief he heard it go into gear and started to drive the truck down the road. Then he heard frantic honking. He looked back and saw that the first lever had released the trailer, which he was leaving way behind along the roadside.

Rayburn laughed. "A few days later I saw Sisney and asked him if he had booked the driver for drunk driving. 'After what you did to his truck,' Sisney said, 'all I could do was charge him with public drunkenness.'" Thus began a life-long friendship between the two troopers.

After the patrol school, K.O. Rayburn was assigned to an Oklahoma City unit where his partners were Otis Haltom and Guilford "Cactus Face" Duggan. Rayburn recalled, "Duggan was the only patrolman they gave leave to play professional football. At that time we worked shifts of three weeks days and six weeks nights. He was a big, strong man. He was the first All American Lineman from the University of Oklahoma, before he went into the pro ranks. The last team I remember him playing with was the Buffalo Bills. He broke his nose while playing at OU, and they set his nose crooked; that's why they called him Cactus Face." [Others remembered that Duggan often refused to shave during football season at OU and that was the way he got his nick-name.]

Rayburn continued, "Cactus Face lived in Nicoma Park. To stay in shape year round, he bought a little one-horse hack used to deliver milk and a walking breaking plow. He used to break gardens during the day. Since he seldom slept during the day, when he worked nights his partner drove. Cactus Face always made a good contact, but sometimes he was not alert to what was happening. One night when we were working together he was dozing as usual. It was his turn to make the contact when I stopped a car near Spencer for running a stop sign. He got out and started up to the car to make his contact. He suddenly stopped and looked back at me. He said, 'What did he do?' I just looked off, pretending not to hear. He walked on up, and the driver got out of the car. Cactus Face looked back at me again, and I just looked off. He took a couple of steps back toward me and said, 'Little buddy, what did he do?'" Rayburn laughed and said, "I finally told him, and he completed his contact. When he came back to the car, Cactus Face said, 'Don't ever do me that-a-way again,' and he meant it. He and Otis were very good partners for me to start working with."

Leonard Kelsoe, a farm boy from Gotebo, was one of the troopers trained in a special patrol school held in 1943. Kelsoe had been in the U.S. Army and had received a medical discharge because of asthma. He was looking for a job when he heard about the need for patrolmen. There were twenty-three men who started the two-week special school in the Armory Building in Oklahoma City and only eight who were graduated. Kelsoe recalled, "In a short while, there were only three or four of my group left. The others had been told that they were hired only for the duration of the war, but they didn't tell me that. I was the only one from that school that stayed on the patrol." He added, "Actually most of them got fired; there were really some lulus."

Leonard Kelsoe was first assigned to Holdenville and then to Wewoka when a car was moved there. He remembered, "When I was in Wewoka, our territory was 100 miles across, from Coalgate to Okemah. One night I was working on an accident at Okemah and got a call on one at Coalgate. I was working by myself." There was no way one patrolman could complete the investigations required for two accidents that far apart. The scarcity of patrolmen often meant that some things would just be left undone.

My dad completed his probationary year on August 23, 1943. He was assigned to a unit in Oklahoma City which meant that he could continue to live with us in Piedmont. He wrote this postcard to his mother:

"Dear Mother,

> Happy Birthday. I have my year of probation in today. I am living at home now and drive our car to the City every day. I work 12 m.n. [mid night] to 8:00 a.m. Like it fine. Dry here everything burned up. We are all feeling fine and hope you are. Lots of Love, C.A."

Since patrolmen were on the road so much, they stopped at meal times or for night breaks at cafes or truck stops along the Oklahoma highways. Troopers established regular stopping places within their territories. Beverly's, a moderately priced restaurant located just north of the Oklahoma State Capitol building on Lincoln Boulevard, became a popular meeting place for troopers assigned to the Oklahoma City area. (24) It also became a familiar stop for troopers who came in to patrol headquarters for meetings, squad car repairs, or to deliver reports and pick up supplies and equipment. Troopers often arranged to meet at Beverly's when they were in "the City."

As the rest of the country continued to change to meet the requirements of the war, Oklahoma also changed. Major military bases included Tinker Field in Oklahoma City and Fort Sill in Lawton. The state also became one of the major areas through which people traveled to get to the places they were needed. Route 66 turned into "a convoy road. Many stretches were filled with jeeps and trucks transporting troops and arms to the many military bases and forts that dotted the length of the highway. Bus and train stations in the big cities on the route were crowded with servicemen shuttling between duty posts. Uniformed hitchhikers were scattered up and down Route 66." (25) The work of Oklahoma Highway Patrol troopers who remained on duty during the war years was certainly affected by these changes.

The entertainment industry played an important role in supporting war efforts through war-bond rallies and moving pictures. In 1942, the hearts of most Americans were touched by the picture show, *Holiday Inn* and the song, "White Christmas," sung by Bing Crosby. This song became extremely popular and was heard on the radio and juke boxes across the country. Through this music and wide-spread advertising, people all across the United States began to give even more importance to spending holidays with their families. K.O. Rayburn reminisced, "I was feeling sorry for myself for having to work on Christmas, instead of celebrating with my family. I was called to a wreck at 36th and Eastern, and after I took care of the drunk driver who had hit a car, I went over to the lady who had been hit. She was sitting in her car with California tags and crying. I had already asked her if she had been hurt, but I asked her again. She told me that she was crying because she had left Oklahoma and moved to California several years before. She had finally saved up enough money to come home to see her family on Christmas, and now she couldn't get on over to eastern Oklahoma to see them because of the wreck. I knew the wrecker driver real well. When I told him the story, he agreed to loan her a car so she could go on over to see her folks. After that, I didn't feel sorry for myself any more. I felt good that I was able to help someone."

It was important to most troopers to feel like they had made a difference in someone's life.

Rayburn described a more serious incident which occurred at about the same time period with a drunk driver. "One evening I stopped a drunk driver at 36th and Eastern. He was a large Negro man, and when he got out of the car, I saw that he had a straight razor in his hand. I could tell he knew how to use it, because he had the handle in his hand with the blade up over the back of his hand. He started coming at me, and I drew my gun. I didn't want to shoot him, but I knew I would, if he kept coming. I told him to stop, because I wasn't going to let him cut me with that razor. About that time a light went on over my head, and I heard a woman scream. She begged me not to shoot him and said he was a veteran who was home from a psychiatric hospital. I asked her if she could control him, and she said she could. She had him drop the razor, and then she begged me not to put him in jail. I left after she promised to call the hospital to come and get him."

Rayburn concluded, "Later I talked to the sheriff and he said they had a similar incident the last time the man got to come home. He went to a club near his house and got drunk then too. The sheriff said that he would check to be sure he got back to the hospital. I was sure glad I didn't have to shoot him."

One of the primary survival rules for patrolmen was to always have two men working in a car at night. From the first days in patrol school, recruits were reminded about their vulnerability in approaching a car, especially at night. The three-man assignments to units supported that premise. However, the shortage of troopers during the war made it impossible for troopers to maintain this practice and many were working alone.

Leonard Kelsoe recounted an incident that illustrates the need for the presence of a second person in the patrol car. "I was down at Sulphur working with Kenneth Will. I picked Kenneth up to start the night shift, and we got a call on a hit-and-run from one of the towns north. After we got into Davis, this car passed us, and we stopped them. The trooper making the contact always walked up to the side of the car and asked the driver to get out. When I got up there, I saw that the guy had a .38 automatic in his hand. I ducked down behind the door and ran backwards. I came out with my gun and told him to drop it or I'd blow his head off. The only thing that saved me was that he kept looking back to see what my partner was doing. When I walked up to the driver's door, Will had walked to the back of the other side of his car. If I'd been by myself, I wouldn't be here today, I know that. They had a car load of burglary tools. We tried to book them for every charge we could, but their lawyer had bond posted by the next day, and they were out on the street. We found out that the guy killed a man in Oklahoma City three months later."

Auxiliary Patrol Activated

To address the problem of dwindling numbers of troopers on the roads, the state legislature created an Auxiliary Highway Patrol in 1943. The legislature passed House Bill No. 441, authorizing auxiliary patrolmen to "assist in quelling disturbances, facilitating the movement of Federal troops across the State and in enforcing the laws of the State and protecting the highways there of." It gave the Commissioner of Public Safety the authority to deputize "such persons as highway patrolmen and permit the same to equip themselves at their own expense with arms, uniforms and insignia now authorized to be worn and used by regular members of the highway patrol. [These] shall not be regular members of the State Highway Patrol, but only as and when called for special duty, and for only the duration of time required to perform the same. [They] shall not claim equipment or expense." (26)

Under this plan, troopers found able-bodied civilians who could be trained in basic police skills and would ride with them as partners. These auxiliary patrolmen served as the second man in patrol cars at night. Otto Rauch recalled "They proved to be very helpful in working accidents by directing traffic and performing other non-law enforcement duties." They also provided the back-up for troopers as they carried out their duties and stopped to assist stranded motorists or made stops of law violators at night.

Unfortunately not all of the troopers turned out to be hardworking and brave. Leonard Kelsoe described a situation that illustrates this point. "There were two deputy sheriffs killed in the southeastern part of the state. My partner and I were sent to the Waurika Creek Bridge to check the traffic coming through. Well, I stood out there all night checking every car. My partner stood over behind the patrol car with our shotgun in his hand. He said, 'I'm not going out there. You're a dead duck if he comes along.'"

Kelsoe continued, "I told him, 'If you haven't got the guts to do the job you were hired to do, you ought to quit.' I was scared—don't think for a minute that I'm the bravest man on earth. I was scared to stop every car, not knowing if that guy was in there or not. The next day, after we were released, I had my partner drive us on back home. I took the shotgun he had been holding and saw that there was a shell up in the barrel. I tried to eject it, and it wouldn't come out. I held it out the window and pulled the trigger. It just snapped; it wouldn't even shoot. He'd 'a been a big help, if I had needed back-up! He had stood there all night with a gun that wouldn't work." Kelsoe shook his head in disgust.

Manpower was not the only problem the patrol faced. A shortage of gasoline and tires developed, and a complete shutdown of automobile manufacturing meant that a fleet of 1940 and 1941 cars would have to survive the war years. In 1943, the legislature added to the patrol's responsibilities by officially assigning security responsibilities to the Department of Public Safety. Protection of the State Capitol Building, the State Office Building, the State Historical Building, the powerhouse, the Governor's Mansion, and the grounds surrounding them came under the jurisdiction of the Department of Public Safety and the responsibility of the highway patrol. During these changes, the Department of Public Safety was moved from the National Guard Armory at 100 N.E. 23rd Street to a building at the corner of N.E. 36th and Eastern.

In order to maintain coverage on the state's highways, troopers were working fifty-four to sixty hours a week; with twelve-hour work days. The families of the patrolmen, like other American families, were affected by shortages and rationing caused by the war. To buy meat, canned goods, coffee, or sugar, families had to use stamps from rationing books that were issued to each person in the family. The rationing of gasoline and tires also impacted everyone. Even people living in cities began victory gardens where they grew their own vegetables. Recycling began as women turned in their silk and nylon stockings to make powder bags for naval guns, children sent their empty toothpaste tubes for scrap metal drives, and bacon grease was saved to be made into explosives. (27)

There were German prisoners of war housed in Oklahoma prisons at this time. Some were in El Reno and some in Okemah. A much repeated story about Cactus Face Duggan involved one of those prisons. The Germans were getting out of hand and authorities called in the highway patrol and others as reinforcements to deal with the anticipated riot. When the various law enforcement officers assembled, they were being prepared to go in with riot guns. Cactus Face Duggan was one of the patrolmen there that day. According to the story, he said, "Aw, just give us each a baseball bat. That's all we'll need." They went in with the baseball bats and the riot ceased. There were different versions of this story concerning whether anyone was seriously hurt or not, but Duggan's reputation as a rough-and-tumble patrolman continued to grow. (28)

There was widespread devastation from floods in eastern Oklahoma in the spring of 1943. The Patrol was involved in helping with traffic control and assistance in moving victims. Chick Clark remembered an incident with a storm back in Oklahoma City at about this same time. "My partner and I were sitting at South West 56th by the airport, and we saw a big storm coming. We were about out of gasoline, and the station where we usually bought our gas was closed. We started toward town and ran right into the storm. We could see a big funnel and two little ones. Then they joined together. It hit at South West 29th. The rain just poured down, and the tornado turned our patrol car over on its side. We weren't hurt. I crawled out and went toward some voices calling for help. There was a ditch filled with water and a wooden bridge across it. When I stepped on the bridge, down I went into the water. I had on boots, and they filled with water. I crawled out of the ditch and kept going toward the voices. I came to an old cistern and shined my flashlight down in it and saw three little shoats [pigs] grunting for me to get them out. I went on to a little grocery store where there was a big man sitting on his legs that had been broken backwards. His daughter and her little kiddies were there, but they weren't hurt much. It was their voices calling for help that we had heard. We could hear an ambulance coming, so it wasn't too long until we had some help." Patrolmen all over the state were helping with whatever problems came their way.

Even though troopers worked twelve- to fourteen-hour days, many of them worked at a second job in order to have additional money for their families. Vernon Sisney, who lived in El Reno, began to work part time in the Caddo Hospital laboratory. Sisney recalled, "Since I already knew how to do blood analyses, they kept me on." He explained, "I didn't want a promotion in the Patrol, because I wanted to keep my second job."

Leonard Kelsoe talked about his efforts to supplement his income. "I had to do something on the side to make a living. One time I bought cars and cleaned and polished them, fixing them up to sell. At Holdenville, during the later part of the war, I got into guns and peddled them. Everybody knew that I bought guns, if they had one to get rid of. I bought pistols. There was a guy who would buy them up and send them to the west coast. I had a family, and the patrol didn't pay that well."

The hard work and extraordinary efforts of Oklahoma Highway Patrolmen did not go totally unnoticed. In November 1943, Governor Robert S. Kerr wrote a letter to Commissioner Gentry which recognized the determination of the patrol in the face of difficulties. He stated that the fine record was "due to the efficiency and loyalty and spirit of your entire organization. I am proud of you and it, not only for myself as governor, but also for all the people of Oklahoma." (29) This compliment from the governor was shared with the hard-working troopers in order to build their morale. Troopers were well aware that there had been at least five bills proposed in the legislature before 1943 to abolish the Department of Public Safety. But the good reputation of the patrol caused those attempts to end in failure. (30)

There was one major area of technological advancement for the patrol during the war. The Department began to convert to a frequency-modulated (FM) radio system, and FM radio receivers were installed in many patrol cars by 1944. Before these FM radios, Department of Public Safety communications personnel had installed radio equipment but did not service it. With experimental FM, however, the patrol had to employ trained technicians to build and service the radios. Charles Hughes was appointed Chief Radio Officer for the Department. (31)

Troopers Join U. S. Navy

In spring of 1944, a group of troopers from the Oklahoma City district were drafted at the same time, and my dad was among them. Troopers in good standing received letters of recommendation signed by J.M. Gentry, Commissioner and J.M. Thaxton, Chief. The letters outlined the training they had received, a personal evaluation of their work, and an offer for them to return to the patrol after their tour of duty with the armed forces. (32) Many of these patrolmen decided to join the U.S. Navy and were sent to San Diego, California. Dad and Vernon Sisney rode on the same train together, and they were both assigned to the Naval hospital. Three others, Dave Faulkner, assigned to the military police; Chick Clark, assigned to teach communications; and K.O. Rayburn, also assigned to the Naval Hospital, joined them in San Diego. In addition, Otis Haltom and Jack Smith were in California in the U.S. Navy. During the next few years these Oklahoma Highway Patrolmen served the United States Navy in various capacities.

Chick Clark remembered his assignment. "My chief had been retired from the China War. He owned a liquor store in San Diego and had a big trailer outfitted to teach communications. I taught recruits how to speak the phonetic alphabet in case they were on a ship. I also worked in the U.S.S. Grant Hotel laundry for 16 months." Vernon Sisney and my dad went through training together in the Navy hospital in San Diego. After the training Sisney was sent to Frederick, Maryland, where he was involved in chemical warfare. He stated, "Then I was returned to San

Diego and worked in the Training Center, Psychiatric Center Lab." My dad became a Pharmacist Mate and was assigned to the rehabilitation hospital at Arrow Head Springs close to San Bernardino, California. The hospital was converted from a resort hotel that had been built in the 1930s. There he assisted with physical therapy and was in charge of the lavish swimming pool, and he took a lot of kidding from his patrol buddies about this assignment. Although Dad did not see any military action himself, he did work with young men who had been severely injured. He also took any part-time work he could get to make money to send home.

On July 9, 1945, twelve of the twenty-five former Oklahoma Highway Patrolmen who were in a branch of the service near Los Angeles formed a Guard of Honor for Oklahoma Governor, Robert S. Kerr, who appeared at a public function with the governor of California. Dad wrote to his parents in Kansas that it was quite an event, "a real blow out," and he had a very good time that day with his friends from the patrol. (33)

Troopers Return After the War

A ruling was passed in 1945, that any serviceman who had three or more children would be discharged. In October, Dad, who qualified for this discharge, returned to Oklahoma and went back to work on the highway patrol, assigned to Oklahoma City. One of the troopers with whom he worked was Charles R. (Ray) Rich. By this time the patrol headquarters had returned to the National Guard Armory.

Other troopers were also returning home to Oklahoma from the armed forces. By this time, existing motor courts and tourist cabins could not accommodate the surge of people on the roads to and from California. Chick Clark described how he was affected by these conditions. "I got out of service in California a little early. Vernon Sisney's wife and children, a boy and a girl, were ready to come home when I was discharged. I drove them back in their car." He added, "We had to sleep one night in the car." Clark returned to the highway patrol and was assigned as a patrolman at Guthrie for two months until he was promoted back to lieutenant for the Clinton district.

Vernon Sisney recalled his return to the highway patrol. "After the Navy, I came back to the patrol for nine months. During that time I set up Civilian Defense Programs across Oklahoma. I often did chemical warfare demonstrations. One of them was the 'English Calling Card.' I used a solution of carbon tetrachloride and phosphorus and soaked a piece of paper in it. In no time at all the innocent looking piece of paper would start to burn. It amazed everyone, and there were a lot of funny things that happened with that demonstration," he added with a laugh.

Sisney concluded, "Then my officer from California called and asked me to take the chief psychologist position at the VA hospital in New Orleans. I resigned from the patrol and went to Louisiana." Other troopers returned to Oklahoma as they were discharged.

At this same time around Oklahoma City, Dad, who was happy to be back at his patrolman's job, was cited in the newspaper for some life saving efforts. He was credited with helping save the life of a day-old infant. According to the report, Kingfisher doctor Ivan Clark was transporting the infant to an Oklahoma City hospital in his own car. When he stopped for the third time to revive the suffocating infant, my dad came along. The baby's father and grandmother rode along in the patrol car as Dad drove and the doctor operated the respirator in the back seat. They made the twenty-five mile trip to Hubbard Hospital in record time, and the baby was reported to be "doing better" the following day. (34)

In another incident, about 1:00 a.m. Dad found a stranded motorist who had driven his car into flood waters in the Santa Fe underpass just south of Britton. As the water lapped at the driver's chin, Dad was quoted as calling out, "Ahoy, what craft, and are you in trouble?" Dad then swam out to the stalled car; pulled out the driver, who could not swim; and paddled with him to shallow water. (35)

Troopers never knew what kind of assignment they might get from headquarters. Otto Rauch remembered being asked to assist with crowd control right after the war. "I got an order to go to Shawnee or someplace around there. There were a couple of American soldiers who were driving a Mercedes Benz that had belonged to Hitler. There was quite a crowd as they explained about the car. The only thing American about it was the gasoline. It had bullet proof glass and a double ignition; it was some car!" he exclaimed. "I escorted the car on to Wewoka," Rauch concluded.

There was a large number of patrolmen transferred in the spring of 1946 to make room for the troopers who were returning to the patrol from military duty and to meet the demands of the roads. Otto Rauch, who now had a wife and baby daughter, Catherine and Mary, was moved from Wewoka to Poteau; this was his thirteenth assignment in the five years since he had joined the patrol. Leonard Kelsoe was moved from Wewoka, where he had worked with Rauch, to Clinton for a few months and then on to Elk City. On November 3, 1946, my dad was transferred from Oklahoma City to Chandler. This was too far for him to commute, and my parents had vowed not to be separated again after their experiences during the war. So we prepared to make our first move as a family to Chandler from Piedmont, where my parents had maintained a home for nine years.

Figure 1—"Trooper C.A. Morris in the
Oklahoma Highway Patrol summer uniform in 1942."

Figure 2—"Trooper C.A. Morris in the
Oklahoma Highway Patrol winter uniform in 1942."

Figure 3—"Trooper C.A. Morris with his patrol car in 1942"

CHAPTER 3

THE POST-WAR YEARS
1946-1951

AT THE CONCLUSION of World War II, economic conditions in Oklahoma started to improve greatly, and this resulted in a period of growth for the highway patrol. The 1946 Oklahoma Legislature not only approved the funds for a patrol school, it gave the members of the highway patrol a raise. For the assistant commissioner and chief, the raises were $300, bringing their salaries up to $4,200 per year. There was also a raise of $900 per year for the other patrol officers and troopers. Troopers now made $2,700 per year, the first raise experienced troopers had seen since the patrol began nine years before. (1) Other supports for the troopers came with the beefing up of car repairs being carried out at headquarters and a new division for driver licenses. During 1946, Chief Thaxton initiated a movement to professionalize the ranks of driver examiners, and the first separate Driver Examiners Division was created. Lt. Charles Rice, an original examiner, was selected to attend a driver examiner's school in California conducted by the American Association of Motor Vehicle Administrators and bring back information to improve Oklahoma's system. (2)

Commissioner Gentry was also able to focus funds on another area of safety education that he believed was extremely important. From the beginning of the patrol, one of the responsibilities of each trooper was to give safety talks at schools and community groups. However, many patrolmen had trouble meeting their vast range of other assigned responsibilities and gave a low priority to speeches. Often they did no more than make a few remarks at community meetings hoping to alert the public to the dangers of the roads and the importance of obeying the laws. Realizing that not enough attention was being paid to schools, Commissioner Gentry was able to allocate funds for a full-time team to work in the area of safety education. He designated Maurice Burson as the first director of Driver Education for public schools in 1946. (3) An organized effort to take safety education into the schools followed.

Experiences in Remote Regions of the State

K.O. Rayburn described his return to the patrol in 1946. "After the service, they assigned me to Enid. I couldn't buy a car, so I was down at the bus station waiting for the bus to Enid. I was paged, and Jim Thaxton, the Chief, said they were starting a patrol school the next Monday. He wanted me to teach in it, so I stayed in Oklahoma City to teach at the school. After the school was over, they asked me to help open a new detachment at the Cookson Hills in Sallisaw. They had me pick up one of the new troopers from the school and an older trooper at Wewoka, named Harry Davis. And we went down to Sallisaw together to start the new detachment." That first post-war patrol school had been held at the National Guard Armory in Oklahoma City, and forty-four new recruits were graduated to begin working on the increasingly crowded Oklahoma roads.

As Rayburn and the other two troopers arrived in Sallisaw to establish the new unit, they found that the Cookson Hills area of eastern Oklahoma remained rather isolated and cut off from other parts of the state. The radio in their patrol car received signals with no problem, but it was not strong enough to send its signals to headquarters at McAlester. The troopers were supposed to go to the top of their highest hill three times a day to call in for information and also to report that they were all right. If the troopers were any place else in their region when they received a call on their radio, as others had done in earlier days across the state, they had to go to a telephone to communicate with headquarters.

People living in that area of the state retained a feeling of independence and did not always cooperate with authority from outsiders. Rayburn recalled, "One day soon after I got there, I was looking for witnesses to an accident. I went over to an old man who was sitting on a porch. I was in my uniform, and I told him I needed his help. He asked me what it was about, and I told him. He said that he would talk to me, but if I had been asking about Pretty Boy Floyd, he wouldn't help me. I asked him, 'Why not?' He pointed to a field with a bunch of old stumps and told me this story:

One hot day I had a mule hooked onto my old plow and was plowing that field. I stopped to wipe the sweat off of my brow and looked up to see a man with a machine gun on his arm step from behind that tree. He said, 'What are you gonna plant there?' I told him cotton. He said, 'How much can you make if your crop's good?' I told him about $50. He reached in his back pocket and pulled out some money. He handed me two fifty dollar bills and said, 'Daddy, turn that ol' mule loose and get yourself over in the shade.' Then he just left."

Rayburn concluded, "That's why most people in the area were not willing to take a stand against Pretty Boy Floyd. His brother was the sheriff, and a good one too. We had to learn how to work with the citizens around the Cookson Hills and to earn their trust."

Many other areas of Oklahoma retained local identities that patrolmen needed to understand and adjust to. The Panhandle, which had been known as No Man's Land before statehood, was another example. Chick Clark had become the lieutenant of this district with headquarters at Enid. In addition to making regular trips to observe troopers' work and carry out routine matters, the district officers tried to be in Guymon for the annual rodeo held in May. Clark explained, "People were different out there than they were anyplace else. They were human. If you were to arrest someone, it didn't matter if they were from Kansas, Texas, New Mexico, Colorado, or Oklahoma, you didn't have to put them in jail. You'd just tell them to be at the courthouse at 9:00 a.m. on Monday morning, and they'd be there. Even if they were drunk when you told them, they'd remember. They'd be lined up outside the door. They were really honest people." He concluded, "They were at the rodeo to have a good time, not to cause trouble."

Not only was it important for troopers to understand the people in different parts of the state, but they also needed to learn quickly about the differences in the climates and natural resources. Rayburn reminisced, "Two troopers from western Oklahoma were called down to southeastern Oklahoma for a roadblock. They were down at a bridge that had a big cottonwood tree. They were there for two days, and it was hot! A farmer's wife fed them, and one trooper said he had eaten so much fried chicken since he had been there, he could almost fly. In the afternoon the shade of the tree moved way over across the creek. One trooper looked at the water and said to his partner, 'It's only a couple of inches deep, just back the car into the creek to keep it in the shade.' He watched as his partner backed it up. The car went down into the creek, and the water came up into the car windows." Rayburn said with a laugh, "They had never seen such clear water and couldn't judge its depth, since most of the water out west is red."

Route 66

Oklahoma's leaders were anxious to broaden the base

for future economic growth after the war. The state had a good climate, abundant fuel, geographic proximity to other growing areas, and a diligent congressional delegation. It ranked eighteenth among the states in war contracts and facilities. Tulsa and Oklahoma City were third and sixth, respectively, among the nation's cities in terms of expanding job rates. Total income in the state rose some 132 percent as a result of wartime expansion. Receipts from agriculture surpassed even those from industry because of the great demand for food and cotton fiber. (4)

Adding to the growing Oklahoma economy was the increase in travelers along its roads. Shortly after the war, Route 66, which was the major highway from Chicago to Los Angeles, became crowded with new vehicles filled with ex-GIs and postwar families on the move. As more automobiles were produced, the traffic count soared. Route 66 entered Oklahoma in the northeast corner near Miami, passed southwestward to Tulsa, and then extended to Oklahoma City and straight west to the Texas Panhandle. The writer Michael Wallis states, "Route 66 became one great big traffic jam. The westward migration surpassed the great numbers of the Dust Bowl era when the highway had been clogged with migrants." (5)

A new era had arrived for the average American family, that of the family vacation by automobile. According to Wallis, "In 1946, in Los Angeles, Jack D. Rittenhouse published *A Guide Book to Highway 66*, a book that became a Bible for road travelers. For only one buck, travelers could follow Route 66 town by town over two thousand miles of fascinating highway. Besides listing the best motor courts, cafes, and tourist attractions, Rittenhouse also offered sage advice and road tips:

Inquire about road conditions ahead at gas stations when driving during November through March.

Be sure you have your auto jack. A short piece of wide flat board on which to rest the jack in sandy soil is a sweatpreventer. One of those war-surplus foxhole shovels takes little space and may come in very handy. Put new batteries and a new bulb in your flashlight.

Carry a container of drinking water, which becomes a vital necessity as you enter the deserts. For chilly nights and early mornings, you'll find a camp blanket or auto robe useful — and it comes in handy if you find inadequate bedding in a tourist cabin." (6)

Wallis concluded, "As the growing number of vacationers gassed up their new postwar sedans and thumbed through Rittenhouse's handy guidebook, they also heard for the first time 'Get Your Kicks on Route 66,' Bobby Troup's bluesy pop hit of 1946 . . . . Nothing captured America's love affair with the road more than this song." (7)

In addition to the increase in number of automobiles on Oklahoma roads, there was also an increase in number of trucks that were needed to transport goods for the booming economy. Trucks were becoming larger to carry more and were traveling faster to deliver the cargo at a more rapid pace. All of these changes put added responsibility on the highway patrol. Both Trooper Kelsoe and my dad had responsibility for long stretches of Route 66 in their new assignments.

Leonard Kelsoe described how he made the adjustment to a new assignment, "When you were transferred in, you just went in and did your job. You'd meet the local officers first thing — especially the sheriff, 'cause we had to use the sheriff's jail. We needed their good will. I have been in places where I'd put a man in jail, and the sheriff would let him out ten minutes after I left. Lots of the sheriffs were jealous of the Oklahoma Highway Patrol 'cause they wanted the 'honor' of doing all of the work in their county. They were elected and needed the votes."

Since married patrolmen usually tried to move their families to their new assignments as soon as possible, it is also important to understand how family members perceived moving to a new community. My mother, talked about making the move from Piedmont to Chandler, which was the first time we had moved with Dad on the patrol. "When we moved to Chandler there were two other troopers there, Mayes Lowrey and Bob Blackburn. Bob was single, and Mayes and his wife, Maxine, had two children, Grady Neal and Sharon Euala. [Grady had been named for one of the original troopers with whom Mayes had worked. Sharon's middle name reflected her parent's Cherokee Indian heritage.] We moved into the upstairs of the big house the Lowrey's were renting until we could find another place. Maxine was a big help in getting the kids into school and getting settled in a new community. Soon we were able to move into a small house, but it didn't even have running water. Then finally, we found an acreage where we could have room for our cow, a pig, and some chickens."

Troopers were assigned away from their hometowns and extended families, so it became the custom for families of patrolmen to welcome and assist new arrivals to their units. Troopers and their wives and children depended on one another for support and usually formed close bonds. Mother recalled, "In Chandler, we became like a big family with the other two troopers. We always had holiday meals together, because one of them always had to work. Bob Blackburn practically lived with us. He came to eat at our house a lot. On our kids' birthdays, he always brought them nice gifts. He was really a nice young man," she concluded.

Leonard Kelsoe recalled similar feelings about his early years on the patrol. "When you lived in a district, the troopers were one big family. On holidays we had to work sixteen to eighteen hours. One Christmas a supervisor and I worked so everyone else could be off. He had Christmas dinner with my family."

The three-man units contributed to the feeling of closeness, according to all of the troopers interviewed. Kelsoe stated with a scowl, "Now three troopers can live in the same town and hardly know one another. Each one of them has a car, so they don't have to work together. They don't even have to associate with one other."

Troopers Address Diverse Problems

When a trooper worked alone, he was on his own to get help if he needed it. K.O. Rayburn described how he dealt with an incident early in his career. "One day I was in a town and knew I needed to arrest two guys who always gave everyone a lot of trouble. I couldn't get any help that day; the deputies were out, and the sheriff was gone. A great big guy came to me and said he knew I was in need of help. He said he was a city policeman in the next town waiting for his wife to finish shopping. I told him what we needed to do, and I approached the two men. I told them they were under arrest. As I faced one, the other one came around to get me from behind. The policeman leveled him. As the one in front of me started toward me, I pulled out my blackjack and whacked him on top of his head. The blackjack had a lead piece on a kind of spring. Although I hit only once, the blackjack whacked him several times. We took them over to the jail and booked them. I should have taken that one to the doctor, but I didn't."

Rayburn continued, "The Federal Marshal asked to have them released to go to see a dying parent. I said he needed to ask the jailer. The jailer let them go, and they didn't report back to jail. They did go to get a haircut, and a policeman was in one of the barber chairs. The barber had a fit over what had happened to the guy's head. Later I heard my lieutenant was coming to see me and to check up on what happened. I hurried up and got the sheriff to issue a Auxiliary Deputy Card for the guy who had helped me. When the lieutenant asked about the incident, I told him that 'a deputy' had been helping me." Sometimes a trooper had to act first, and then think the incident through later, doing what he could to make it acceptable.

Rayburn remembered another incident where he had been creative. He had stopped one young man many times for a variety of driving violations. He paid his fines, but his driving didn't improve. "This one time I got so tired of stopping him that I decided I had to do something else. So I told him that I had been authorized to revoke his driver's license. He gave me his license, and I took him home. His folks were really glad that I did it. But when the lieutenant found out about it, he wasn't so happy. He told me never to do that again. And I didn't," he concluded with a chuckle.

The unique position of highway patrolmen in communities coupled with the personalities of a few of the troopers sometimes led to some rather questionable behaviors. Rayburn told the story of a trooper in southeastern Oklahoma who really over-stepped his authority. "One evening the trooper stopped at a parked car where a young couple was very much involved in expressing their deep feelings for one another. He had them get out of the car. After telling them that it was dangerous to be out on the roads alone at night, he told them that he had the authority to perform marriages. So, right there on the roadside he performed a 'marriage' ceremony. A year or so later in one of the small towns, the trooper saw the couple walking down the street with a small baby. He stopped to talk to them and said, 'You know, I do divorces too,'" Rayburn said, laughing.

Throughout the state, the problem of drunk drivers continued to add to the dangers of the roads. Otto Rauch recalled an incident in which he and his partner were run off of the road. "One night in Wagoner County, an eighteen wheeler weaved over and ran Harvey Hawkins and me off onto the shoulder. I put the car in reverse and turned around and caught up with him weaving all over the road. He had a semi loaded with rice he had picked up in Arkansas. And that wasn't all he'd picked up. In the cab of the truck was a bottle of muscatel wine. He had a lot of the wine in his bloodstream too." Rauch said matter-of-factly, "We arrested the driver." Rauch told of two other incidents in which he was run off the road in the patrol car but then was able to catch up with and arrest the intoxicated drivers without ever being hurt.

Leonard Kelsoe wasn't so lucky chasing a car near Elk City. He described an incident that troubled him for the rest of his career. "My partner was driving; we didn't have seat belts. My partner was a fast driver, and when our car stopped, I went through the windshield. It really messed up some lower vertebrae in my back. My back gave me fits the rest of the time I was on the patrol."

By the end of 1946, the Department of Public Safety published *Oklahoma Highway Patrol Calamity Catalogue: A story in Black and White that Reveals in Red What Took Place on Oklahoma Streets and Highways in 1946*. It listed eight divisions of the highway patrol; #1-Claremore, #2-McAlester, #3-Coalgate, #4-Lawton, #5-Clinton, #6-Enid, #7-Pawnee, and Headquarters. The publication organized statistics regarding fatalities for the years 1943-1946. Not only did it give the number of fatalities, but gave information about the month, hour, and days of the week of the accidents. It analyzed the accidents further by listing the ages of the victims, role of the person who died, type of weather, type of roadway, and location. The figures showed that the number of deaths on Oklahoma highways was steadily increasing. There had been 267 fatalities in 1943, 309 in 1944, 414 in 1945, and 500 in 1946. The number of pedestrians who had been killed by vehicles in the state showed a similar increase: 62 in 1943, 77 in 1944, 122 in 1945, and 118 in 1946. By the end of 1946, there were 573,820 registered vehicles in Oklahoma, and 427,036 were automobiles.

At the beginning of 1947, Roy J. Turner, who had been

elected the previous fall, assumed the governor's position and appointed Paul J. Reed commissioner of the Department of Public Safety. J.M. Thaxton moved from the position of chief to that of assistant commissioner; and H.B. Lowrey, who had been assistant commissioner during Governor Kerr's reign, became the new patrol chief. Under Commissioner Reed "the patrol again assisted the Oklahoma Crime Bureau in raiding the illegal whiskey traffic. Governor Turner favored using the patrol to raid places which flagrantly violated the laws of the state." (8)

During the legislative session the troopers received some added benefits as the legislature created a death, disability, and retirement fund for the employees of the Department of Public Safety and their dependents. The state put $25,000 a year into the fund, and the state treasurer could hold no more than five percent of a trooper's salary for the fund. With the post-war economic boom, it was becoming increasingly difficult to find enough men to join the patrol and difficult to get troopers to stay in the jobs. This was the beginning of a series of employee benefits that was designed to make the patrol more enticing to new recruits.

The Woodward Tornado

On April 10, 1947, a devastating tornado ripped across the Texas Panhandle and hit Woodward, Oklahoma. After the tornado leveled half of the city, killing hundreds of people, troopers from all over the state rushed to the scene to coordinate rescue and relief measures. Many troopers worked nonstop for three or four days with little sleep or rest. In certain sections of the city, destruction was so widespread that cars could not drive down the streets, and troopers patrolled the city on foot.

Chick Clark remembered his role in the disaster. "I went to Woodward and worked seventy-four hours before I had a chance to go to sleep. I finally went to sleep on a cot in a house in Woodward that hadn't been hit. The breakfast the next morning was the best I ever had. The woman made hot biscuits, sausage or bacon, and eggs. It was sure good to get some home cooking," he said as he licked his lips. "I remember that 108 people were killed. It was terrible. After three days, I went back to headquarters. I was the lieutenant and thought I should get back," he concluded.

K.O. Rayburn recalled his experience. "We started from Sallisaw and drove straight through to Woodward. Devastation was everywhere. The other troopers had worked fourty-eight hours straight, so we went to work to give them some rest. We were watching for looters. I saw a dark complexioned man over in the area of the remains of homes pulling up boards. When I tried to talk to him, he couldn't speak English. I took him to the central command center and asked for anyone who spoke Spanish. A translator talked to him and found out that the man had got off the train and was picking up things that he could use. He had on two pair of shoes, slippers and lace-ups, two or three shirts, and layers of pants. It was in the heat of the day, although the nights were still cold. I put him in what was left of the jail; there were holes in the roof. When I got ready to leave Woodward five days later, they asked me to take the man to Oklahoma City, since they weren't going to prosecute him. So we dropped him off at the bus station and hoped he found a way home." Rayburn shrugged and concluded, "My heart really went out to those poor Woodward people."

My dad was sent to Woodward soon after the tornado hit. Since he had received medical training in the Navy, he volunteered to help at the hospital. Soon they determined that he could be the most help by using his fast driving skills for transporting blood and medical supplies from the airfield to the hospital. He worked for five days racing between the air field and the hospital trying to save lives. Dad also worked with the news media. We were very surprised when we heard his voice on the radio one evening as he gave an interview about the tornado damage to a news reporter from WKY radio in Oklahoma City. (10) After he returned home to Chandler, Dad told my mother about his disappointment with another patrolmen who had been sent to Woodward to help. "The other trooper was supposed to meet C.A. and take over the driving assignment, so he could get some rest. C.A. started looking for him and found out that the trooper was in one of the tents with a Red Cross nurse." Mother sighed and said, "The trooper was single, but C.A. thought he should have been more considerate of the people who had lost their loved ones in the tornado."

Troopers' Varied Responsibilities

My dad's first aid training was often put to use in his role as a patrolman on Route 66. Mother recounted an experience when he assisted one of the Chandler doctors with surgery. "One night a man had been in a wreck, and C.A. took him to the doctor's office. 'Doc' Mileham decided the man's arm had to be cut off, but there was no one else around to help. So he told C.A. what to do, and they sawed it off right there in the office." At another wreck, the victim was not so lucky. Mother said, "He came home very upset early one morning. There had been a bad wreck in which a woman had her face smashed in. C.A. had sat with her waiting for the ambulance. She was badly hurt, and as she tried to swallow, her teeth kept coming out. He removed the teeth from her mouth so she wouldn't swallow them. C.A. said that she was so kind and gracious and had thanked him for everything he was doing for her. But before the ambulance arrived, she died. He usually didn't talk too much about his work, but that really bothered him. He came home that night shook up."

On a lighter note, my mother recalled an accident near

Chandler that involved Les Paul and Mary Ford, professional musicians who were quite popular at that time. Dad worked the accident and said that neither of them had been badly hurt, and they had been very cooperative. When they got back to California, they sent him a thank-you letter for what he had done for them.

Leonard Kelsoe was working on the western part of Route 66. "I worked twenty-one injury accidents on 66 highway one year. Back then, the road bed was an eighteen foot concrete slab on the sandy soil. So there'd be a two to three inch drop-off at each side of the road. Later they put blacktop along the sides. We had more people from California who would drop off the edge of the pavement and turn the wheel, fighting to get back on the road. When they came back on, right across the road they went. If there was any body coming, they hit them. That was treacherous right west of Sayre in that sandy country."

He continued, "One accident had three fatalities. I worked all night and couldn't find out who the people were. I went on home and went to bed. I didn't call in to headquarters because I didn't have anything to tell them. I really got eat out over it. I still don't know what they expected me to tell them. The commissioner really ate me out!" This incident seemed to continue to puzzle Leonard Kelso many years later.

Troopers were not only responsible for working the accidents and dealing with the people who were involved, but they were also responsible for follow-up afterward. Contrary to how they felt, troopers were not working in isolation. It was important to keep headquarters informed through calls and written reports, so that the commissioner's office could deal with the news media and politicians who maintained control of the patrol's budget. Patrolmen also had to file charges with the county attorney's office and go to court after arrests had been made. Dealing with this aspect of the job was often difficult for troopers.

Otto Rauch recounted, "A young county attorney just out of law school wants to make a record for himself. I remember that in Miami, Charlie Chesnut was elected in the fall of 1940. He was one of the best I ever worked with. Edgar Boatman in Okmulgee was another good one. He wanted to win cases, and he tried many of them. He wasn't afraid to take a case to court. One trooper I worked with said that the county attorney in Muskogee came into the office shaking hands with both hands. He was an indifferent prosecutor," Rauch said with a smile. Getting the county attorney to take a case to court was one problem, but appearing in court was another.

Kelsoe described one of his early experiences. "My partner and I were in court as witnesses against a drunk driver. The defense attorney had no witnesses for his client. To help the man at all, all the attorney could do was disqualify the officers. I hadn't been on the patrol too long, and the attorney could tell I was getting mad as he questioned me in court. When we broke for lunch, the attorney came over, put his arm around me, and said, 'Let's go eat.' He told me that there were two officers saying his client was drunk, and no one saying he wasn't. The only defense was to disqualify them. He said, 'There's nothing personal about it.' That taught me something. From then on I didn't get mad when the attorneys defended their clients."

In 1947, after a year's preliminary work, Lt. Charles Rice set up the first driver examiner's academy. To support the newly formed Driver Examination Division, uniformity was the theme both for training of driver examiners and for the testing of driver license applicants across the state. Examiners Glenn Carmichael and Levurn Dryden set the pattern for written driver testing and continued to seek more and more professionalism in their ranks. Although efforts were being made to improve the status and conditions for the examiners, manpower was never able to cope with the ever-increasing workload, and harried examiners found themselves driving 40,000 to 50,000 miles each year to conduct driver tests. (11)

A Driver Training Course was held at Oklahoma Agricultural and Mechanical College in July. The new Department of Public Safety safety education staff worked with the College of Education at the university in Stillwater to develop this training program for individuals who would be teaching driver training in schools and communities. My dad was one of the patrol troopers who attended. At the completion of the session, he received a certificate dated July 11, 1947.

During this time in Chandler, Dad and his partners were working very long shifts. Even after a trooper had gone home to bed, he was sometimes called out to help in an emergency. Mother described one particularly memorable incident. "C.A. was working nights, so he was asleep when they called for help in finding a boy who was lost while swimming in Bell Cow Creek. He got up, put on his bathing suit, and drove our car out to the creek. The father was there with the others looking for the boy. C.A. was a good swimmer and was able to stay under the water for long periods of time. He found the boy's body caught on some underwater brush. When he brought the body to the shore, the boy's father, who was standing in the water, keeled over. They had a real hard time getting the father out of the creek before he drowned too." The young man's drowning was a shock to our small Chandler community. The creek was a popular hang out for kids, and many mothers subsequently became concerned about the safety of their children, especially those who could not swim well. Some of the mothers got together and took turns driving their kids over to learn to swim at Shawnee, the closest public swimming pool to Chandler.

Leonard Kelsoe remembered that it seemed like a trooper's life was never his own. He remarked, "While I was working on 66, many a night when the snow was flying, I'd just get into bed and get good and warm, and I'd get a call to go out on an accident."

It was often difficult for a patrolman to get enough rest. At that time, troopers who were working night shift were not supposed to go out of service until the traffic slowed down on the roads and potential problems had been eliminated as much as possible. If there were ball games, or parties going on, troopers waited until they were over and the participants had time to get home off the roads.

K.O. Rayburn laughed as he told a story illustrating how one trooper tried to get his shift to end a little earlier. "This trooper had to work a double shift and was very tired and wanted to go home. It was a Saturday night, and the people in a night club showed no sign of leaving. Finally he went to the patrol car and got out a tear gas canister. He took it over to the air intake fan for the club and set it off. The trooper jumped into his car and drove up the road. In about five minutes, he drove back to the club. He found the patrons outside coughing and crying. Asked what he did next, the trooper said, 'I got out and cried with them.'"

Traffic fatalities had increased in December 1947. According to a newspaper article with the headline "Woman, Child Die Following Luther Crash," the state traffic deaths in December 1946 had been twelve for the month and was already twenty-seven, by December 15,1947. The article described an accident on Route 66 and featured a photograph of my dad looking at the crashed car. (12)

Not all highway patrol responsibilities were connected with the loss of life but sometimes with the beginning of life. Chick Clark remembered a snowy night he was working in Enid. "One winter a couple was on their way from Covington to the Enid Hospital. Red Arthur, who was riding with me, and I found them stuck in the snow. She was about to have a baby, so we put her over in my car. It wasn't long until she had the baby right there in my car. I was scared to death." Clark looked off into space, smiled and said, "That was quite a deal."

Politics and the Patrol

Since the state legislature was directly involved in funding, and in many cases administering, the Department of Public Safety and the patrol, state and local politics played an important role in every trooper's life. Economic conditions continued to improve in the state, yet the appropriation the legislature made to the Department of Public Safety for 1946 was $700,260, an increase of only $260 more than the allocations for 1938 and 1939. (The appropriation for 1941 had been the all-time low of $624,852) There was an emergency appropriation of $148,750 in 1947 to help cover the costs of the added divisions and increased responsibilities. By 1948 and 1949 the legislature appropriated $1,015,080 to the Department of Public Safety, which included another round of raises. Yearly salaries reflected the raises in the following ways: commissioner from $4,800 to $5,400; assistant commissioner $4,200 to $4,500; chief $4,200 with no change; (2) captains $3,600 to $3,900; (8) lieutenants $3,000 to $3,300; (10) sergeants $2,820 to $3,120; (135) experienced troopers $2,700 to $3,000; and (66) inexperienced troopers $2,400 to $2,700. There had been no patrol school in 1947, so there were only two salary steps for troopers. (13)

The increase in appropriations also resulted in some additions to the patrol's technology. Lt. Art Hamilton became the first trooper-pilot of Oklahoma's Air Patrol in 1948. Oklahoma was the first place in the country to use aircraft in traffic control. "An officer in the air could see miles of highway, enabling him to observe traffic patterns and better detect violators . . . . Working alone, Hamilton added a new dimension to enforcing traffic laws. From the air he could spot ten violators for every one detected from the ground." (14)

Politics also impacted how a trooper did his job. Chick Clark remarked, "When we first started, you could arrest the governor, if he broke the law. But then politics got so bad we had to watch ourselves. We'd arrest someone, they would complain to the politicians, and then it would come down from the commissioner onto us."

Mother described an example of the influence of politics on my dad. "C.A. got in trouble in Chandler. A prominent doctor was an alcoholic. He would get out on the highway and just barrel down the road. One time when C.A. caught him, he took him back to the County Attorney's office. C.A. made the remark, 'If my own mother were on the highway in this condition, I'd arrest her too.' The doctor was a strong politician and a strong Democrat. He got by with it. The word came to C.A. that he should not bother the doctor any more," she said with a sigh.

My dad didn't seem to allow these kinds of things to change the way he worked. Over the years he learned the power of the press, and much of his career was chronicled in local newspapers. An article titled "Patrol Prisoner Tries Suicide" reported, "A 30-year-old man wanted for questioning in Muskoge[sic] and Tulsa for alleged forgery, was being held in the Lincoln county jail at Chandler Wednesday night after he attempted to commit suicide by jumping out of a highway patrol car. Troopers C.A. Morris and Joe Dobson of the highway patrol recognized the suspect's car in a Meeker gasoline station and, after investigation, arrested him. The man surrendered without a struggle, the officers said, an[sic] while they drove him to Chandler he boasted he was wanted for forgery 'all over the country,' and was paroled from California and Texas jails. During a lull in the conversation the prisoner suddenly opened one of the car doors and announced that he was going to kill himself by jumping out." According to the article, Dad said that while he was driving, he grabbed the man by the hip pocket and pulled him back inside. (15)

On March 8,1948, Trooper Joe Dobson and Dad appeared on the front page of the *Daily Oklahoman*. They had worked a wreck in which a person had died, bringing the yearly death toll up to seventy-six as compared to sixty-three the year before. The wreck, which was caused when a car side-swiped a house trailer, had happened at 4:45 a.m. on U.S. 66, nine miles west of Chandler.

Dad often provided information to newspaper reporters in an attempt to get something he thought might be an important lesson for people into the newspaper. A filler article described how he had quit smoking. Dad threw away his cigarettes after thirty years of smoking and was quoted as saying that he quit "mostly just to see if I had the willpower." (16) My mother remembered that Dad had been pulling my brothers on a sled after a snow storm, and when he had trouble getting his breath, he realized what smoking was doing to him. He had begun smoking as a very young man, and his kicking the habit started what was to become a lifetime effort of trying to get others to follow his example and quit smoking. This sometimes caused discomfort and friction when he worked with patrol partners who smoked.

Special Programs and Plans in 1948

The Department of Public Safety placed an increased emphasis on the area of safety education and the number of safety programs in Oklahoma schools began to grow. In 1948, Lt. O.B. Patterson, a trooper who had been associated with public schools as well as public safety, was appointed to head the safety education programs of the department. The number of schools participating in driver education programs increased from 18 to 100 by the end of that year. When a school system began a course, the driver education staff trained teachers to conduct it. Once personnel were trained, the department staff set a curriculum for the course and assisted the instructors occasionally. (17) Although Dad was not a member of the Department's staff, he played an active part in driver education in schools located near Chandler. He started what eventually grew, as additional programs cropped up cross the state, into a state-wide drivers' contest for students from the driver education classes.

Another one of the state-wide educational programs was called Safety Junior. It was aimed at elementary school age children and was carried out in a quiz kid format. In Chandler, the teachers of the three grade schools each selected two pupils who then competed in a preliminary contest conducted by my dad. All ten of the grade school teachers were judges to select one representative and one alternate from each grade. I was one of the second graders chosen. Two articles about the contest appeared in the Shawnee *News-Star*. A photo of Dad in front of a group of twelve children with our hands raised to answer a question appeared with an article titled, "Chandler Safety Kids Perform for Lions Club." (Figure 4) The article stated that the Safety Jr. radio quiz team and alternates both scored 100 percent in an exhibition contest at the Lions Club. It continued, "Chandler's quiz team has bested Tecumseh and one of the two Shawnee teams in two Saturday broadcasts over station KGFF in Shawnee. This Saturday the safety team will meet Stroud." The article continued, "The 'Safety Junior' contests are sponsored by the highway patrol and state safety council in cooperation with KGFF. It includes nine schools in Lincoln and Pottawatomie Counties. Trooper Howard Flanigan, Oklahoma City, is in direct charge of the program." Parents of the pupils were invited to attend the Safety Jr. contest at the studio, and the public was encouraged to tune to KGFF, 1450 on the dial. (18)

I remember how my dad's brown eyes would twinkle as he asked trick questions to prepare our team for the contests. One question was, "Should a bicyclist ride on the sidewalk on the right or the left side of the street?" When he called on me, I wasn't fooled, I knew that no one was supposed to ride a bicycle on the sidewalk. Participating with my dad in the Safety Junior contests was one of the highlights of my elementary school experience.

Some of the plans developed by the Department of Public Safety included other state-wide agencies. The devastating tornado at Woodward was not the only natural disaster Oklahoma had experienced in the 1940s. There had been floods in the east, forest fires in the southeast, and gas and oil explosions in the central part of the state. Paul Reed, Commissioner of the Department of Public Safety was appointed to organize state agencies into "a plan for coordinated action in the event of a disaster . . ." On April 1, 1948, the *Oklahoma Disaster Relief Plan*, published by the Department of Public Safety was presented to the public. The plan described the role of the American National Red Cross and each of the state agencies in a disaster situation. The forty-three page document listed the responsibilities of the following agencies: Oklahoma Highway Patrol, National Guard, State Agricultural Department, State Board of Funeral Directors & Embalmers, State Health Department, State Game & Fish Commission, State Board of Education, State Division of Forestry, State Welfare Commission, and a Citizens' Committee.

An organizational chart of the highway patrol in this document showed the following individuals in leadership positions: Commissioner, Paul W. Reed; Assistant Commissioner, J.M. Thaxton; Chief, H.B. Lowrey; South District Captain, F.D. Petty; Oklahoma City Lieutenant, R.R. Lester, Sergeants, O. Haltom and J. Herbert; McAlester Lieutenant, C.T. Raley, Sergeant, A.G. Bidwell; Coalgate Lieutenant, E.L. Bumpass, Sergeant, W.H. Bailey; Lawton

Lieutenant, W.D. Hamilton, Sergeant, C. Awtrey. North District Captain, N.C. Holt; Claremore Lieutenant, W.S. Abbott, Sergeant, E.C. McIntosh, Tulsa Sergeants, H.J. Harmon and D. Faulkner; Pawnee Lieutenant, Joe Boyce, Sergeant, W.J. Smith; Enid Lieutenant, E.S. Clark, Sergeant, Taylor Lain; and Clinton Lieutenant, Ralph Thompson. Each of the headquarters had its own radio call letters. Oklahoma City—KOSO, McAlester—KOSW, Coalgate—KOSC, Lawton—KOSY, Claremore—KOSU, Pawnee—KOSP, Enid—KOSR, and Clinton—KOSX.

The organizational structure of the patrol had not changed much since 1937. The state was divided into the two administrative districts, North and South, headed by captains, and further divided into divisions. Each division was numbered and had a lieutenant and one or more sergeants who had supervisory responsibility for the patrol units located at their headquarters as well as in outlying towns. Headquarters at Oklahoma City had five patrol units plus Chandler, Shawnee, Norman, and Purcell. McAlester had one patrol unit and Okmulgee, Poteau, Sallisaw, and Wewoka. Coalgate had two patrol units plus Pauls Valley, Durant, Idabel, Ardmore, Hugo, Ada, and Sulphur. Lawton had one patrol unit with Anadarko, Chickasha, Altus, and Duncan. Claremore had two patrol units and Pryor, Talequah, and Muskogee; Tulsa had three patrol units with Nowata, Vinita, and Miami. Pawnee had two units and Ponca City, Pawhuska, Bristow, Sapulpa, Cushing, and Guthrie. Enid had two units plus Watonga, Woodward, Alva, and Guymon. Clinton had two units and Hobart, Elk City, and El Reno.

One persistant problem troopers had to contend with, yet the department took no steps to address, was that of the stiffling heat in the patrol cars. The long hot summers of Oklahoma had always presented discomfort, and having to sit in a hot patrol car for hours on end only made it worse. As troopers came to Oklahoma City for meetings, they enjoyed the newly remodeled Beverlys "Chicken in the Rough" Restaurant on North Lincoln Boulevard. By 1948 it had air conditioning. Although some businesses, like Beverly's, had addressed the severe heat of Oklahoma's summers by installing air conditioning, there were no air conditioners in the patrol cars. To make matters worse, troopers were still required to wear the long sleeved wool uniforms adopted in 1937. Leonard Kelsoe shook his head as he stated, "We got $50.00 per month for cleaning, pressing and eating out. In the hot summer time we wore those long sleeved wool shirts, and we'd have big rings of sweat in just a few minutes."

Some troopers attempted to deal with the issue of extreme heat and long sleeves on their own. There was a gleam in Rayburn's eyes as he recalled, "We wore those long sleeved uniforms winter and summer. One day I was over in Ft. Smith, Arkansas, and saw some brown short sleeved poplin shirts with epaulets. They wore them at Fort Chaffee. So I bought a couple and started wearing short sleeved shirts when I worked alone on day shifts, but I always carried my other one with me. One of the other troopers saw me and got one for himself. Well, one day I heard the lieutenant was coming my way, so I put on my regulation shirt. He got there and just smiled as I got out of my car to meet him. 'Nice shirt,' he said. He drove on over and caught the other trooper in his short sleeved shirt. He ordered him to get back into uniform. It was the mid-1950s before we got to wear summer uniforms with short sleeved shirts."

In the summer of 1948 the patrol school was moved to the campus of the University of Oklahoma where it would remain until a new facility was built. At the conclusion of that school, twenty new recruits joined the ranks of the highway patrol.

Troopers were assigned to provide protection and traffic control when well-known people appeared in public anyplace in the state. Candidates campaigning for the United States presidency created such a circumstance. Otto Rauch described one of his experiences. "When President Truman was running in 1948, my partner, E.B. Lynn, and I were assigned to go to McAlester where his campaign train stopped. We were to mingle in the crowd and listen to Truman speak from the back of the train. Bess and Margaret were both with him. Then the train pulled out and went to Eufaula. We had to drive FAST to keep up with that train. But we got there just as the train did. After we listened to Truman's speech again, we went back home."

When President Truman arrived in Oklahoma City on September 28, 1948, his campaign party left the train so he could make a speech at a Democratic gathering held at the Oklahoma State Fair grounds. Dad, who had retained his athletic abilities, was one of the troopers who was assigned to security. Mother remembered seeing him running along beside Truman's car, holding on to it as it transported the President into the area where he was to give his speech.

Troopers in Communities

Being a highway patrol trooper in a small community was not an easy job. In addition to traffic law enforcement and traffic control, troopers also held an important place in the structure of the community. Leonard Kelsoe recalled, "Oklahoma Highway Patrolmen were highly thought of. They were thought of as the leading citizens of the district. Everybody respected them. Any more, kids have no respect for any officer. We were out there to help the public. We talked to people nice and treated them nice."

However, there was another side to the way troopers were treated in some communities. Otto Rauch said, "Any public official is under constant public scrutiny—especially if he wears a uniform and carries a gun and wears a badge. I have been called Gestapo, Hitler's brown-shirted troops, sometimes by an attorney in court. That's about the worst thing someone could call an officer," he said with a sigh.

Many times a trooper's personal life and his professional life became intertwined. One such incident found its way into the newspapers and became an important part of the foundation of the "straight-arrow" reputation that my dad built in the Chandler community. "Farmer Delivering Hay to Patrolman Winds Up in Court" was the headline of an article describing an accident that occurred as a farmer with a load of hay for us attempted to deliver it to our home on Route 66 in Chandler. The article stated that Dad gave the farmer a court summons as a result of the accident. Fifty years later, a childhood friend of my brother's remembered the incident. "He even arrested the poor old farmer delivering his hay."

I believe that this inter-relationship of a trooper's personal and professional life is important in understanding what it was like to be an Oklahoma Highway Patrolman. My dad's own journals, which were started in 1951, became a major source of information for the next chapters. They reflect this infusion of personal with professional views and give a richness to this document that would be greatly diluted if only the professional data were recorded.

As soon as we arrived in Chandler, my parents had become involved in the community. Mother, who had been a one-room school teacher before my parents were married and a substitute teacher at Piedmont, welcomed the role of home room mother for our classrooms. To involve my younger brother, Tom, in scouting, she also became a Cub Scout Den Mother, working with Hope Vassar, an attorney's wife, who had three young boys, Paul, Joe Sam, and Bill.

Dad became an active Boy Scout leader with my older brother, John's group. Even with his busy schedule, Dad made sure he was available to challenge the young scouts with merit badge activities and camp outs. Dan Erwin, a good friend of John's and the son of an attorney, stated, "I remember as a kid that his schedule impressed me. I was used to Dad going to the office and coming home at a certain time. And that just didn't fit with a patrolman."

John remembered a camp out when our dad's authority was challenged by the exuberant scouts. "We had gone out on an overnight. We had our tents pitched and a little fire built. I guess he decided it was time for us to go to sleep. But we didn't want to; everybody was all wound up. After a warning or two, we broke camp, and he marched us back to town in the dark." Dad took the boys right home. From then on they knew he meant business when he took them anyplace.

Dad often involved the scouts in activities of high interest. One year Dan Erwin and his brother, David were preparing to go to the Boy Scout Jamboree in Valley Forge, Pennsylvania. Dad encouraged the boys in the scout troop to capture some of the then plentiful horned toads to send with the Erwin boys for trading. Dan Erwin recalled, "We put a bunch of those horney toads in shoe boxes that we had poked holes in. They traded really fast when we got there. They were a pre-historic type animal that would flatten out when they were scared." Dad also helped the scouts make neckerchief slides out of briar roots. "That was the one area in Scouts where you could be an individual. You could have whatever kind of neckerchief slide you wanted. No two roots were alike," Erwin remembered. Dad didn't put up with any nonsense, but he enjoyed the young scouts and often tried to incorporate safety education into their scouting activities.

1949 Legislature Authorizes Many Changes

Between January 2, and February 19, 1949, there was a great blizzard that hit the middle of the United States reaching as far south as New Mexico and Arizona. On twenty-five of these forty-eight days there were big storms with temperatures below zero. The Air Force dropped food, blankets, and medical supplies to people and feed for animals in many remote areas. (20) Oklahoma was not spared. During this time period, highway patrolmen made many emergency runs for hospitals transporting vital life saving materials, such as blood and equipment. Assisting stranded motorists became an around-the-clock responsibility.

The 1949 state legislature was kept busy with many issues related to the highway patrol. Senate Bill No. 274 provided additional benefits to troopers and their families. It provided for retirement after twenty years of service at three and one-half percent of the total salary he received during his service employment. The bill also covered dependents at full retirement pay at the death of the retired trooper. Group medical and hospital insurance was also added to the benefits package. (21) These changes were designed to attract more men looking for a job with security for themselves and their families.

The legislature also passed a Uniform Traffic Code which clarified old laws and added new ones. Until this time, the Ten Rules of the Road passed in 1915 and revised in 1927 (Appendix A) were the only traffic laws troopers could enforce. With stronger and stricter laws to enforce, the patrol's efforts were more effective. Otto Rauch stated, "One of the most important changes was when we got the Uniform Traffic Code. Until then there were just too many things that were left up to a trooper's judgment. Then the local authorities could change things if they disagreed with you."

A Size and Weights Law was passed by the 1949 Legislature in response to the booming trucking industry that put semi-rigs capable of transporting three or four more times as much cargo as ever before on Oklahoma roads. This law was designed to protect highways and bridges from oversize and overweight abuse by setting size and weight limitations. The Department of Public Safety was named to enforce the law and establish the Size and Weights Division. Eight troopers, one supervisor [formerly called sergeants], and one lieutenant were designated to enforce the new law. Thirteen permit clerks were assigned to issue oversize and overweight permits. The troopers teamed with eight Oklahoma Tax Commission officers to patrol the highways. (22)

This legislature also reviewed the Driver Examiners Division which had been under-funded and under-staffed since its beginning in 1937. The legislature authorized a personnel increase of more than 200 percent. Fourty-four positions were added, and funding was granted for a training academy to be held along with a patrol trooper academy the following summer. Recognizing the need to have more patrolling of Oklahoma's roads, the legislature authorized the number of troopers to be raised from the 155, which had been in effect since 1941, to 214. (23)

Another area that emerged as one that needed to be dealt with at the state level was that of vehicle liability insurance. Uninsured motorists were becoming a problem for those with whom they had wrecks. The Department of Public Safety became aware of the need for drivers to become financially responsible for any damage that they might cause. Lt. Carl Tyler researched and developed the plan for a financial responsibility law. He worked with the commissioner and key legislators as he guided the bill through the 1949 legislature. "The bill provided that drivers involved in accidents should be financially responsible for the total damage resulting from accidents in which they were involved. Those who had no liability insurance came within the jurisdiction of the financial responsibility law." (24)

A Safety Responsibility Division was formed as a result of this law. One of the first tasks was to sell the safety responsibility program to troopers, district attorneys, judges, and the public. Carl Tyler worked with assistant, Paul

Rudell, and five clerical helpers to publicize specific provisions of the bill explaining both benefits and liabilities to citizens. As the new division got underway, every accident report involving damages exceeding $50 was processed and reviewed by the division personnel. The reviewing procedure was totally manual and was intended to identify drivers involved in accidents who had no liability insurance. A letter was then sent to the uninsured motorist informing him that either a bond covering the cost of repairs would have to be filed or he would be subject to having his license tags revoked. Each stage of enforcement required additional reviewing and paper work, a task which grew through the years. (25)

For the new Safety Responsibility Division to be effective, the patrolmen had to turn in complete accident reports and collect the license tags that were revoked. K.O. Rayburn described the process that was used for patrolmen's reports: "Each trooper completed a report on every accident. The lieutenant was to analyze these reports and make decisions about assignments of personnel in their district. Troopers also completed a summary of their activities — contacts, time on duty, etcetera. Supervisors and lieutenants also summarized and analyzed these. All reports and summaries were sent into headquarters where more analyses and summaries were made. Many officers thought that too much time was spent on reports, keeping men off of the road."

Otto Rauch gave his viewpoint as a trooper out on the roads. "I didn't like filling out all of those reports. It seemed like the harder you worked on the road, the more reports you had to fill out."

As office staff was working on reading, analyzing, and summarizing reports, they sometimes found some humor in the way a patrolman had completed his report of an accident or incident. The following statements were attributed to a report completed by my dad, "The subject was arrested for driving while drunk and transported to jail. While being taken to jail, he got sick and threw up and went to the bathroom in his clothes, and stunk up the patrol car something awful. Before I could take him into jail, I took off his overalls and hosed him down." The officers at headquarters had laughed about Dad's report, but said that they could always depend on Morris to tell it like it was. (26)

By 1949, the radio communication system, which had been poor for many troopers across the state, was completed with an FM transmitter and receiver at every district headquarters and one in every patrol car. Finally, every trooper could transmit and receive messages, and district command personnel could know where all of its units were. Coordination of efforts such as roadblocks, manhunts, and disasters had finally become a fairly simple matter. (27) I can remember many times Dad would come home to eat dinner with us while he was on duty. Rather than go out of service, he would park the patrol car near the open back door so he could hear the radio. We would all listen closely, but none of the rest of us could understand the voices that were interspersed with static. I do remember the sign off "KKC-883."

Another change at the Department of Public Safety in 1949 was the establishment of the Public Information Office. A civilian, Jerry Marx, was appointed to the job as public information officer. Marx was in a wheel chair as a result of a bout with polio. He had the responsibility for issuing press releases, responding to questions from the press and public, and working with officers in the department to maintain a positive image.

1949 Patrol School

A five-week patrol school was held in the summer of 1949 on the University of Oklahoma campus in Norman. The first examiner's school was also held there at the same time. At the completion of the schools sixty new patrolmen and thirty-five new examiners emerged. The examiners were assigned to one of the four new geographic districts with headquarters at Oklahoma City, Lawton, Enid, and Tulsa, with a senior examiner heading each district. Examiners went out to all major towns in each district where they conducted their tests in the local tag agency, a retail store, or another facility, when necessary. Testing included a vision acuity test, a written examination, and the final road test in the applicant's own car. Training and tools were being used that insured a uniformity of testing would exist from Miami to Altus, and from Guymon to Broken Bow. (28)

Two new troopers from that patrol school were Don McDaniel and Nat Taylor. Taylor, with five older sisters, had grown up in western Oklahoma where his father was a teacher and also a member of the state legislature. Nat Taylor Senior had been a member of the House of Representative in 1930 and 1931, and a member of the Senate from 1932 until 1940. He had played a key role in the establishment of the highway patrol. When Nat Junior returned from the Navy in 1946, he stopped by the patrol headquarters in Clinton to get his driver license renewed. The dispatcher asked Nat if he would consider taking a job as a dispatcher. The dispatcher explained that he was the only one working after the others had quit when they got better jobs. Taylor recalled, "I told him I wanted to be a trooper, but I was only 21 years old." After talking to the dispatcher for a while, Taylor decided to take the necessary tests. He said, "One test was for operation of a radio, and I hadn't done that before. So they helped me get by that one, and I became a dispatcher. I stayed three and a half years." Taylor described the role of dispatcher. "He kept all records in the district headquarters. He made weekly breakdowns of reports for the department; did dispatching on the radio, sending cars where they need to be; and took messages by telephone." By 1949, Taylor was old enough to become a trooper.

Don McDaniel, a native of Shawnee, described his joining of the patrol. "Jerry and I got married in Corpus Christi, Texas. After I was discharged from the Navy, I needed a job. I got in on one of those on-the-job training deals with a tire company. They weren't really training me, they were just getting cheap manual labor. I began looking around for something else. I had admired the troopers who worked around Shawnee, so I went down to patrol headquarters in Oklahoma City. At that time Bob Lester was in charge, the district commander. We talked at length. They were just getting ready to have a patrol school, but it had been filled up. Bob Lester and K.O. Rayburn tried every way in the world to get me in, but they couldn't. Bob Lester hired me as a dispatcher, and I worked for him for two years. Then I got into the 1949 school."

Since they had both worked as dispatchers, McDaniel and Taylor became friends at the patrol school. They remembered their five-week training vividly. McDaniel explained, "The school was tough. It seemed to me like they were trying to make it so tough you would leave. In fact, during the first two weeks we lost about ten people. It did teach us a lot. Even though I wasn't sure how much I was getting out of it at the time; later, out on the road, it would come back to me." He continued, "It taught me more than anything else, wherever you were stationed to get acquainted and work with the people in charge of that county, the county or district attorney and the judges. Because they are the ones who worked with the laws; they would file your cases or they wouldn't."

Taylor recalled, "Since I had been a dispatcher, I already knew most of what they taught. But there were so many who weren't familiar with what the patrol did. They had us work a few accidents and fill out reports. I had checked a thousand reports as a dispatcher looking for flaws — spelling or facts. I'd put a note on them for the lieutenant, so he didn't have to read 'em all. They were trying to get as many troopers on the road as they could with the little money they had. Most of the instructors were from the patrol—most from Oklahoma City and maybe one from Tulsa. They were just trying to acquaint us with how it was to be an officer. In those days courtesy and assisting disabled motorists were a big deal. We'd never pass a woman or a man on the road without stopping to help them."

As the new troopers took to the roads in 1949, Oklahoma motorists were driving more than they had ever done before. They drove six and one-half billion miles, an increase of 400 million from 1948. (29) Additional troopers were definitely needed.

McDaniel described his first assignment as a trooper. "I was sent to McAlester and Nat was sent to Okemah. We were in different districts, but our territories came together. Nat and I would arrange to meet at the county line. We stayed in close contact; we always had a feud going. I had made the highest grades during the school, but he got the lowest badge number. He got 205 and I got 207. He always brought that up and said that it proved that 'the brass' knew he was smarter than I was," McDaniel said as he laughed.

Promotions within the ranks continued to be something that mystified and angered many members of the patrol. At this point there were no required procedures for promotions, demotions, or transfers of troopers. The commissioner, who was appointed by the governor, appointed the chief, who was free to make assignments as he saw fit, but all decisions were subject to the commissioner's approval. Leonard Kelsoe described his opinion about promotions within the patrol. "Troopers were supposed to stay away from politics, but promotions were all politics. A person's ability had nothing to do with it. It was just who had done the most 'brown nosing.' Except for a few men. There were a lot who didn't [brown nose], but there were more that did, especially in the upper echelons. They kept adding higher officers to make room for those who climbed up," he said in disgust.

K.O. Rayburn's description of his first promotion supports the idea that these decisions may not have been based on fair and even criteria. "There were four on the panel deciding on the new supervisor for McAlester, the chief, two captains, and the lieutenant. I was one of the two being considered. Later I found out they took four votes during the day, and each time it was a tie vote. At the end of the day they went to the commissioner. He said he didn't know either of us. But he had heard from Jerry Marx who went through Sallisaw once a month as his wife took him to Hot Springs,[Arkansas] for treatments, that on each trip he saw me out on the road. The commissioner voted for me, and I got my first promotion."

In addition to being promoted to a supervisor position, K.O. Rayburn continued to teach at patrol schools; he taught at all three of the patrol schools from 1946 through 1949. Rayburn stressed, "We tried to teach troopers that how they made their contacts was very important. They needed to have spotless uniforms, wear their hats, not smoke or chew gum or anything else. They needed to be friendly but professional."

As much as the training staff tried to prepare the new troopers, there was still much to learn when they went to work. In McAlester, where Rayburn was supervisor and Don McDaniel reported to work, there was a much repeated story about how McDaniel dealt with one of his first arrests. Rayburn recounted with a gleam in his eye, "One day Don arrested a woman he had stopped in town and was attempting to put her in the backseat of the patrol car. But she refused to bend over to get in. An old deputy was watching and started to laugh at the new trooper. He said, 'Son, do you want me to show you how it's done?' Don said that he did, and the deputy walked up to the woman, pulled out his blackjack, hit the her across the head, and gave her a shove into the backseat of the patrol car. The deputy slammed the door and said, 'It works every time!' Don couldn't believe his eyes at what had just happened. He sure took a lot of kidding about that." Rayburn laughed as he finished telling the story.

Nat Taylor recalled some issues he dealt with as he started to work as a patrolman. "In the beginning, I had the worst time giving old people a ticket. They don't deliberately do stuff. The accident reports stated, 'did knowingly and willfully do' so and so. I didn't think they knowingly or willfully did something, they just accidentally did it. My original partner, Wallace Strang, broke me in that way. A ticket is a penalty. How can you penalize a poor ignorant soul? You know, we didn't have turn signals then; we used arm signals. I wasn't going to stop some little old lady for not sticking her arm out in the rain. I've seen people signal with their right arms inside the car. At least they signaled." Taylor concluded, "The biggest no-no for a trooper was to run by someone who was broke down. Old time patrol was just common sense."

Another new trooper from the 1949 patrol school was Kenneth Payne, who was assigned to work with my dad in Chandler. Payne's introduction to the realities of a patrolman's job was sudden and swift. On September 22, he and my dad had an experience that was one of the most unnerving of their careers. According to a newspaper article, the incident began when the patrolmen chased a car which was swerving erratically along the highway. They stopped it at a beer tavern and attempted to arrest the driver, Don Hughes. The other man in the car, who was his brother, Dewey, intervened and a fight followed. Dad followed Don as he ran into the tavern, went behind the bar, and came out with a gun. With his hands up, Dad backed up to a window and yelled to Payne to get some help. Dad wasn't sure what Payne would do since he was a new trooper. However, Payne returned to the patrol car and radioed for help before he too was forced into the tavern. Troopers Ray

Rich and M.D. Samuel arrived and were standing by when Dad was able to talk Dewey into taking the gun away from Don. My dad commented later that the end of the gun barrel had looked like a cannon as he talked to the brothers. (30) On October 3, 1949, Commissioner Paul Reed wrote a letter of commendation to Dad that said in part, "Inspector Petty informs me that you acted in a most level headed manner and that you upheld the highest traditions of our Department in the finest manner possible. I am pleased to make this commendation a part of your official record."

Their territory in Lincoln County was a busy place, and Dad and Kenneth Payne were featured in newspaper stories on three other occasions later that year, one for capturing a car thief, another for investigating the death of a carnival worker who fell from a speeding truck, and the third for investigating an accident in which a hitchhiker was driving a car which he wrecked and injured three people. (31)

At home, their wives, Helen and Wanda, had become good friends. My mother was fifteen years older than Wanda and tried to help her adjust to the strange working hours and the stresses on the family that went along with the job of a state trooper. Wanda and her son, Steve, spent many evenings at our home, where we younger children played together and our mothers cooked, sewed, or just talked. Mother tried to help Wanda understand the life of a patrolman's wife, and they gave comfort to one another when there were dangerous incidents like the one at the tavern. It was a difficult adjustment for any young wife to watch her husband get dressed up in an attractive uniform and leave home at dark not to return until early the next morning. In addition to worrying about their husbands' getting hurt or killed in the line of duty, many troopers' wives wondered if their husbands were working the whole time or carousing. In fact, some marriages broke under the strain, and more than a few troopers left the patrol to preserve their marriages. (32)

Events and Efforts of 1950

Not all of the emergency situations patrolmen were called to assist with were related to law enforcement. On February 25, 1950, Leapy the Leopard disappeared from his "escape proof" pit at the Lincoln Park Zoo in Oklahoma City. The wild cat had been brought from India only a week before. For three days and nights the Oklahoma City Police Department, zoo officials, big game hunters, wildlife experts, U.S. Marines equipped with M-1 rifles and walkie-talkie radios, and some members of the Oklahoma Highway Patrol searched for the 175 pound animal. Families were terrified of the leopard, and as far away as Chandler, parents wouldn't let their children outside after dark. Almost every hour there was news that a sighting of the leopard had been made some place around the center of the state. Dad drove to Oklahoma City from Chandler to join other officers and assist with the hunt. Sixty-one hours after he escaped, the leopard was found near his pit, dead from an overdose of tranquilizer in the horse meat left as bait. (33) During this time our imaginations had run wild. My brothers and I were sad that the leopard was dead but relieved that our dad was no longer out hunting for the wild animal. We were also happy that we could once again go outside at night without being terrified of being attacked by a wild cat from India. (34)

Records from the Department of Public Safety Information Office for 1950 give additional information about some of the pertinent activities going on in the department during that time. The reports that troopers were required to complete resulted in a mountain of paper work. A March 1950 Department of Public Safety Press Release reported that there was an average of 3,000-3,500 accident reports completed and sent in by highway patrol troopers each month. It also reported that in January of that year, there had been 5,000. The release explained that the 207 officers' reports were reviewed and tabulated every ten days and processed each month for reporting to the legislature and to the public, and all of this was done by hand. (35)

In small towns, particularly those that were located far from one of the larger cities, the Oklahoma Highway Patrolmen were seen as tangible evidence of the extension of the State government into small towns and communities. Citizens saw them as sometimes helping and sometimes interfering with their lives. Nat Taylor recalled a situation that illustrates this point. "My partner, Wallace Strang, and I went to a little old place called Paden, this side of Okemah. We pulled up in town and the city marshal came up to us. He said, 'They're having a picture show tonight. Are you all going to go?' We asked where, since the town didn't have a movie theater. He pointed down the street and said, 'On the side of that building down there—see those chairs?' People just brought their chairs and set them out beside the building once a week for the picture show."

Taylor concluded, "Just about dark we came back by and sat there and watched the show. When it was over, nobody left. Finally the marshal came over to us and said, 'They're not gonna leave until after you do 'cause none of 'em have a driver license.'"

Obtaining a valid driver license continued to be a problem for many Oklahoma citizens; there had been no license requirement until 1937. The fact that funds for license examiners' training and salaries were only sporadically provided by the state legislature made it seem that there was little legislative commitment or consistancy in requiring that all drivers in Oklahoma be licensed. After 1949, there were license examiners assigned to every area of the state, but troopers continued to provide testing when needed. However, making sure all drivers were licensed was an on-going task for law enforcement officers. Troopers Taylor and Strang returned to Paden to give driver license tests shortly after their experience at the picture show.

Within two weeks, the Department of Public Safety sent an examiner to Paden to finish testing those who wanted to become licensed.

Taylor recalled another aspect of the driver licensing problem. "When we first moved to Okemah some of the older ladies were staying home. One of 'em came over and asked my wife, Betty Jo, if I'd give her a driver's test. The license examiner who was coming there was failing everyone, she said. Well, I gave that lady the test, and she passed. Then a bunch more ladies came for me to give them the tests. Most of them passed on the first try." Taylor shook his head as he said, "The license examiner got really mad at me."

He explained, "Those ladies had never parallel parked in their lives — there was no place around there where they even needed to. They could all drive just fine and none of them would drive away from their town." The state regulations were designed for all drivers, and there were no provisions for those who had been driving for years, but couldn't meet some of the requirements. The license examiners were charged with providing consistent standards throughout the state. However, Taylor felt that there should be some exceptions depending on the circumstance, such as not requiring elderly women to pass a standard for parking in a manner they would never need to.

It was important for troopers to enforce the law and follow patrol procedures, but it was also important for them to make sound decisions based on the community in which they worked. K.O. Rayburn, who had provided instruction in patrol schools since 1946 and had become a supervisor in 1949, was involved in some aspects of trooper assignments and transfers. He described some of his thoughts about matching trooper's skills and needs with the various settings throughout the state. "I always thought we should try to match troopers to the communities. Some troopers needed very little supervision or support. They could be trusted to make good decisions and not step over their authority. Other troopers needed lots of support and closer supervision. When we made assignments to remote areas like Guymon, we should have considered this, but we didn't when I was there," he concluded sadly.

According to the records of the Department of Public Safety Information Office, May 1950 was designated Vehicle Inspection Month throughout Oklahoma. Jerry Marx's Press release stated, "The Department of Public Safety has started its Vehicle Inspection month in compliance with the nation wide program inaugurated in 1946 by the President's Safety Council. All Patrol units and License Examiners of the department are participating in the program in an effort to inspect as many vehicles as possible." (36) Drivers throughout the state could expect to be stopped in roadblocks, where their vehicles would be inspected for safety violations. Ensuring that vehicles were safe continued to be one of the most important responsibilities of the Department of Public Safety.

In every trooper's memory, one of the worst experiences was that of coming upon a wreck that caused deaths of innocent people. The memories were even more painful if children or young people were involved. For my dad, the most memorable crash occurred near Chandler in the early morning of May 26, 1950. A car filled with teenagers was struck broadside by a heavily loaded gasoline transport truck owned by one of our neighbors in Chandler, Glen R. Key. The force of the impact drove the truck completely through the automobile carrying the right side doors all the way through the car. Four teenagers were killed and one was seriously injured. (38) Hoping to make an impression on his own children about the fragility of human life and the importance of safe driving, Dad took us to see the wreckage early the next day. Many years later, all three of us could still vividly recall seeing traces of flesh and brain matter from the teenagers on the front of the truck. Our family joined the rest of the community in mourning the loss of the young people and the tragedy with the transport truck.

While working with the press in Chandler, Dad had become good friends with reporter, Jim Bradshaw, who wrote for the Shawnee *News-Star* newspaper. Dad continued his practice of giving him information related to patrol business and also provided him with personal information that might be humorous or light in nature. An article that illustrates this was titled, "Trooper hunts quail with radio aerial." The newspaper article stated:

"Trooper Clarence Morris wasn't too busy arresting motorists Thanksgiving day but what he had time to do a little quail hunting—with a radio aerial. Cruising U.S. 66, Morris saw (does he ever miss anything?) a group of bobwhites fly across the road above his patrol wagon. One of the birds clipped the long antenna and fell off to the side of the road. Morris stopped, climbed out and pursued the crippled quail into the wilderness, finally winning the chase." (39)

Near the end of Governor Roy J. Turner's term, in 1950, there were several changes in the leadership of the patrol. Patrol Chief H.B. Lowrey had been replaced by Ralph Thompson in 1949; Commissioner Paul W. Reed was replaced by Carl Tyler and then Coble Gambill in early 1950. J.M. Thaxton remained as assistant commissioner through the term. The election in the fall of 1950 brought Johnston Murray to the governorship formerly held by his father, the colorful previous governor, Bill Murray. Dixie Gilmer was appointed commissioner; Coble Gambill, assistant commissioner; and Carl Tyler, chief. All of this created waves and ripples of change throughout the Department of Public Safety and the highway patrol.

The patrol was once again seeking new troopers and hoped to attract men who had some college education through the G.I. Bill. In March of 1950, newspapers across the state ran articles from one of Jerry Marx's press releases, encouraging college students to apply for the patrol school to be held that summer. They listed the requirements as : "Residence in Oklahoma for two years; ability to meet physical and mental requirements, weight of at least 165 pounds, height of at least 5 ft. 10 in.; and the ability to pass a character investigation." The press release continued with some facts that would attract men who were seeking some job security. "Troopers on the patrol receive $250 a month plus longevity after two years of service, and there is also a pension plan for those who complete 20 years of service." (40)

The tenth patrol school held in the summer of 1950, was thirty-two days long and brought an additional seventy troopers into the ranks. The legislature had appropriated additional funds for the operation of the patrol bringing the total allocation in 1950 from $1,015,080 the previous year to $1,680,895. These funds were used to pay sixty-seven additional troopers and give raises in salary to all officers above the patrolman level. Eleven new units were added at Antlers, Tishomingo, Marietta, Lawton, Elk City, Fairview, Hominy, Tulsa, Wagoner, Seminole, and Oklahoma City. Repercussions resulting from all of these changes—shifts in leadership, raises going only to the higher officers, addition of new troopers, and establishing of new units—were felt throughout the patrol ranks.

Patrolmen learned to anticipate changes after gubernatorial elections, when a new commissioner was usually appointed. But sometimes it was not only the commissioner and his appointed officials who could directly affect a patrolman's life. K.O. Rayburn remembered with furrowed brow, "The thing about the patrol that bothered me the most was how politics and political appointments affected the organization. There was usually a shake-up when a new commissioner came in, but one governor had it in for a trooper. He had him transferred every month for a year." He described another way political pressure was put on highway patrolmen. "The state legislature retained much of their original control of the Department of Public Safety. Many of the state representatives come in with their only view of the organization based on their personal experience with troopers stationed in their communities. Then they exerted their influence based on their limited view." A state legislator could not only affect the life of an individual trooper, but one with enough political clout could propose legislation that would affect all troopers. Many patrolmen did not understand the importance building good relations in a community even if they disagreed with the local politicians. Rayburn concluded, "The trooper's job was hard enough as it was."

Transfers, demotions, and promotions within the patrol continued to be at the discretion of the commissioner. Patrolmen had no appeal process, and their only recourse was to resign if they disagreed with the decision. Chick Clark recalled, "I was lieutenant in Enid, and they just busted me. They wanted to put a friend up there, so they said I was too easy on my men. And they busted me down to a supervisor. I had never been called on the carpet. I believed we needed to make our work as enjoyable as possible, or we would just get hardened." Clark was transferred to Oklahoma City where he worked until his retirement in 1958. During the twenty-one years he worked for the patrol, he was transferred thirteen times.

During this same time period, K.O. Rayburn was transferred from McAlester to Oklahoma City remaining at the rank of supervisor. Rayburn described his next promotion in the early 1950s: "The Public Education Officer was Bill Large, a former minister. At a meeting in Kansas City, Bill fell dead. He had some radio programs, so they asked me to cover them. As I left the studio in the First National Bank Building, the commissioner, Dixie Gilmer, who was quite ill, was sitting in a patrol car outside. He said that he had listened to my program and as of right then, I was the Public Education Officer."

Although most of the responsibilities of a trooper involved reacting to actions of law-breakers or investigating accidents, many patrolmen looked for ways to make a difference by preventing accidents. During 1950 a former highway patrolman, Clinton Riggs, was successful in getting the first "Yield Right of Way" sign installed at a Tulsa intersection. He had conceived of the sign while attending Chicago's Northwestern Traffic Institute in 1939. Riggs was responsible not only for designing the new sign, but for establishing the concept for it and getting it to be a part of state and national traffic control systems. After leaving the highway patrol Riggs worked for the Tulsa Police Department for many years.

In the fall of 1950, the Department of Public Safety began a campaign designed to make the state's highways safer through a series of press releases from the office of Jerry Marx, Public Information Director. A November press release stated, "October has taken its place as the bloodiest month of 1950 on Oklahoma highways. For the first time this year, 50 persons were killed in traffic mishaps in one month.... For the first month in more than two years, no fatal accidents occurred on hazardous, heavily traveled U.S. Highway 66, on which 7 persons died in September." The release credited the new policy of selective enforcement with this change on Route 66. (41)

In an effort to decrease the number of accidents during the Thanksgiving holiday week-end, newspapers were asked to announce the following on November 22: "The patrol has canceled days off for troopers Thursday through Sunday.... The extra duty schedule was drawn to handle Thanksgiving holiday traffic and that connected with the Oklahoma—Nebraska football game in Norman Saturday." The release also advised the public that all traffic troopers and size and weight troopers would be patrolling during this time. (42)

During December of 1950, the patrol used a Christmas theme to emphasize their efforts toward greater safety on the roads. The December 13 press release posed the question, "Would an accident spoil the Christmas season for you? Comply with all traffic laws and safety is your reward." The press release continued, "This is the question posed and the answer given by the OHP in specially printed messages to be given an estimated 24,000 out-of-state motorists entering Oklahoma on major highways before Christmas." The release called these "border stops" and noted that forty-two and one-half per cent of motorists killed in November had been from other states. The distribution of *Give Safety for Christmas* bumper stickers was also announced.

On December 20, the public was informed that "The Oklahoma Highway Patrol is combining holiday greetings with its written warnings during the month of December. Every written warning issued contains a Christmas message on the reverse side. It's all a part of the patrol's December safety drive." The release also noted however, "Those motorists who receive arrest summonses will not receive the greetings." By the end of 1950, only 501 people were killed in traffic accidents as compared to 523 in 1949. In contrast, 9,661 were injured in 1950, where only 6,870 had been injured in 1949. (43)

C.A. Morris Transferred

According to most of those interviewed, patrol personnel matters were decided by a few at the top of the organization with little consideration given to the trooper's or his family's wishes or the problems a move would cause them financially or personally. The expenses for the relocation of a trooper was covered by the department, but any expenses for his family were his own responsibility. The tradition, begun in 1937, that a trooper would be assigned away from his home community to a place anywhere else in the state at any time, continued to be followed. On January 12, 1951, my dad was notified that he would be transferred to another assignment, beginning February 1. The following Monday, he was told that he would move to Shawnee located in Pottawatomie county, twenty-eight miles south of Chandler on State Highway 18. With only a two-week notice, our family had to move from our home, make arrangements for our live-stock, and enroll us in new schools, if our family was to remain together. At the same time, Dad had to wrap up his work in Lincoln county and adjust to a new assignment in a new county. This was expected of every trooper with no questions asked. Actually, our family had been fortunate. Many troopers were moved around frequently. For example, Otto Rauch, who now had been at Poteau since 1946, had been transferred twelve times in the eleven years he had been on the patrol.

Regardless of the fact that other troopers had been transferred more frequently, this was an unwelcome blow to our family. Why had Dad been transferred so suddenly, with no hint that it was coming? No official records were found to show how decisions were made about transferring troopers. However, my mother's memories, his own journal, and newspaper articles help to give several perspectives to the answer of that question.

In Chandler, Dad had built a reputation as a no-nonsense law enforcement officer. This did not make some of the local citizens happy when their paths crossed. He had no tolerance for drunk driving and took the offending driver right to jail or the county attorney's office. Some of these citizens were influential in the community. At this time, Chandler's state senator, Boyd Cowden, served as president pro tempore of the state Senate and had a great deal of political clout. He had the ability to exert political pressure on the Commissioner of Public Safety. Mother always believed that the transfer from Chandler was a result of some of her remarks about Mr. Cowden. She had often been outspoken and usually said what she thought. She recalled that when her neighbors asked her to work in Boyd Cowden's reelection campaign, she had declined. She told them that she didn't think he should be reelected because he was doing such a poor job. Later she found out that the neighbors were related to the head of the Democratic party in Lincoln County. Mother reported that if Dad had ever been told why he was transferred so suddenly, he had never shared that information with her.

My parents had become very involved in the community from the time they moved to Chandler in 1946. Mother had worked in our schools, helped with Cub Scouts, and kept us active in the Methodist church. In addition to his patrolman duties and community involvement, Dad incorporated safety speeches into his work with the Boy Scouts and had begun to travel all across the west-central part of the state speaking to Boy Scout groups. It was difficult for our family to say good-bye to their many friends in Chandler. John was in the eighth grade and had a group of good friends with whom he hunted, fished, and participated in Scouts. He also played on the junior high basketball team. Tom, who had learning difficulties, was in the fifth grade. He had made good friends in Cub Scouts and had just started to participate in Boy Scout activities. I was a fourth grader who loved school and had several close friends I would miss. We had settled into a comfortable life and felt like an integral part of the Chandler community. This unexpected move made us feel like our roots were being ripped from our grounding.

There had been community reaction to Dad's transfer even before it was officially announced. During mid-January the following appeared in the local newspaper: "TALK: Agitation is brewed we're told, by a few here for the transfer of Highway Patrolman CA Morris. There's nothing official on this, but the rumor is hot. Frankly, we think Chandler would lose a solid citizen if it lost Morris." (44)

Dad's own thoughts about his transfer to Shawnee were chronicled in the journal that he had begun keeping on January 1, 1951. (45) On Friday, January 12, he wrote, "Day off. Helen and I went to Shawnee and got boys bedroom spread. Got notice to move Feb. 1, 1951. Thanks Mr. Cowden. 9:30 pm." This notation indicates that Dad believed Mr. Cowden had influenced his transfer in some way. His summary for the week indicated his discomfort with the news, "Notice to transfer came Friday—don't know where to."

The following Monday's journal entry shows that his concern about moving did not distract him from his work or interest in his son's basketball team. "Worked split with 67. Car washed. I drove. Went to O.C. for new assignment—chose Shawnee. One arrest R.O. negro jailed. J.R.H.[junior high team] lost 1st game in tournament. Prague to Okemah J.R.s." Two days later, John Eddleman, the trooper being transferred from Shawnee to Chandler, came to look at the rented house our family would be vacating. On Friday, Dad's day off, he and Mother went to Shawnee house hunting. "No luck" was in his journal entry. "Hectic week thinking of moving, house hunting, and answering questions—" summarized his feelings about the week.

By Sunday, John Eddleman came to request the house we were living in. The following Friday on his day off, Dad began to pack. On Saturday he went to Shawnee to look at another house and found one that would meet our family's needs, at least temporarily. His summary for the week showed his positive and resilient attitude and had a very different tone from the previous one: "Nice week, parties, gifts and farewells. Have place to go." On Wednesday, January 31, we moved. "Moved Chandler to Shawnee. Snowed, turned cold. Got moved O.K." His summary for the week was, "At Shawnee—we all like it."

After his move, Dad's friend, Jim Bradshaw, wrote a lengthy article for the Shawnee *News Star* titled "Trooper plays no favorites." The article said in part:

"Clarence A. Morris, Shawnee's new highway patrolman, is the kind of officer that couldn't be elected sheriff but once in most Oklahoma counties. He'd be too good when it comes to doing what he was supposed to do."

Bradshaw cited some pieces of information about my dad's activities as a trooper in Chandler. Some of those are listed below:

>-Morris began patrolling Lincoln county's 250 miles of highway in 1945.
>-Morris hasn't missed a workday yet. Fifteen different troopers came and left while Morris stayed in Lincoln county.
>-He has moved black-and-white cars about 400,000 miles in his nine years as a trooper.
>-Morris has preached safe driving in nearly every school building in Lincoln county.
>-Morris started the state and district driver's training contests.
>-He played Santa Claus for a while last Christmas at Crippled Children's Hospital.
>-Morris has arrested over 1,500 people since he joined the state police in 1942.
>-In one month Morris ushered 35 to the county jail or to the nearest justice of the peace.
>-He's jailed men and women for everything from carrying concealed weapons to committing immoral acts.
>-During a recent 6-month period, Morris and Troopers Roy McIntosh, Kenneth Payne and Vernon Anderson arrested enough offenders to dump $6,000 in fines into the various court cash barrels over the county.

Bradshaw included other events in Dad's career. "A beer tavern cut-up at Davenport would probably have bled to death if Morris hadn't brought his first aid kit to the scene. Morris repaired the scuffler's arm gashes and then locked him in jail for disturbing the peace. . . . Morris and Payne trailed an armed robber at 95 mph from Meeker to Prague, and Morris was about to run out of gasoline when Payne shot all four tires off the hijacker's late-model Oldsmobile."

Bradshaw described some of the many sides of my dad. "It was said many times during Morris' six-year tenure in Lincoln county that the frank and husky trooper would arrest his own grandma, if grandma persisted in making the wrong hand signal for a left turn. . . . He got a letter from a New Jersey lady he arrested for no driver's license — asking him to help her find a job in Okla. . . . In October, 1949, he passed up a chance to make an arrest. When called out of bed at 2:00 a.m. to help city police round up robbers who highjacked a big crap game after a fish fry, he said, 'Well they went down there to lose their money, didn't they?' And he went back to bed."

Bradshaw concluded, "Arresting people isn't a hobby with Morris. It's the unpleasant duty of every officer. He has reams of warning tickets to prove he has let hundreds off easy." (46)

Apparently my dad's transfer from Chandler had been based on some political reasons; he had arrested a lot of people. However, there also appeared to be many in the community who were very sorry to see Dad and our family leave. There were other indications that Shawnee needed a strong, experienced patrolman to help resolve some problems that had plagued the county for some time. C.A. Morris seemed like a good candidate for that job.

Although Dad had been older than the other troopers with whom he worked when he first went to Chandler in 1946, the others had more experience on the job than he did. When he moved to Shawnee at forty-four years of age, he was not only many years older than the other troopers, but also had many more years of experience on the patrol. Mother reported that Dad had felt like a big brother when he began to work with Don McDaniel and Nat Taylor at Shawnee. Dad began this difficult new assignment as a highway patrolman in Shawnee just as his own family began to deal with the challenges of raising teenage children.

Figure 4 — "Trooper C.A. Morris with members of Chandler's Safety Junior quiz kids in 1948. His daughter, Donna, is third from left on front row."

CHAPTER 4
THE THREE-MAN UNIT AT SHAWNEE
1951-1955

SHAWNEE IS THE county seat of Pottawatomie county, known for its whiskey towns and lawlessness during pre-statehood days. Although by the 1950s, the town had developed into a center for business and had built a reputation for valuing family life and education, serving as the site for both Oklahoma Baptist University and Saint Gregory's College, out in the remote areas of the county an anti-law enforcement attitude continued to exist. In addition, there was a great deal of commuter traffic that passed through the county as workers traveled to and from Oklahoma City on the west and the oil field areas to the east. All of these factors created special types of problems that needed to be addressed in the early 1950s.

Don McDaniel, who had been at McAlester during his probationary first year as a patrolman, described his move to Shawnee in 1950. Contrary to information from others interviewed, McDaniel's story reflects that some consideration was given to his personal feelings and family situation in deciding on this transfer. "Bill Hamilton asked me if I had a preference for assignment. My wife, Jerry, had been having some health problems, and we had a new baby. He asked what would help us. I told him that it was no use, a trooper never got to go back to his home town. He said, 'Why not try it? If it's never happened, it could happen.

Ask for it.' So I put in for Shawnee so Jerry could be near our families. And that's where I was assigned."

Since there were no provisions to help troopers move their families as assignments were changed, each man had to figure out how to do it on his own. McDaniel recalled the day of his family's move, "We didn't have any money to move. The wrecker company in McAlester offered us his wrecker truck and trailer to move in. Everything we had was in pasteboard boxes on an open truck and trailer. It was cloudy, and we were scared to death it was going to rain and ruin everything we had. It was a mess!"

Nat Taylor, McDaniel's buddy from patrol school days, had moved from Okemah to Edmond in June 1950, and then was assigned to Shawnee that September. Taylor remembered that the situation in Shawnee and all across Pottawatomie county was not like the Okemah area in which he had worked his first year. "There were more fatalities in the Shawnee area than any other concentrated place in the state. With Seminole, Holdenville, Wewoka, and Tinker Field employees coming through three times a day and two-lane, poor highways, there were lots of wrecks."

Based on what he heard from his and his wife's families who lived in the area McDaniel knew that the troopers before he went there had not been very successful. For whatever reasons, the troopers were not consistantly enforcing traffic laws, and "the district attorney wouldn't file cases in the county," McDaniel said.

Taylor explained, "The troopers there before us hadn't really done their jobs. They were good guys who just got in with cliques." Citizens were beginning to complain about what was happening in their county, and information from troopers' reports indicated that more prevention activities needed to be carried out.

According to Taylor and McDaniel, the patrol leadership recognized the need to bring in some strong and enthusiastic troopers to deal with the problems that existed in Pottawatomie county in the early 1950s. McDaniel described the meeting he and Taylor had with Lieutenant Bob Lester before they reported to their assignment in Shawnee, "He said he wanted us to go over there, make some friends, and begin to do some work in that county."

"The Oklahoma City 'brass' pulled everybody out and put me with McDaniel and gave us three different troopers before C.A. came," Taylor remarked.

When they went out on their newly assigned roads, the two young troopers found out that the methods they had used to accomplish their jobs in their previous assignments didn't always work in Pottawatomie County. Consequently, the methods they sometimes resorted to were not what they had been taught to do in patrol school, but they did seem to be effective. "If you got ready to stop someone and turned the red light on, the younger people would just take off," McDaniel remembered. "The other troopers had just let them go. From the first, whenever we'd try to stop somebody, we'd have a chase on our hands — night or day. Sometimes when a car would stop, we'd pull up behind 'em and bump 'em along. We told 'em to get the runnin' out of their system, and then we'd tend to business." Taylor described the actions he took when drivers refused to stop. "Pretty regular I'd shoot out a tire. Some old boy wouldn't stop — he was runnin' everybody off of the road. You're by yourself, and you don't have any other way to make him stop. So you shoot at something that will make him stop." Even after many years had passed, Taylor sounded frustrated. "You don't shoot at a driver, you shoot at tires," he explained.

Morris Arrives in Shawnee

The situation as former troopers McDaniel and Taylor described it supports the idea that my dad's transfer to Shawnee was not made for purely political reasons. It appears that his experience and skills were needed to develop an effective public safety program there, although there was no documentation that he was advised of this. McDaniel explained, "When C.A. got to Shawnee, he made it clear that he was going to work with the county attorney, but he also made it clear that he was going to enforce the law. They found out pretty quick that he wasn't going to bring in any 'green' cases — they were going to be good cases and stand up in court. It was rotten when we got there." He continued, "Nat and I were kind of renegades as compared to C.A. He'd been on a while, and we'd only been on a year. He tried to control us, more or less. We were doing things he didn't approve of, a lot of times. He was kind of ornery, but he kept us out of trouble," McDaniel concluded with a laugh.

When Dad arrived, he started to work right away in the areas of community safety education. His journal entry for February 1, 1951 stated, "First day working at Shawnee. Speaking at Seminole Boy S[couts]. Adults. supper 1.50 with Palmer, Potter, Curley Parsons." During his first week, Dad made eight arrests and worked two wrecks. Also during that week he had his photograph taken by the Shawnee *News-Star* newspaper.

McDaniel said, "C.A. worked closely with the newspaper. He knew that if there was a story in something we were involved in that they would like to have it. And they appreciated it too." Laughing and shaking his head, he added, "Nat and I did a lot of things we hoped the newspaper never got ahold of."

An undated clipping from the *News-Star* used some humor to introduce their newest trooper to the public and warn them what to expect from him. "C.A. Morris, the county's new highway patrolman, doesn't have much patience with drivers who commit several offenses. 'You know, we only pick up a fellow about one out of the 50 times he makes a violation,' he declared. 'For example, how many times have you failed to signal on turning?' he asked me.

'Pretty weather we're having now, isn't it,' I replied. Moris[sic], by the way, is almost as good a newspaperman as he is an officer. He never misses a story, our Chandler correspondents always said when he was stationed in Lincoln county."

Dad had taken some notes as he prepared for his new assignment. In the front of his journal, he listed his two new partners' names and their telephone numbers: "Don McDaniels[sic], 1143M and Nat Taylor, 3271R." He also noted: "OS 41, Art 47 Sec 369, patrolling, attending court, special ass., maintenance of equipt," a reference to the Oklahoma Statute or law related to the need for keeping records to claim reimbursement for expenses incurred while on duty. In addition he recorded, "Conoco Credit Card No. P-628-56," which he would use to gas up the patrol car in Pottawatomie county.

With such short notice, we had moved into a small rental house in a residential area of Shawnee. Mother and Dad immediately began looking for an acreage to buy. They felt strongly that their pigs, chickens, and milk cow were a necessary part of our lives, insuring that we would be well-fed and we children would learn the rural work ethic they both valued. On February 13, 1951, they went to see an acreage at 1805 North Harrison Street. There was a house, a garage with two rental apartments, a small barn, and a ten-acre pasture with a pond. The following Saturday, Dad and Mother signed a contract on the property. On Monday, February 19, they paid $1,000.00 down on it, and on February 28, we moved into our new home on North Harrison. By this time the state provided a van that patrolmen could rent to move their families. Dad wrote, "Moved with Bill Roal's pickup and new State Moving Van. $9.00. First day in new home, worked with Nat."

The move to the house on North Harrison helped ease the pain of leaving Chandler a bit for my brothers. A friend of Tom's, Joe Sam Vassar, recalled that his and his brothers' hearts had been broken when Tom and his family moved to Shawnee. But when they came to visit him on the acreage they discovered that there was a pond where they could go fishing and swimming. "It was almost like going to camp," Vassar said. He also remembered that our dad had played a joke on him and his brothers on one of their first visits. Dad had been getting out-of-date candy bars from a candy salesman to feed to the pigs we were raising. Vassar said that Dad had asked the boys if they liked candy and of course they said yes. He made a big to-do and then gave them some candy bars which turned out to be wooden samples used for displays. After the joke Dad gave them some real candy bars. Vassar laughed as he told how surprised they had been.

Patrol Routines

In a three man unit, which was what the patrol tried to have in the most populated parts of the state, there continued to be a requirement that two men work together at night for safety reasons. "The day man would go on about 7:00 a.m., and he'd pick up the evening man about 5:00 p.m. He'd work until about 8:00 p.m. and pick up his partner. They would work until they'd get through with traffic," Taylor stated.

McDaniel explained, "About 2:00 a.m. the two men would take the patrol car to the day man's house and leave it. The police department would pick the two men up and take them home. Any call-outs would go to the day man." He continued, "Sometimes the wives would have to go and pick up their husbands after they left the car for the day man." The rotating schedule was worked out among the troopers and then was sent in to their headquarters to have it approved.

Making a stop of an unknown driver was a very dangerous thing, especially at night. Troopers had been trained to be cautious and to look out for their partners as well as themselves. Taylor described the equipment in the patrol car that they used when stopping cars at night. "There was a red spot light on the left so the trooper driving could use it to keep a driver off him. The white spot was on the right. The partner kept that light right on the driver to make sure he didn't come up with a gun or something. He would also shine it over to the shoulder of the road to show the driver that it was safe to pull over, off the road. On top was a little blinking red light and a siren. There were amber lights in the back window."

Taylor described the procedures they followed when making a stop at night. "Partners took turns. If I was driving, I opened my door and watched traffic and held my flashlight while he went to the car. The next one, I'd get out and my partner would look over the car with his flashlight while I talked to the driver. If it was a young person, I'd ask him to get out of the car—didn't want to embarrass him. If it was 'Mother'—you didn't tell her to get out of the car."

McDaniel shared a slightly different version, "We always had the driver get out. That way we could always keep our eye on 'em to see that they didn't make any moves or anything. We'd take 'em back to our patrol car to write a ticket. They taught us in patrol school to get 'em out of the car away from their family or company—where they wouldn't be embarrassed about what was being said."

The three troopers, McDaniel, Morris, and Taylor, began to systematically patrol their assigned roads and consistently stop drivers who were breaking the law. According to his journal, during his first month in Shawnee, Dad made thirteen arrests. McDaniel reported, "The word got around and within a short time people started respecting us, and we didn't have so many chases [when we stopped cars]."

In addition to the high volume of traffic that passed through the Shawnee area, there were night-time activities that caught the troopers' attention. "They had lots of dances going on—especially on Saturday nights. We had to work those beer joints quite a bit. You didn't have to worry about going into a beer joint with C.A. You always knew where he was and what was gonna happen if someone did get out of line. He didn't tolerate too much," McDaniel said.

Taylor recalled an incident in which things didn't go at all the way they thought they would. "One night C.A. and I ran a couple of guys a couple of miles. I was shooting at their tires. I shot one of the back tires off. Then I hung out of the window with my .38 pistol and took some more shots. I hit our spotlight and shot a hole right through it. While I was shooting, the car missed a curve and landed in the ditch. I ran up there, and one old boy jumped out and made a run on me. I hit him open handed and just knocked him for a loop. The other guy jumped out and threw both hands up. He was twice as big as I was, and he kept saying, 'I'm not gonna fight! I'm not gonna fight!'"

Taylor continued, "I motioned to the guy I'd knocked down and told C.A. 'Now you watch this guy, I had to slap him.'"

"C.A. said, 'Oh, come over here,' to the guy. That old boy just ran right over and hit C.A. right in the mouth, breaking his false teeth in two. C.A. beat the whey out of him. The old boy got up and escaped C.A. I had to knock him down again, but he tore my jacket off. The other big old boy just started bawling like a baby. He was about six-six, and we hadn't touched him." After this incident Dad had to get his teeth fixed right away. Taylor could wait a little longer to get his jacket repaired. They teased one another for months about who was responsible for the damage to the spotlight, and who was to blame for the destruction of their property.

Taylor reflected back on fighting, "Some troopers liked to fight. I hated to fight because you always got your clothes dirty and tore up. Then you hated yourself for whacking somebody. Sometimes I would hit someone with my gun, but I always hit him on the shoulder or hand or wrist. It hurts so bad that a guy kind of freezes and stops fighting. It doesn't break anything, but boy, does he get crippled up for a week or two. If I got in court and they asked me about it, I'd say I hit him with my pistol. If you answer honest, the lawyer didn't make anything out of it," he concluded matter-of-factly.

Troopers never knew what to expect when they went to work. In fact, for many troopers, this sense of the unknown and possible dangers were the very characteristics of their job that drew them to the patrol. During some shifts everything was quiet and peaceful, and sometimes things were chaotic. McDaniel recalled one night when things took a strange turn, "One Saturday night Nat and I were working. After the traffic died down we would usually go out on the back roads. A lot of times drunks would be taking those instead of highways. We were involved in a lot of embarrassing things with people. Earlier an FBI agent had seen us in the sheriff's office and had given us each a box of .38 tracer bullets. They'd light a fire when they hit so you could tell how close you came to something. Well, we were driving down this county gravel road, and we saw a jackrabbit. Nat said, 'Stop, I want to see how close I can come to that rabbit.'"

McDaniel continued his story with a gleam in his eye, "He put a couple of tracers in his gun and leaned out the window. He shot and hit right in front of the rabbit, and the bullet ricocheted off the gravel. The fire was just a flyin' as the bullet hit a tree up ahead. All at once, a car started up and took off. We liked to have wrecked the car chasing them — we couldn't see a thing, there was so much dust. A mile or two ahead, we hit pavement. Nat said to let 'em go, but I hit the red light as I slowed down. The car just pulled right over and stopped. An old boy jumped out of the car without a stitch of clothes on. We jumped out and tried to get him back in his car as fast as we could. By then traffic was a mess, with everybody slowing down to gawk at what was going on. The guy said that they had thought it was the woman's husband shooting at them. You just never knew . . ." McDaniel concluded with a hearty laugh.

One of the parts of the job that most troopers continued to dread was the completion of reports. In addition to filing a report for every accident, there were also reports for arrests and warnings. Information from reports indicated how troopers were spending their time and what kinds of problem drivers there were in their areas. Each trooper was aware of expectations regarding numbers of arrests he was to make and numbers of warnings he was to give out: a type of quota system. Near the end of a month, troopers often tried to get their numbers into better alignment. McDaniel smiled as he remembered, "One shift C.A. and I decided that we had plenty of arrests, but we were short on writing warnings. So that shift we decided to write some warnings. Weeds had grown up about hip-high on the shoulders of the roads. I was driving, and we stopped a car. This time it was C.A.'s turn to make the contact. So I pulled over, and he opened the door and stepped out. He went right out of sight! I could hear someone struggling in water. I had pulled the car right up on the edge of a bar ditch drain. If I had been over another foot, we'd have turned the car over. When he stepped out, he fell right into about six feet of water—it was over his head. That's the maddest I ever saw him. He swore I had done it on purpose. He was even wanting to fight me. I had to take him home; his uniform was ruined."

Dad had some good reasons for thinking McDaniel had played a trick on him. Taylor and McDaniel often tried to pull one over on him, and then he would get back at them. McDaniel described one such incident: "C.A. didn't smoke, and he was on Nat and I all of the time. To make it worse, we were smoking cigars—it was stinking the patrol car up.

He'd jump on us about once a week about it. Sometimes when Nat and I were working the night shift and we took the car over to leave it at C.A.'s, we'd both light up cigars just before we left the car. We'd roll the windows up and leave it filled with smoke, just to aggravate him. Then he'd have to go out early and warm the unit up with all of the windows down, trying to get the smoke out of that car." McDaniel continued, "One evening Nat and I went over and picked the unit up from C.A.'s. It was getting cold so we turned the heater on. As it warmed up, there was this awful smell, and it just kept getting worse. We liked to 'a never found what was causing the smell. C.A. had stuck some limburger cheese in the heater." McDaniel laughed and said, "He really got back at us that time."

Our family settled into life in the Shawnee community fairly quickly. Mother became active in helping at the schools and in the Methodist Church's Sunday School programs. Since John mirrored our dad's ability and interest in athletics, he and Dad began attending the end of the basketball season's games at the high school. Dad continued to give speeches to Boy Scout groups, schools, as well as community groups. Shortly after we moved to Shawnee, Dad played in a fundraising basketball game that was held at the high school gym. Mother fashioned a costume with a pointed cap to cover his bald head and long stockings that looked like tights. Although Tom and I laughed and thought he looked great, John, who was just entering high school, was very embarrassed that his dad would look and act so ridiculous in front of his new friends. To make matters even worse for John, Dad's photograph in his costume appeared in the newspaper the next day.

Safety Speeches

Safety speeches continued to be a required part of every trooper's job. Some troopers enjoyed this contact with the pubic and some did not. Taylor reflected on his feelings, "I couldn't believe that they'd take us off of the road to go talk to a bunch of adults who treated it like a joke. I hated having to go to make a talk. With children I didn't mind so much, but with adults . . . . One day I got a call from Oklahoma City to go to Tecumseh to make a talk. They were the biggest bunch of drunks. They all worked at Tinker Field, and I had put most of 'em in jail at one time or another. I was by myself, so I had to go. It was the Kiwanis, I think. When they introduced me, they said that everybody knew me."

"I said, 'Yeah, you all know me; I've had all of you in jail. You all look like jail birds to me, everyone of you. You must have called me over here to punish me, 'cause I don't like any of you. The reason I don't like you is because you don't believe in obeying the law. You set the poorest example for our kids that anyone could. And each one of you has a houseful of kids. I'm gonna be up here talking to you about one of your kids getting hurt or killed in an accident.'"

Taylor concluded, "You could have heard a pin drop. I talked to them for about ten minutes and accused them of everything I could think of. Then I asked if there were any questions. One of them said, 'I believe you have answered every question already.' And I left." After many years had passed, Nat Taylor seemed to still resent being forced to make safety talks to adults as a part of his patrolman's job.

Taylor added, "C.A. liked to make talks. He'd go at the first of every year—in his own car—make every school in the county and make a talk. That's pretty dedicated. He'd let them see his pistol and shotgun and everything he had. He had a little bitty box filled with stuff—his 'Lost Kit.'" My dad was a bit of a ham, and he enjoyed being in front of groups. According to his journal, during the month of March 1951, he gave speeches to Boy Scout groups in Shawnee, Norman, Edmond, Clinton, El Reno, and Oklahoma City. He also was a guest on Shawnee's KGFF radio station once; spoke to a total of 1,865 students in schools; and gave a speech to a nurses' group in Norman.

While Dad was working in the Boy Scouts with my brother, Tom, he had decided to find out how many useful items he could pack in the smallest container. He called it his "Lost Kit" and often used it as the focus of his talks on safety preparedness. He started with an aspirin box and changed to an automobile fuse box with a sliding lid, when the aspirin box lid kept popping open. Using his vivid imagination and creativity, Dad wove a story of survival in the woods to go with each item in the box, from tiny fishhooks to 100 feet of fine wire to matches and a striker. At one time he even included a $10.00 gold piece in the kit. He enjoyed talking to groups and sharing his thoughts on safety and always being prepared for anything that might come along. At home, from the time we were small children, he had us discuss many aspects of safety and being prepared. He made sure we knew how to exit the house in case of a fire, we had learned where to go in case of a tornado, and we frequently identified what we needed to take with us in case of a disaster. He strongly believed in educating his own children as well as others about the importance of being prepared.

Dad made a real effort to build a good relationship with Pottawatomie county officials. He and our family became good friends with the county sheriff, Leroy Flinchum. The fact that Flinchum had been a cowboy with the 101 Ranch and told tales of traveling and performing all over the world was a fascination to us, especially John. After a few months of consistent patrolling, the county attorney seemed to change his stance toward the patrol troopers. McDaniel recalled, "Before long we had the county attorney riding with us to see what a mess it was [in the county]."

In February of 1951, another dimension was added to the Department of Public Safety, the Chaplain's Corps. In this auxiliary of the Oklahoma Highway Patrol, a number of ministers representing various church denominations and areas of the state volunteered their religious services to members of the patrol, their families, and others who may have encountered tragedy while traveling through the state. (1) While on duty, a chaplain was dressed like a trooper but instead of the OHP on his collar, he had a cross. (2)

With the exception of his probationary year in Cushing, Dad had worked the rest of his career in the Oklahoma City District. He was well acquainted with the leadership of his district and with most of the leaders of the patrol. Although he sometimes lost his temper and liked to play jokes, for the most part he was a dedicated highway patrolman who was concerned about doing a good job. He wanted to please his bosses and maintained many friendships he had made during his career.

From the time he arrived in Shawnee, Dad had assumed the role of unofficial leader of the unit. McDaniel remembered a time when Dad thought he had really done the wrong thing. "C.A. and I were working this night and got a call of an accident out on a county road where there were personal injuries. We finally found it, and a drunk was involved. As soon as we drove up he started running, and he took off down the road. C.A. was running ahead of me, but we weren't gaining on the old boy. So I pulled out my pistol and fired a shot into the ground. At that same time, the drunk hit a barbed wire fence, and he dropped to the ground. C.A. just froze—he thought I'd shot the guy. He looked at me and turned just as white as a sheet and said, 'Now, you've got us in a lot of trouble.' I started laughing, and when he found out what had happened, he liked to have never got over it. He thought I'd shot and killed a drunk driver!" said McDaniel, laughing gleefully.

One of the shared responsibilities of troopers in a three-man unit was to keep their patrol car washed and serviced. McDaniel explained, "We got the car serviced on our off time. And that was something about C.A.—he wasn't any help at all. He hated getting that car cleaned up worse than anything. He'd work two shifts, if one of us would get the car serviced. We just did it when it got real dirty. One time we got a new unit, we took it down to the garage and had the motor wiring, and all under the hood sprayed with lacquer. Then all we had to do was turn a hose on it, and it would sparkle. Our 'secret' finally got out, and everyone in the state started doing it. About every three months, they'd have a state-wide troop meeting in Oklahoma City where they had an inspection. Sometimes they had them in other towns and city and county officers would be on call. Then they started having meetings in regions of the state, so someone was always working."

Taylor related a story about an inspection that caused Dad great embarrassment. "One time we were running late to an inspection in Oklahoma City. We had worked all night, and I was really pushing it to try to get there on time. I pulled up to the armory, and everyone was already inside. I sounded my siren for them to open the door and let us in." Taylor continued with a chuckle, "As we pulled in, everyone was all lined up, and the 'Brass' was inspecting units. Just as I pulled up into a place our radiator hose broke, and old rusty water spewed out all over everyone. C.A. said, 'Boy are we in trouble now!'" The Shawnee unit took a lot of ribbing about this incident, but there were no formal reprimands.

Troopers' Families

The three troopers' families became good friends. Since Don and Jerry both had their own families in Shawnee, they did not spend as much time with the other troopers' families. Jerry worked, and they lived in an apartment with their two little girls, Donna and Linda. Nat's wife, Betty, was a full time homemaker taking care of their two small children, Linda and Johnnie. Betty and my mother had both come from rural areas of western Oklahoma and seemed to have a lot in common. They got together often.

Mother recalled a time when she and Betty had been really scolded by Dad. "One evening about 5:00 p.m. we were on the porch waiting for the patrol car to pick him up for work. C.A. said, 'If this wind were from another direction, I'd think we were going to have a tornado.' He went on to work, and sure enough about ten miles north of us there was a bad tornado—at Meeker."

She concluded, "The next morning Betty and I were talking, and we decided to go to Meeker to see the damage. C.A. [and Nat] had been out all night and had not come back home yet. We loaded the five kids in our car and started on the ten-mile trip. We saw cattle dead along the road and houses blown away. About five miles up the road, we met the patrol car with C.A. driving. He stopped, gave me a good lecture, and sent us home. He didn't get home until the next day. Now we knew better than to go into an area where there had been a disaster, but we just wanted to see it for ourselves," she explained. Dad always expected us to do the right thing and to serve as an example for others.

Mom and Dad were always searching for ways to stretch their money to provide for three growing children. For entertainment our family took advantage of free passes given to troopers by the local picture show and the carnivals and circuses as they passed through Shawnee. We also attended Indian Pow-Wows held in Pottawatomie county. Our family drove the 1947 Chevrolet that my parents had bought new for $1,215—including the trade-in for their 1936 Chevrolet. After making adjustments to our life in Shawnee, we settled into a very busy life with family and new friends.

During their long night shifts, the younger troopers often talked to Dad about money troubles. In 1950 and 1951, Dad was making $3,000 a year and Don McDaniel and Nat Taylor were each making $2,700 a year. Since my parents had learned to be very frugal during their nineteen-year marriage, Dad tried to get his partners to follow their example. McDaniel chuckled as he described an incident that brought a lot of laughter for many years after it happened. "Jerry and I had bought something, maybe a car. We couldn't really afford it, but we had bought it. Well, when C.A. and Nat talked about it, C.A. said, 'Why in the world did they buy that? They should have bought a cow.' C.A. didn't approve of it one bit. He told Nat, 'I don't want you kids to say anything else to me about hard times.'"

McDaniel continued, "Well, old Nat couldn't wait to get over to our place to tell us what C.A. had said: that we should have bought a cow! Jerry told Nat to get right back in his car and go over to C.A. and tell him if he could find a place to put a cow in the apartment we were living in, we'd buy a cow. C.A. was always trying to get us to save a little money. We got a kick out of that. What in the world would we have done with a cow?"

According to his journal, in late April of 1951, Dad began conducting high school Driver's Training contests in the Shawnee area. He spent the 24th in Maud preparing for a contest, and the next day Taylor and McDaniel assisted with it. Central High School won first, Chandler second, and Midwest City third. On the 27th Dad moved on to Norman to prepare for the regional contest to be held on May 2. He assisted with the state contest on May 9, and Shattuck won. These contests were only a small part of the many safety education programs sponsored by the highway patrol. Later in 1951, the National Safety Council awarded top educational honors to the Oklahoma Department of Public Safety for school safety education. (3)

During May and June, Dad was called to court in Oklahoma City four times to testify in a case resulting from the wreck between the Glen R. Key truck and the teenagers in Chandler. On June 23, my dad, who had never missed a day's work for illness, was taken to the hospital in Shawnee for an emergency appendectomy. The McDaniels took care of us children while Nat Taylor went to the hospital with Mother. Dad could not go back to work for about five weeks. He stopped keeping his journal on a daily basis while in the hospital and made only a few entries during the rest of the year. (No additional journals were found from 1951 through the middle of 1955.)

On July 24, 1951, tragedy struck the Oklahoma Highway Patrol as Trooper Theo Cobb, who had joined the patrol in 1937, was killed by a hit-and-run driver while he was investigating a minor collision on State Highway 76 north of Fox. A twenty year-old Fort Chaffee, Arkansas soldier turned himself in to the Healdton city marshal a few hours later and said that he had been afraid to stop. He was charged with manslaughter. Only two other troopers had been killed in the line of duty in Oklahoma, and Cobb's death was a stark reminder of the dangers of the job.

Korean War Impacts Patrol

Although seventy new troopers had been added to the force in 1950, the Oklahoma Highway patrol was having trouble keeping men since problems in Korea were escalating. The U.S. armed forces were building up their troops rapidly as President Truman sent units to help in South Korea. Between June 25, 1950 and July 27, 1953, Oklahoma Highway Patrol Chief Carl Tyler withdrew twelve patrol units from the force for lack of manpower. (4)

While waiting for Dad to return to work, Taylor and McDaniel continued working their territory with the help of other troopers who were assigned to work with them on a temporary basis. Taylor reflected on his feelings about being a trooper. "I felt like I was doing good. My dad was a school teacher [and also in the state legislature], and he said his greatest reward was when a kid, he had thought would never make anything of himself, would come back and be a professional of some kind. I think that is true." Like his father, Trooper Taylor didn't expect immediate rewards for his work on the patrol. He continued, "I never dreaded a shift. I always loved going to work. So many times you just went out and wrote warnings, went into a cafe and sat down at someone's table and visited with them. I'd always order a cup of coffee, but I didn't drink it. You really didn't *do* anything. It was dead, but I liked it. You really developed good friendships with people. Out on the road by myself, I might need some help. Those friendships I had made might save my life sometime."

Taylor's experiences growing up and living in rural areas of the state gave him a perspective that wasn't always in agreement with the the way things were supposed to be done according to the department. He described a situation with accident reports in which the Department of Public Safety requirement for information to use in their statistical analyses was counter to his view of what should have been happening in a community. "They'd use statistics for all kinds of things. I believed a warning was as important as an arrest. Sometimes when I'd work an accident, I'd investigate and then give them both a warning. I got into trouble over that. But often two drivers in the country had known each other as kids. There was no need to arrest someone. They just wanted the insurance company to know that they were not at fault. Paying a fine wasn't going to help anybody. The lieutenants would just throw a fit." He concluded, "I think they finally put the option of giving both parties a warning on the reports." Although most troopers, like Taylor, disliked some aspects of the reports they were to fill out, information from these reports created the data upon which many state-wide decisions were made, ranging from where patrol units were assigned to which roads would be repaired. The accident reports also formed a critical link in making drivers financially responsible for their actions.

The Safety Responsibility Division processed and reviewed every accident report with damages exceeding $50. "The reviewing procedure was totally manual and was intended to spot drivers involved in accidents who had no liability insurance. A letter was sent to the uninsured motorist informing him that either a bond covering the cost of repairs would have to be filed or he would be subject to having his license tag revoked. Each stage of enforcement required additional reviewing and paper work, a task which grew through the years. The division had to depend on already overworked troopers for collection of revoked operator's licenses and car tags during the fifties." (5)

Our family had taken a summer vacation since we moved to Chandler. Over the last four years we had gone fishing in Minnesota for two weeks with my mother's sister and her family, the Louthans, who lived on a farm near Chester. Dad and Uncle Art loved to fish. We always returned from our vacations refreshed, ready for us kids to return to school, and in time for another of Dad's passions: football. In the fall of 1951, John was a member of the Shawnee High School Wolf Pack junior varsity football team, and Dad never missed a game. In addition, he managed to draw the duty assignment to work traffic at the OU Sooners' home games in Norman as often as possible. His journal entry for Saturday, November 17, read, "Norman OU vs Iowa State Wrecked Unit 30 Dinner 1.25 Supper 1.75." He didn't give any details about his wrecked patrol car. However, Dad's journal entry for Saturday, November 24, 1951, was, "Sig. 93. dinner 1.30 Ate at Beverly's with Capt. Bob Lester." Signal 93 meant to report to Oklahoma City garage for car repairs or exchange. Apparently Unit 30, which had been wrecked at the ball game, had been repaired.

That Christmas, Dad received what was to be the first of many gifts from Shawnee businessman, Shorty Reid. One year it was an electric cooker oven, another a kitchen food mixer, and other useful items followed. Reid owned a gas station that operated a wrecker in Shawnee and gave a nice gift to each patrolman every Christmas. (Reid's phone number, 3128, was listed in Dad's 1951 Journal.) Troopers called him whenever they needed a vehicle towed near Shawnee. It was common practice throughout the state for troopers to identify one or two companies they would call when a vehicle needed to be towed. There was another listing in the journal for Young's Salvage, also in Shawnee.

Dealing With Emergencies and Issues

Holidays were often a hectic time for patrolmen. Taylor described a memorable one. "On Christmas Eve, McDaniel relieved C.A., and before he picked me up he worked a three injury accident. He called me and told me to get my uniform on because the next accident had a fatality. It was a misty, heavy air night. The wreck was a mile north of the drive in. It was a three-fatality accident. That accident made eleven fatherless children, three widows, and two of the widows never regained their faculties. The children were all torn up. There were eighteen Signal 82s, or injury accidents, around the area that night." Taylor shook his head as he commented, "It was the worst night of my life!"

Because there were so many other accidents, Taylor and McDaniel had to call for help from several places before they could find enough ambulances to transport the injured people. Taylor continued, "We had used ambulances from Norman to Edmond to Seminole. It took us a week to sort out where everyone went. People would locate their children, and they'd be so relieved to find them. But they wouldn't call us. Mac and I smoked a whole box of cigars that night," he said with a sigh. Troopers had to follow up on every individual who was involved in an accident and include their condition on the report they filed.

On New Year's Eve of 1951, two reporters, Frank Leslie

and Jack Reese, from the Shawnee *News-Star* rode with McDaniel and Taylor. The next day a long article appeared on the front page titled, "Patrol's job is to protect you from yourself." The reporters stated that Troopers Taylor and McDaniel stopped twenty-four cars and worked one accident during the time they rode along. They wrote, "In all instances the highway patrol worked with courtesy and efficiency. Whenever motorists were stopped they were treated politely, but firmly, as troopers explained just what violation of the traffic code had occurred." They also noted that the three Shawnee patrolmen had put 180,000 miles on the patrol car (an average of 200 miles per day) in the previous eighteen months. (6)

Dad could get fired-up when he felt that he or someone he cared about was being falsely accused. In late January 1952, he responded to a citizen who criticized the highway patrol for their delay in issuing driving permits in a Sunday newspaper column titled, "Public Pulse." Dad wrote a lengthy response for which he received a $3.00 check as first prize and had his letter published. In the letter, he emphasized that driving was a privilege not a right and described the many efforts the state had underway to make the roads safer. He stated, "The $3 that you pay for this driving PRIVILEGE is NOT used by the state highway patrol, but goes into the state's general fund and the money used by the department is appropriated by your legislature." He charged, "Mr. Strickland, you implied that our present highway patrol is no longer a service to the motoring public and no one can expect help if in trouble on the roads today. But I am sure that a great percentage of the people of this state will not agree with that implication."

He explained, "I noticed that the average old age pensioner in Lincoln county received $50.10. With my family of five, I received a take-home check of $251.75. This included nine years of longevity in addition to my base pay. Simple arithmetic reveals that I received $50.35 for each member of my family. Is this loose handling of state money? The license examiners receive even less money than patrolmen."

Dad concluded, "Now, in closing, let me assure you Mr. Strickland that the OHP is still serving the people, still giving away gas, fuses, lifts, information, etc., doing everything it can for the motoring public in distress. Yes, we're trying to make this PRIVILEGE worth $3 every two years and make the highways a safer place for you and yours."

Not all of a trooper's work was filled with tragedy or negative events. McDaniel described a time he and Dad went out of their territory for a little fun. "One evening C.A. and I were working, and he suggested that we slip out of our district and go to the Kolache Festival at Prague. He asked if I had ever eaten a kolache, and I said, 'No.'

He said, 'They're good, a kind of sweet roll with fruit in them.' We got over there, parked the car, and elbowed our way into a restaurant. It was full. Someone moved from a table, and we sat down. C.A. ordered a cup of coffee and two kolaches. I had already looked around and knew I didn't want to eat one of those things.

So I said, 'Bring me a cup of coffee and a Hostess cupcake.'

C.A. blew his fuse. I got a lecture when we got back to the car. He said, 'That embarrassed me to death. I take you to a Kolache Festival and that's what they are eating, and you order a Hostess cupcake!'" Dad had always been proud of the Czech delicacy, since my mother was Bohemian, and she and her family made kolaches. According to McDaniel, Dad never asked him to eat a kolache again.

One of a trooper's responsibilities was to appear in court to testify in criminal cases after an arrest. This was done during work time, in uniform, and in a patrol car. Often a trooper was called to testify in civil court when there were lawsuits resulting from an wreck he had worked. Taylor commented, "After an accident, one person would sue the other one. The trooper would make out an accident report, and it may have been obvious that one of them was wrong. But the trooper would be called into court, and everybody in there would call him a liar. So most troopers started carrying a camera with them. At an accident scene they'd take some pictures, and when they got called to court, they had a picture to back up what they said. C.A. taught me how to testify in court. It got 'em scared when we'd show up. You could not testify in a civil action while on duty. If we got subpoenaed to court and we were on duty, we'd have to take leave, change out of our uniform, and drive our own car. Then we could charge for our time and expenses. We would be an 'expert witness.' We wouldn't take too much, or we would lose credibility."

My mother remembered some of Dad's experiences with taking photographs to court. "He got a 35 mm camera and began to take pictures of wrecks as he worked them. We didn't have auto insurance like we do now. When they would get to court to try to prove that the wreck wasn't their fault, it was the other fellas', all they had was the pictures C.A. had taken. C.A. made a lot of money for a while. There were a lot of lawsuits; when someone didn't have insurance, they would go to court. There was one attorney who was very good to C.A. He would subpoena him and have him bring his pictures to court. He would give him as much as $300.00 after court. Gee, that was a lot of money for us. We were trying to pay for our house. C.A. didn't know very much about that attorney. One night the attorney called, and he was recovering from some kind of surgery. He did some sweet-talking and asked C.A. to come and spend some time with him. This was the first time C.A. realized the attorney was gay. C.A. said, 'No, I cannot come in to see you.' That was the end of the big money; he had gone to court three or four times for that attorney," she stated coldly.

Dangers on the Job

Although troopers had learned to be alert constantly while they were working, there were times when they didn't realize the danger they had been in until after it was over. McDaniel told about one such incident. "One night Nat and I were chasing a stolen car with a bunch of kids. We finally got them stopped and while we were talking to them, one of the kids said, 'I was scared to death when they started shooting at you with that rifle.' Sure enough, when we went back down the road we found it in the bar ditch. It was empty, and they threw it out of the window. We didn't even know they had been shooting at us," he said incredulously.

Being a highway patrolman was not a nine-to-five job. Troopers were expected to work long hours and be resourceful and self-sufficient. McDaniel gave an example, "We might be sent out on a road for a bank robbery or something. We'd set the roadblock up, and the FBI would get all of the information and keep it flowing. We would check every vehicle. It was time consuming and really messed up your routines. We won more than we lost. If anyone left, it just weakened the chain, and that's where they got through, usually. There would be two troopers or a trooper and a sheriff's deputy. No one was to be alone. No one ever checked on us. They didn't check to see if we had food or anything else. The patrol was so well thought of that the farmers would make sure we had food. At that time we might be out a week and never get to change clothes or anything else. You can imagine how dirty and smelly we were by then. We wouldn't have survived if [the farm folks] hadn't helped us. We were never reimbursed for all of the overtime we worked. We couldn't even call home." McDaniel added, "The good way our kids turned out was due to the wives. It wasn't due to the men. We were gone too much."

Although they dealt with people and problems every day, patrolmen needed to be continually reminded of the dangers of their jobs so they wouldn't get lulled into carelessness. McDaniel's voice broke as he recounted an incident that could have been tragic. "You never knew when something was going to happen. One night C.A. and I were working together. We had stopped a car for speeding and it turned out to be an escapee from Texas. He was in for life. The car had been stolen, but they hadn't got the information out on it yet. It was C.A.'s turn to make the contact, so we got out of the car. I stepped behind our car, and C.A. walked up to the car and asked him to step out. Well, when he did all hell really broke loose. He opened the door and kicked it open into C.A. and knocked him off balance. He jammed a .45 automatic into his stomach and pulled the trigger. The gun misfired. As soon as I saw what was going on, I tried to get up there to him. But before I could get up there, that old boy had been well taken care of. C.A. almost beat him to death. I pulled C.A. off and called an ambulance. We still didn't know who he was until we got to the hospital. It was a big trial there in Shawnee. They filed attempted murder charges. It happened so fast, I couldn't do anything. C.A. went to the bar ditch and threw up." McDaniel concluded in a soft voice, "There wasn't a thing I could do, it happened so fast. Even though I was backing him up, it happened before I could even move. It taught me a lesson." This was a story that I had never heard before. For whatever reason, my dad had not told any of our family about this brush with death.

But patrolmen couldn't always count on emergencies to happen when they were working with partners; sometimes they were working alone. Taylor explained, "Troopers were different than most other law enforcement officers, because they were by themselves so much out on the roads. They didn't have anybody to help them if they got in trouble. They had to depend on being a good officer and having people help them." In July 1952, near Poteau, a life-theatening incident happened to Trooper Otto Rauch which illustrates this point.

The Poteau News, dated July 24, 1952, reported under a photograph of Rauch, "Victim Otto L. Rauch, Poteau state highway trooper, was severely beaten by Denver and H.N. Baker jr. last Thursday when they suddenly turned on him and attacked him as he was bringing them in to jail. Rauch had arrested the brothers on U.S. 271 near the state line. They had been drinking and Denver was driving without a license. Rauch was taken to the Poteau hospital in a serious condition after the incident. His condition is much improved now and he is expected to be able to leave the hospital today."

Otto Rauch described his view of this incident. "I have to admit that I was careless with those two. Denver Baker was one of the meanest men who ever trod the earth. He had shot the Poteau police chief in the knee a few months before. He got a suspended sentence. I only had one pair of handcuffs, that's all the department furnished, and I didn't buy another pair. I had driven thirty miles before they attacked me. We were all sitting in the front seat with Denver in the middle and his brother on his right. About a mile from jail, Denver took the metal helmet he was wearing and swung it right across my nose and face several times. He had just jammed his foot on the brake. He told his brother to get my gun. They tried to shoot me, but I grabbed the barrel of the gun and the bullet went through the windshield. A Fort Chaffee colonel, D.M. Zeiss, came along and stopped. He started honking his horn. Kenneth Williams, who lived nearby, stopped and came up to the patrol car. I said, 'Kenneth, these boys are beating me to death, help me!'"

"Denver said, 'Kenneth, this is none of your business.' Kenneth walked away toward his car." Rauch said in a hushed voice, "That was the darkest moment of my life, when I saw him walking off."

He continued, "The next thing I knew I was moving

rapidly across the seat and out of the door. They were pulling me with the gun that I was still holding by the five-inch barrel. Then I heard Kenneth saying, 'They are leaving now.' Kenneth had turned around and had come back. Kenneth took me to the hospital."

Rauch concluded, "The next thing I remember was Dr. Bill Cotton sewing me up with the nurse standing there. My nose was smashed all over my face. The nurse told the doctor that she didn't feel any pulse. Dr. Cotton said, 'He's shocking to beat hell.' I stayed in the hospital for a week, and I was in recuperation for another week."

According to the newspaper article, the Baker brothers made their way to a butane company five miles south of Fort Smith from where they called their sister, who begged them to surrender. They were unaware of the massive search that was underway for them, including the use of the patrol plane flown by Art Hamilton.

Taylor remembered the search, "When the sheriff asked who had hurt Otto, the farmer told him it was the Baker brothers, and they had taken off east. The sheriff called ahead, and by the time he got to the Arkansas line, there were about forty patrol cars there. The troopers had heard about it and had left their districts without permission, to help. They wanted to kill those two. Some of the Baker family got word to the brothers to turn themselves in at Fort Smith, or somebody would kill them. They sent the crime bureau chief, the district attorney, and a judge to Fort Smith to protect them on the way back."

Rauch described the aftermath to the incident. "My superiors and fellow troopers always supported me completely. However, in Poteau, the county attorney would not recommend the maximum sentence. He was an old county attorney who was just marking time until he could retire. The commissioner, Dixie Gilmer, sent Lew Wallace from the State Attorney General's office to assist with the prosecution. The Bakers pled guilty and were held for sentencing. Mr. Wallace asked the county attorney to recommend the maximum sentence for second offense for Denver. But he wouldn't do it." Rauch stated flatly, "Denver got six years and his brother got four." Rauch continued to live and work in Poteau until he was transferred to Okmulgee in 1953.

Troopers Helped Others

Taylor described the feelings among the troopers during this time, "It was a good patrol then. Everybody knew everybody. There were some sorry scamps, but everybody knew who they were. They might be sorry, but each of them had some good traits. Old Duggan did things everybody else would have been killed for. But if he ran onto a family that hadn't eaten that day, he'd put them in his car and take them in and feed them. He'd do anything for you. Everybody liked to work with him because you never had to worry whether he'd help you if you got in a fight. He was just great. If you couldn't trust somebody, he was pretty sorry." Taylor continued, "If you went out to eat, and you saw an old boy sitting over there and you knew he was hungry but didn't have any money, you just bought his dinner. It's always been that way."

Taylor described how Oklahoma Highway Patrolmen tried to help other troopers' families in case of an untimely death from any cause. "When we were working in Shawnee, they had a thing—when a trooper died, they collected $25.00 from each trooper and gave it right to the family within three hours. During that time McDaniel and I didn't have any money, we were broke. We never did worry 'cause C.A. would pay for all three of us, and we'd pay him back when we could. But one time three troopers died in one month. C.A. said, 'I don't think I can stand for all of it this time.' He would always try to help us, he was just that kind of a guy. But, in those days, many troopers did that kind of thing for one another."

Taylor gave an account of another veteran trooper who helped younger ones. "At Edmond there was a trooper who was kind of a scamp. He drank a lot and did lots of things he shouldn't have done. Everyone knew he was good for his word, even if he did drink a lot. Troopers who went through Edmond would stop at a cafe and charge their meals to him. They'd just write down their badge numbers. [He] would go by and pay the tickets. One time I asked him if he ever lost any money. He said, 'Oh, no, they always pay me.' He did that for years," Taylor recalled.

An article and photograph of Don McDaniel, Nat Taylor, and my dad standing beside their patrol car appeared in the Shawnee *News-Star* near the end of 1952. Under the photograph was, "Highway patrolmen keep busy making county roads and highways safe for travelers. During 1952, the troopers stopped 11,782 times to aid drivers who were having car trouble." (7) (Figure 5)

Taylor cited an example of a special way that Dad helped travelers: "C.A. always kept the old highway patrol tires from our unit. I've seen him tell a person who was stranded that he'd get him a tire. And he'd go to the house and get him one of those tires. Everybody respected him." Dad always remembered what it was like to have very little money and couldn't stand to see anything go to waste. He also carried painful memories of our family's trip home from California during the war when he had trouble getting tires and saw this as a way he could give immediate and direct help to people who needed it.

Although many other patrolmen went out of their way to help motorists, another example of Dad's assisting a family appeared in the newspaper. An article dated August 19, 1953, had the title of "Silver Lining". It stated that a woman in Tecumseh had "lost control of her car and overturned with three children yesterday. The only casualty was a piggy bank. It burst open and scattered silver dollars all over the highway. Highway Patrolman C.A. Morris said it took him two hours to retrieve the coins."

In the fall of 1953, Dad and his partner were called to an accident on Kickapoo Street south of town. It was Dad's turn to work the accident, and he was surprised and distressed to find that it was his own son. John, who was with a date, had missed the curve and run off the road. Fortunately no one was hurt and it caused only minor damages to his car. Later John and the other trooper said that Dad had dealt with him as patiently and courtiously as he would have done with anyone else's son. It was all handled through the legal system, and there were no further punishments given out at home.

Although they often felt isolated, the Shawnee troopers were not totally alone as they patrolled their district's roads. In 1953, the Shawnee *News-Star* published a photograph and article to inform its readers about the use of the patrol airplane for traffic control. The photograph showed Captain Gene Bumpus, head of the southern half of the state, A.M. Hamilton, pilot, and Dad standing in front of the patrol airplane and a patrol car. The Article, titled "Plane patrol spots violators of road," said in part, "Oklahoma holds a unique spot among the 48 states by being the only one to use an airplane consistently for highway traffic control. The 1952 Beech Bonanza plane, which helps put the finger on traffic violators, has a little more than 109 hours flying time now. When the plane is in this area, Troopers Nat Taylor, Don McDaniel and C.A.Morris cooperate with the pilot in spotting violators. Oklahoma has been using the airplane techniques for the past two years." (8)

The procedures used in clocking speeds of cars from aircraft included a stop watch and mile markers painted on roads or section lines. Hamilton checked the time it took a driver to get from one point to another, then he would compute the speed from the results. After confirming the results, he would radio the troopers to stop the speeder. From 1948 to 1952, Hamilton had assisted in stopping over 7,000 speeders. He also aided in the apprehension of three bank robbers, three rapists, ten kidnappers, 100 escaped prisoners, and hundreds of car thieves. During that four-year period, Hamilton flew the equivalent of twenty-four times around the earth while on duty with the patrol. (9)

Variety of Assignments

Once in a while the Shawnee troopers became involved in a life saving effort unrelated to highway accidents. A newspaper article stated that Dad and McDaniel were making routine highway checks on the Saturday evening before Labor Day. About 8:00 p.m. they were notified that a young man was being transported to the hospital after being bitten by a rattlesnake. The doctor requested help in getting the needed serum, since it was a holiday and the usual methods of transportation were not available. By 11:00 p.m. the wholesale firm had been contacted and an Oklahoma City patrol unit picked up the serum by 11:10. Dad and McDaniel met the unit at the county line and within forty minutes had the serum at the hospital for the snake bite victim. (10) Afterward, the troopers continued with their usual late Saturday night duties.

McDaniel remembered that hard and fast driving was one of Dad's trademarks. "C.A. would be driving down the road at ninety miles an hour just like he was going forty. We would come to a bridge meeting a car, and he wouldn't slow down a bit. He'd just hold it steady, stay on his side, and go right on over the bridge without blinking an eye. At first it scared me to death, but I got used to it. But I'll bet those other drivers were always scared out of their wits." Mother remembered that Dad was frequently called on to help in emergencies such as transporting blood or organs for transplant.

Often troopers were ordered to interrupt their busy schedules and add wear and tear to their already over-worked vehicles to do something that they didn't think was very important. Otto Rauch said, "I put over 500 miles on my car one day to lead a bunch of movie stars around. They wanted to drive faster than the speed limit, but I didn't. We drove around in Le Flore and Latimer counties. It was a lot of nonsense. The leader of the group was Broderick Crawford [who starred in the television program 'Highway Patrol']."

Up until this time troopers were still required to wear the same wool uniforms all year round. In the hot summers, they roasted in the long sleeved wool shirts with neck ties and leather Sam Browne belts across their chests. But after many years Oklahoma Highway patrol troopers finally received summer uniforms. Rauch recalled, "We got to wear short sleeved shirts, no ties, and no Sam Browne shoulder belts, just the waist belt." The troopers felt like they had been set free.

As in most organizations, there were stories that went around through the "grapevine" in the highway patrol. Oklahoma Lieutenant Governor James E. Berry, who had been in that office from 1935 through the early 1950s was a colorful subject. He lived in Stillwater and was known as a heavy drinker. One of the highway patrol's responsibilities continued to be to provide transportation for the governor and the lieutenant governor. At times there were no specific troopers assigned to this detail. The Oklahoma City dispatcher would send whoever was unassigned when a call came to transport the governor or lieutenant governor; troopers referred to either of them as "the governor." Nat Taylor recalled, "Anybody they could talk into it had to drive for the governor. All of the troopers hated that job. [Governor] Turner had the reputation of being obnoxious and hateful. Troopers started asking to get their orders in writing before they'd go get him. But [Governor] Murray would just ride with anybody who came by to get him. He didn't drink and was an easy going guy."

Taylor continued, "Most troopers hated to have to go

and get Lt. Governor Berry. At night he'd sit on the right side and work the white spot light. He'd blind people you were meeting. One night he called for a ride, and a trooper had to go pick him up. Berry came out and was about half drunk. He told the trooper, 'I'm ordering you to get on the other side of the car. I'm going to drive!' They started to Oklahoma City, and down the road about ten to fifteen miles, Berry ran off into the bar ditch and turned the patrol car over.

The trooper got out and went to the side of the road, stuck his thumb out, and caught a ride to Oklahoma City. When he got back to headquarters they said, 'Where's the governor?'

The trooper said, 'He's up there with my patrol car where he wrecked it, and I'm not goin' back after him!'" Taylor concluded.

Since it was difficult to find troopers willing to drive for Berry, the "brass" thought they had the perfect solution to two problems. "The story was that Pop Snelson, who lived in Edmond, was sometimes known to drink too much; so they decided to give him to Lt. Governor Berry as a driver. Berry would call him to pick him up, and they became great friends. Sometimes Pop would borrow money from him, and no matter how drunk he was when Pop borrowed the money, as soon as he sobered up, he'd ask for the money back. Berry was a banker, and Pop would tell this on him," Taylor remembered with a laugh. Troopers always enjoyed hearing the latest "Poop" about what was going on around Oklahoma City, and some of the best stories at that time, involved Berry.

Dad continued to make speeches at schools, Boy Scout meetings for adult leaders as well as the scouts themselves, and at civic organizations. The *News-Star* reported, "The Washington PTA heard Trooper C.A. Morris, a former school teacher and father of three teen-age children talk on 'Juvenile Problems' at the Monday afternoon PTA meeting at the school. Trooper Morris paid high tribute to the young people of Shawnee and Pottawatomie county stating: . . . Young people, as a whole, are better than we give them credit for being. Let's try praising them more and condemning them a little less . . . . The highway patrolman suggested that the youth problems are more likely to be adult problems which they inherit through precept and example." (11)

Dad was having his theories tested at home. John and one of our distant cousins, who was staying with us for a while, were working at the gas station together. One day they decided to go fishing out at the lake. It was Shawnee's water supply, but there was a place to rent boats with motors. After they got out in the middle of the lake, the motor stopped working. Since they had no oars, the boys decided to jump into the water and push the boat back to the marina. Just as they were both soaked to the skin and had managed to get the boat angled toward the right direction, the lake patrol arrived. They were ordered to get back into the boat and were towed back to shore. The patrolman radioed Dad who went to the lake and picked up the drenched and scared boys. Although they realized they had broken the law, the boys had a hard time accepting the idea that they were supposed to just sit in their boat and wait for help since there was to be no swimming in the lake for any reason. When they found out that no charges were filed, the boys were very releaved.

Sponsors of school safety programs could always depend on Dad to attend and represent the patrol. When the Shawnee Jaycees presented bike-lighting packets to school children, he joined them. A photograph appeared in the *News-Star* showing Dad with Bill Cowen, Jaycee representative, and Franklin School pupils. (12)

In the spring of 1953, Dad's parents came to visit us from Fredonia, Kansas. In Grandmother Morris's journal, she recorded that on many evenings at dinner Dad would conduct driving safety quizzes. This was a usual routine for us; Dad continued to use every opportunity to practice some of his speeches while trying to teach us about driving safety.

Jim Thorpe, the well known athlete and member of the Sac and Fox Tribe, died while my grandparents were visiting. His funeral was held in Shawnee on April 13, and he lay in state in Shawnee for several days before the funeral. Our entire family went to the viewing, but only John and Grandpa Morris attended the funeral. Dad was kept busy handling traffic resulting from the many well-known guests and officials who came to Shawnee. Later, the high school football stadium was renamed for Jim Thorpe.

To assist troopers in their attempt to decrease the number of speeders, the Highway Patrol began using radar. There were only a few radar units at the beginning of 1953, and they were taken around the state to train troopers and the public about what was coming in the line of speed regulation. (13) At first radar was used in high accident areas in the state. Later the use of radar would become routine.

In May 1953, the Turner Turnpike opened. The eighty-six mile stretch from Oklahoma City to Tulsa was the first turnpike completed following legislative creation of the Oklahoma Turnpike Authority in 1947. It was the first toll road built west of the Mississippi River. (14) Troopers from the decreasing ranks were needed to patrol the new turnpike and would be needed later on the Will Rogers Turnpike which was authorized in 1953. Although the Turnpike Authority paid expenses for the troopers, the patrol was responsible for their equipment, supervision, and training. (15)

Leonard Kelsoe, who had been in Lawton for four years, was one of the troopers assigned to work on the newly opened turnpike. His family, consisting of a pregnant wife and small daughter, continued to live in Lawton. About nine months later, he moved to Fairview, where his family with a new baby daughter joined him.

The post-World War II economic boom and the Korean War were making it more difficult for the Department of Public Safety to attract and keep capable men as patrolmen. In addition to expanding the insurance program in 1949 to include group medical and hospital coverage and retirement after twenty years of service, a credit union was begun in 1953. "Members of the credit union could borrow up to $200 on unsecured loans and up to ten percent of the total assets on secured loans at one percent interest." (16)

By this time K.O. Rayburn had become one of the primary instructors at the highway patrol schools. The eleventh patrol school was held the summer of 1953. Forty-eight new patrolmen were graduated and joined the troopers on the roads just as the Korean War ended. A truce between the U.N. and North Korea was signed on July 27, 1953. Some troopers who had left the patrol to serve in the war returned.

Unrest Among Shawnee Troopers

The three troopers continued to work very hard in Pottawatomie county, and often felt like they were not appreciated by the higher officers in Oklahoma City. Whenever they did something wrong or did something to aggravate someone, they heard about it. But they rarely heard about the things they were doing right. During this time great emphasis was being placed on getting unsafe vehicles off the roads of Oklahoma, and the troopers in Pottawatomie county were doing just that. Taylor sounded frustrated as he said, "C.A., Mac, and I would stop people for everything—headlights, taillights; we tried to get everything fixed. We wrote lots of warnings; we didn't set out to arrest people. But when we made the stops, we found drunk drivers, armed robbers, and such. But the whole bunch at Midwest City, which is where most of the 'brass' lived, made fun of us. There were lots of snitches who would tell us what they said about us. But we had everybody's taillights working. When we stopped someone, he'd know we meant business. And about 800 cars that went by while we had him stopped would know we meant business too." Taylor continued, "Mac and I both requested to get out of Shawnee. We were both new troopers. We worked more accidents than anyone else, and they worked us to death. They took no pity on us."

It was about this time that Dad developed a plan to make a little extra money for our growing family and also assist with law enforcement in Seminole. He had worked with an attorney in Seminole named Frank Seay on a number of civil cases resulting from traffic accidents. Mr. Seay liked the way Dad worked and suggested that he could use some help on a regular basis from a special investigator. The two men developed a detailed proposal that clearly defined the role and showed that there would be no conflict with Dad's job as a patrolman. Dad did not subscribe to the notion that it was better to ask for forgiveness afterward than to seek permission before, so he submitted the proposal to his superiors and waited for a response. He was terribly disappointed when the proposal was denied with no further discussion allowed. John remembered that our dad felt like he had been slapped down when his request was denied, and yet he knew that other patrolmen were making extra money doing a variety of things. Dad just let the idea drop.

In 1953, Don McDaniel was transferred to Midwest City where he stayed for only a short time before quitting the patrol. Taylor described the events that led to his leaving, "Mac worked a wreck at a little ole town called St. Louis, Oklahoma. The town had a narrow road down a steep hill. Right in front of the school a salesman for Reed Roller Bits had a wreck. He sold bits to oil drilling companies. He was going west, and an old boy was coming the other way on his side of the road. The salesman waited as long as he could and then swerved to the other side of the road to try to miss him. The old boy saw what was about to happen and pulled back on his side, hitting the salesman on the back door. Mac did a good job working the accident. There were several people hurt. Mac arrested the guy who had been on the wrong side and pulled back at the last minute. After everything was settled, Reed Roller Bits offered Mac a job. They tripled his salary and gave him a car." Taylor concluded, "Mac thought he was going to make a million dollars, but it was tough to sell those bits."

Bryce Wilde, a graduate of the 1953 patrol school, was assigned to Shawnee. He and his wife and two little boys moved there to join the tight-knit troopers' family group in the McDaniel's place.

On Monday, September 14, 1953, Trooper Johnny Whittle, a ten-year patrol veteran, was shot and killed by a youth he was taking to highway patrol headquarters. The headline on the *Daily Oklahoman* front page was, "State to Demand Death for Confessed Slayer of Highway Patrolman." According to highway patrol records, the murderer was arrested approximately two hours later some three miles away as he was trying to hitchhike. He was sentenced to a sixty-five year prison sentence following a first-degree manslaughter conviction. (17) There was mourning across the state for the popular trooper who had been killed in the line of duty.

Drunk drivers continued to cause problems for themselves and other people who might encounter them on the roads. Many incidents occurred which were made more dangerous and complex for state troopers because one or more of the people involved was drunk. There continued to be state wide efforts to stop the flow of illegal liquor into the state. An Associated Press item from Shawnee stated, "Trooper C.A.

Morris has two dogs to thank for uncovering 166 pints and six fifths of contraband liquor. The hunting dogs, in the back seat of an automobile he stopped for speeding, began playing around while he wrote a ticket for the driver and uncovered the liquor under blankets." (18)

On New Year's Eve 1953, Dad and Nat Taylor made another large haul of illegal liquor. After they chased down and stopped a speeder, who had raced by them at eighty miles per hour, they discovered the whiskey valued at $780.00. A photograph of them with county sheriff, Leroy Flinchum and the 174 pints and three fifths of whiskey appeared in the newspaper the next day. (19) (Figure 6)

Later in 1954, Nat Taylor's request for transfer from Shawnee was granted. He moved to Oklahoma City for a few months and then on to El Reno where he was assigned for a year. George Moore arrived in Shawnee in Taylor's place. Later Trooper Moore was replaced by Lee Sardis.

Morris Stays at Shawnee

Dad continued to take the lead in public safety awareness campaigns in Pottawatomie county. His photograph, along with a citizen in an automobile and some members of the Naitonal Guard, who were helping with safety lane operation, appeared in the May 9, 1954, Shawnee *News-Star* Sunday paper. The accompanying article described the 31-day motor inspection program being conducted through the month by state troopers, aided by safety minded civic groups. There was a state goal of inspecting 7,500 vehicles during the month. According to the article, brakes, lights, steering, horn, windshield wipers, glass, and muffler of each vehicle were inspected.

There were times when Dad was rewarded for his work through an unexpected event. A letter from Oklahoma City written in pencil on Hotel Black stationery dated June 15,

1954, which arrived at our home on North Harrison Street, was one that brought tears to his eyes. The letter said,

"Dear Mr. Morris

I am Robert Worseck whose auto accident case was on trail June 15th. You testified in this case. I was ashamed that I didn't shake your hand after you testified. I didn't shake your hand because of the onlooking jury. Why I wanted to shake your hand was not because you was[sic] our witness and not because we won the case.

I wanted to shake your hand because you was[sic] kind to a scared kid who was in an auto accident one and a half miles north of Asher in 1952. You didn't know me from Adam. You drove me to the Shawnee hospital. You answered my foolish questions. You turned on your auto heater when I was shivering with shock. You dropped me off at the Aldrige Hotel because I didn't know where a hotel was at. In Feb 1954 my lawyer Mr. Green drove me out to your home. You was[sic] working in your garden. I acted conceited and hardly spoke. That was because I didn't want you to think I was trying to influence[sic] you. Once again I was ashamed of myself.

Today on the stand you said you can't remember specific things about a certain accident. You probably don't remember me even after you saw me for a moment today. But believe me I'll remember you and your kindness to a scared young kid.

What I want to say is thank you and "God Bless You."

Yours truely [sic]
Robert Worseck"

This letter was found with other treasured mementos from Dad's career on the Oklahoma Highway Patrol. For him it served as hard evidence, that his actions had carried the messages that he was trying to send.

By this time in 1954, John was a junior in high school. He continued working at his after school job in the gas station to help with the expenses of his old car. He also was participating in track and basketball as well as football. It wasn't easy for a popular athlete to have a dad who was a strong law enforcement officer in the small community. Although John never did get into serious trouble, he continued to cross the line a little as he spent time around the area with his friends. I would sometimes overhear conversations between John and our parents about the need for him to spend more time and energy on his school work. "You can't get the knowledge from your school books by just sitting on them," was a comment our dad made on several occasions.

Through the state legislature responsibility for the School Bus Safety Program and Driver Training was given jointly to the State Board of Education and the Department of Public Safety and Oklahoma Highway Patrol. Newly appointed Pottawatomie county superintendent, Esther Hairston worked with Dad on several cooperative projects that were featured in the *News-Star*. One had to do with his visiting forty-one of the county's forty-six schools which put him into contact with 4,381 teachers and pupils. He truly enjoyed working with children. An article describing this program stated, "Hoppalong [sic] Cassidy himself could hardly have had a warmer welcome than Trooper C.A. Morris of the highway patrol on his recent tour of the county schools. Nor could Hoppy have done a better job convincing kids that their best friend is the law. They tried on his badge for size, got locked up in handcuffs, took respectful peeks at his gun. But along with this eventful visiting they got a through drilling on 'school-going safety.'" During the visit he also showed the teachers and pupils films on safety and juvenile delinquency. (20) That fall Lieutenant B. Wages joined Dad and Mrs. Hairston for a photo opportunity while inspecting the county's forty-eight school buses. (21)

Not all citizens with whom Dad came into contact were pleased about it. A newspaper article described a hearing resulting from a complaint signed by a student at Oklahoma Baptist University, located in Shawnee. G.C. Howard had been arrested by Dad for speeding 75 to 85 miles per hour and had paid $23.50 fine and costs in a justice of the peace's court. The complaint charged that Dad had "backed a vehicle without a flagman", breaking an antiquated city law that was still on the books. Dad appeared at court to defend himself with his partner, Bryce Wilde. But before he was given a chance to say anything, the city attorney Randel Pitman jr. asked to have the charge dropped. However, Judge Clarence Robinson replied that he had already dismissed the case. The article concluded, "Howard didn't show up to press the complaint. And Morris' career of crime was over." (22)

DPS Leadership Shifts Result in Changes

Commissioner of Public Safety, Dixie Gilmer died in 1954, and the patrol chief, Carl Tyler, served as acting commissioner until Lawrence Bellati was appointed in his place. Bellati brought in a new assistant, Bill Blood, replacing Coble Gambill. They made an organizational change keeping the concept of two state divisions, north and south, but beginning a trend toward centralizing command of the patrol in Oklahoma City. In this change, all administrative duties of the Department of Public Safety were put under the command of patrol officers. Two field captains were brought into headquarters and put under direct command of the Chief of the Patrol, Jack Rollins. According to a Department of Public Safety publication, "This move was designed to foster coordination among all districts for the single purpose of promoting public safety." (23)

Officers of the patrol realized that they needed some formal training programs for troopers in the field. Troop meetings and small group instruction as officers made the rounds to see troopers in their home districts were not adequate to keep troopers trained in all of the areas in which they needed to be knowledgeable or skilled. The patrol schools were designed to get civilians prepared to go on the road with seasoned troopers, who then taught them how to deal with day-to-day events. However, some seasoned troopers were not as competent as they should have been, and some had just been out in the field too long to fully understand some of the new methods they were supposed to use and some of the new priorities of the Department of Public Safety.

To help address these issues, an *Oklahoma Highway Patrol Operations Manual* was published in 1954. The introduction stated, "As a means of harmonizing the activities of the Patrol and for the betterment of the Department, this operations manual has been compiled." The thick booklet was encased in a brown leather-looking cover. It spelled out for troopers what the official position was on many matters that had been formerly determined by word-of-mouth or by trial-and-error.

In the front of the manual, 1954 salaries were listed:

First year of service — $3,600 per year
Second year — 3,900 per year
Third and up — 4,200 per year plus longevity
Longevity — At the completion of each 3 years, increase of 3% over present salary is allowed.

Also in the front of the manual was the following "Call of Honor," which reflected the continued high ideals and expectations that existed within the Oklahoma Highway Patrol since its formation in 1937.

"I am an Oklahoma Highway Patrolman, a soldier of the law. To me is entrusted the honor of the force. I must reflect the friendliness and hospitality of the great southwest, and at the same time be courteous but firm in the discharge of my duty. I must serve honestly and faithfully, and if need be, lay down my life as others have done before me, rather than swerve from the path of duty. It is my duty to enforce the law without regard to class, color, creed, or condition. It is also my duty to be of service to anyone who may be in danger or distress, and at all times to conduct myself so that the honor of the force may be upheld."

Some of the sections of this lengthy manual directly addressed actions or issues that framed many of the "stories" related earlier in this book, especially those of Troopers Taylor and McDaniel and my dad in Shawnee. These sections are cited to illustrate that the patrol was making a strong effort to correct some problems that existed, establish some consistancy, and give troopers written directions for all to follow. Some of these items may seem trivial or too constraining for today's standards, but they reflect the priorities and time period of 1954.

Outside Work

"It is expected that members of this Department will devote their entire time to the service of this organization to the exclusion of any other business or calling."

Payments of Debts and Family Support

"Members must be prompt in meeting financial obligations and shall be required to support their family properly."

Use of Tobacco

"Members shall not carry, either in hand or mouth, a cigarette, cigar or pipe when approaching a violator or in lending assistance to any person."

Treatment of Persons and Prisoners

"Members shall not willfully mistreat or use unnecessary violence toward any person, prisoners or otherwise. He shall not strike a prisoner or person except when absolutely necessary as a last resort to overcome resistance, escape or in defense of his own person."

Shooting of Persons, Prisoners, and Automobiles

"A. A member shall not shoot at an automobile, a fleeing person, an escaping prisoner, or anyone else unless in pursuit of a felonious person, or to the officer's best knowledge, a person is about to commit a felony, or to protect his own or some other person's life.
B. It is rare for an officer to be justified in shooting a misdemeanant."

Rewards and Gifts

"The department expects that activities of its members, whether routine or especially meritorious, are conducted in the line of duty and are therefore not to be rewarded by any other material means.

A tender of reward for services, by gratuity or gift of any kind, shall be met with a polite refusal on the member's part."

Patrol Policy in Civil Subpoenas

"The OHP is a public service organization and through custom the public has become accustomed to troopers' backing up their investigations of traffic accidents in civil court by appearing in person in response to civil subpoenas. This service has done much toward establishing good public relations. It will be the policy of the Patrol that uniformed personnel should honor civil subpoenas when the following requirements have been met by the lawyers requesting testimony:

1. Serve trooper and Chief's office with subpoena at least 3 days before date of hearing.
2. Make satisfactory arrangements with trooper subpoenaed for expenses."

The manual continued with eleven points about the troopers' responsibilities in civil matters including need for district commander's permission to use patrol car, wear uniform, take time off from duties, or honor out of state subpoenas. It addressed not charging excessive fees and stressed not attempting to collect fees themselves. Troopers were to refer unpaid fees to the district commander who would then inform the Office of Chief. The next section gave directions and suggestions for how to testify in court in criminal or civil cases.

Other relevant sections of the manual were:

Intoxication/ Drunk Driving

In order to determine if a driver were drunk, troopers were advised to check for the following:

1. Condition of speech and eyes
2. Odor of breath

3. Condition and arrangement of dress
4. Manner of conduct

"Under the assumption it has been established the person is intoxicated, further complete your evidence with:

1. Substantial witness' statements, if available.
2. Apply drunkometer test, if available and secure result of report.
3. Where serious accidents are involved, attempt to take subject to a physician for a blood or urine test (only with written consent)."

Working Hours and Reports Filed

"It is expected that members will be available for duty on a twenty-four-hour basis. They will be subject to call when emergencies exist to work whatever hours the situation may demand."

Responsibility for Night Calls

"The night shift will be responsible until 1/2 hour before sun up. Both troopers on the night shift shall go . . ." It was clear that troopers were expected to work in pairs at night. If alone, the trooper was advised to "pick up other salaried enforcement officer or call district headquarters."

To assist troopers in getting along better with their working partners, there was the following section:

Consideration of Riding Partner

Troopers were advised to:

> Cooperate
> Veterans, teach recruits; Recruits, learn from veterans

Share duties (talk about dividing them up)
Set example for partner in personal grooming
Go beyond halfway in unpleasant duties
Be on time
Socialize, if it fits
Don't gossip

In addition to the new manual, the Oklahoma Highway Patrol began to hold training sessions for troopers at the campus at Stillwater. In late September 1954, Dad joined forty-three other patrolmen at Oklahoma Agricultural and Mechanical College for a forty-hour course in Advanced Patrol Procedures. It was described in a newspaper article as "a rigorous and versatile five day retraining course for troopers and officers." This course was the second of six to be held and was designed for the more experienced patrolmen. "The idea was to exchange ideas among the veteran officers in order to incorporate them into later schools," Dad was quoted as saying, "It was a good experience, everybody including the commissioner and assistant commissioner marched through the same chow line." Studies of law, journalism, psychiatry, investigation of accidents, language study, and shotgun and pistol firing were all part of the class work. Each participant got a certificate dated September 24, 1954, at a steak fry at Isaac Walton Park in Stillwater at the end of the week. (24)

It was difficult to know how to handle a trooper who was not doing a good job, even with the training and supervision that was being given. Rayburn recalled, "A lot of times, if they didn't know what to do with a trooper, they would assign him to the turnpike. He might have got in trouble in his community or just refuse to do much work." He cited an example, "One trooper was assigned because he didn't make enough contacts. The captain announced one day that the trooper had just broken his own record.

He had gone two months without making a single contact," Rayburn concluded as he shook his head.

The fall of 1954 was a busy one at the our home. John was a senior at Shawnee high school and much to our father's delight was starting center on the football team. Tom, who was finally beginning to enjoy living in Shawnee, had entered high school, and he continued to participate in Boy Scouts.

I had just entered eighth grade. I would frequently spend time at the public library while waiting for our school bus to pick me up at the junior high school. Because Mother thought I spent too much time reading, she began to limit the number of books I could check out each week. I continued with one of the household chores I had started several years before: polishing Dad's uniform brass every Saturday. When he returned from work on Friday night or early Saturday morning, Dad would remove his gun and, as he had done since joining the patrol, place it on the top shelf in his closet. He would then leave his Sam Browne belt on the kitchen table. That morning I would lay out newspapers and carefully remove the cartridges from their loops on the leather belt, unfasten all of the buckles, and use a soft cloth with a can of brass polish to clean and then polish all of the brass pieces. After each buckle and cartridge was gleaming, I would put everything back together again. This process was a source of satisfaction and pride for me as well as a way to earn my small allowance that was always tied to helping with chores around our home. Dad always cleaned his own gun and polished the leather on the belt, keeping it as shiny as he did his shoes.

Politics and the Department of Public Safety

The election held in the fall of 1954 brought a new governor, Raymond Gary, to the state. Once again, troopers braced for changes as they waited to hear who the new commissioner and upper echelons of the Department of Public Safety would be. Although Bellati had been in office less than a year, Governor Gary replaced him with Jim Lookabaugh as the new commissioner, H.J. Harmon was brought in as assistant commissioner, and Jack Rollins remained as chief of the patrol. The new governor wanted a campaign of stricter traffic enforcement putting more emphasis on arrests rather than warnings. (25) Even more than the usual changes rippled through the patrol ranks as these new men came into office in 1955.

Bob L. Blackburn, the son of Trooper Bob Blackburn who had worked in Chandler with my dad, completed an analysis of the Oklahoma Highway Patrol in his Master's Thesis in 1976. His view of the situation at this time follows: "As Lookabaugh took office, he announced that any new policies would come out of round table conferences with his old friend Gene Holt, former Stillwater police chief, and T.B. King, the assistant commissioner—another friend of Gary. In early February, Lookabaugh announced that all patrol captains would leave their desk jobs at headquarters in Oklahoma City and return to field duty, working with lieutenants and troopers in the performance of actual duties of patrolmen. According to Lookabaugh, the captains had been taken from field work by Commissioner L.F. Bellati . . . , making the new change actually a return to established policy . . . . By moving captains to widespread posts in the state, Lookabaugh removed their direct influence in the formation of administrative policy."

Blackburn continued, "Two weeks after this move to limit the influence of captains in the administration, Lookabaugh announced a major change in the organization of patrol districts of the state. Instead of two divisions, North and South, with four districts each, the patrol would operate from five divisions with two districts each. This was a move to weaken the power of the patrol's officer class by decreasing the area of each captain's responsibility.

Lookabaugh was successfully reorganizing the patrol to strengthen his position as the formulator of policy. Indicative of the growing breach between Lookabaugh and officers and troopers in the field was Lt. Bill Hamilton's promotion to captain; he was to serve as a liaison between headquarters and men in the field. Lookabaugh apparently considered an intermediary necessary between himself and the uniformed patrol." (26)

As he was leaving office in early 1955, Governor Johnston Murray made statements about Oklahoma and problems he perceived that were featured in a *Saturday Evening Post* article. This airing of the state's dirty laundry in a national magazine shook the citizens of Oklahoma. He denounced the legislative apportionment that allowed rural politicians to govern an urban state now undergoing industrialization. He believed too much power resided in the hands of the county commissioners, who retained narrow views. Their vision was especially narrow, he claimed, when it came to building roads that ultimately served the whole state. The tax system, especially earmarked revenues, was backward and inhibitory, he said. The whole approach fostered haphazard and wasteful government, in which local voters sent representatives to Oklahoma City with instructions to "chop down a Christmas tree and drag it home." In a survey following the publishing of the article, it was found that seventy-five percent of Oklahomans responding agreed with it. (27)

However, the statements seemed to have little effect on the Oklahoma legislature, which continued with business in it's usual way. The legislature passed a law in March of 1955 outlawing the use of unmarked patrol cars. According to the law, every patrol car had to be uniformly marked to indicate to the public the purpose of the car, although the use of unmarked cars the preceding summer had proved to be effective. So effective, in fact, that public clamor called for their prohibition. That same month radar was restricted, again due to public opposition. This cutback likely explains an all-time low in traffic convictions. The preceding October, when both unmarked cars and radar had been used, troopers had made 4,881 arrests and had won 4,116 convictions, a ninety percent conviction rate; after the two bans, troopers arrested only 3,648 violators and won 1,875 convictions, a fifty percent conviction rate. The time the patrol could devote to patrolling the major highways was decreased when Commissioner Lookabaugh ordered patrol units to cruise county and farm roads in order to diminish the growing rate of fatalities on these roads. At this time there were 93,000 miles of state and county roads. (28)

If troopers on Oklahoma's roads weren't discouraged enough about the legislative bans on two of their most effective weapons against deaths due to speeding drivers, they were also dismayed by the order to do even more patrolling. An incident that occurred in Lawton added even more fuel to the fire of discontent in the patrol ranks. In March of 1955, Trooper Bud Williamson of the Lawton district was called to investigate an automobile accident involving a local resident reported to be Lawton's most notorious bootlegger, Lincoln "Step" Wade. When Williamson arrived at the scene, people in the crowd directed the trooper's attention to liquor dripping from the caved-in trunk of Wade's automobile. Trooper Williamson allowed Wade to take his vehicle from the scene of the accident and transfer the liquor to another car, which made the public believe that Williamson was connected with illegal whiskey traffic. Then, to make matters worse, the trooper gave a ticket to the local citizen who had been driving the other car involved in the accident. Concerned citizens from the area called for an investigation of this apparent conflict of duty, opening the incident to public scrutiny. (29)

Lt. C.T. Raley and Capt. Norman Holt were the two officers in charge of the Lawton district at that time, and they began to follow up on the complaints and the incident.

Any wrong-doing on the part of a trooper would be bad publicity for the previously untarnished patrol. The patrol leadership at the state level called for a hearing on the incident and quickly found the trooper not guilty of illegal or unethical handling of the accident. However, the concerns about the incident did not end.

The two officers, Raley and Holt, who had attempted an investigation, were demoted soon after the commissioner's exoneration of Williamson. Raley blasted Lookabaugh and patrol headquarters in retaliation, claiming that he and Holt had been demoted and transferred because of their conscientious investigation of a case which patrol leadership wanted hushed up. Raley even claimed that Governor Gary and A.B. Green, Gary's appointee to the Highway Commission, were controlling policy at the Department of Public Safety and had played a large part in his demotion. According to Raley, because Green had given $50,000 to Gary's campaign fund the Lawton district was unjustly controlled by Green. In addition to the Lawton controversy, Lookabaugh's personnel committee began an extensive plan of demotions, promotions, and transfers which involved almost every section of the state." The Williamson case, the Raley allegations, and a wholesale shake-up of the highway patrol would result in a senate investigation beginning in September of 1955. (30)

Although there were a number of controversies at the upper levels of the patrol, for most troopers on the road their difficult job continued as usual. In an effort to decrease the growing number of highway fatalities in the spring of 1955, Oklahoma joined with other states in the "Slow Down and Live" program. This campaign had originated in eleven northeastern states in 1953, and thirteen southern states joined in 1954. There had been a 12.2 percent reduction in traffic deaths in the participating states during that time period. The campaign, also called "the 101 days," began on Memorial Day and lasted until Labor Day with emphasis placed not only on observing speed limits, but also on following all traffic laws all of the time. The *News-Star* published a photo of my dad with Mayor Adam Hornbeck and Police Chief Bill Holt of Shawnee to kick off the campaign. The accompanying article began, "Trooper C.A. Morris is up to his old tricks again—trying to save lives and slice the accident total in Pottawatomie county." The article stated that literature such as bumper stickers, posters, and billboard material were available for local civic groups to purchase. Shawnee, one of 118 state towns involved, began its campaign with a local insurance company purchasing 500 bumper stickers urging folks to go a little easier on the accelerator—and live. (31)

With the stricter enforcement of traffic laws, the Department of Public Safety adopted a demerit system, in July 1955, that was based on an accumulative negative point system. The Driver Improvement Division, headed by Elmer Bishop, would send a warning letter when a driver's record showed four points had been accumulated through arrests or accidents. When the total points exceeded five, the driver would be called in for an interview, reexamined, and placed on probation or suspended from driving. The system was designed to provide an incentive for driver self-improvement before departmental action was taken. (32) "Demerits could be removed from a driver's record only by a twenty-four-month period without an accident or arrest. After five years of safe and lawful driving, the violator's record would be wiped clean." (33)

Morris Promoted to Supervisor

During the highway patrol shake-up of 1955, Red Etheridge, a size and weight trooper from El Reno, was appointed Lieutenant of the Size and Weights Division. He did some reorganizing and began to try to bring in some new troopers to help implement the changes he wanted to make. One of the troopers he moved to his division was Nat Taylor.

My dad was also directly involved in the patrol shake-up that year. According to a newspaper article, during 1955 the highway patrol conducted "one of the most thorough screening processed in the patrol's history to 'get the top men in the top jobs.'" Assistant commissioner H.J. Harmon was quoted as saying that twenty-eight troopers had been recommended for the four vacant supervisory jobs. Selection of the four men had been based on their records, personalities, and number of years of service with the department. Dad was one of those selected, and he was assigned to the Enid district; Jack McKenzie was assigned to the Oklahoma City headquarters district, Pendleton Phillips to the Durant district, and Lyle Baker to the Edmond district. The new assignments were to take place in August. (34) An article published in the *News Star* stated in part, "C.A. Morris, Pottawatomie county highway trooper since February 1, 1951 and a 13-year veteran with the state highway patrol, was promoted Wednesday to the rank of supervisor, effective today. The promotions were announced by Jack Rollins, patrol chief . . . In the meantime, the county unit will be manned by Bryce Wilde and Johnny Edwards, recently transferred here to replace Lee Sardis, who went to a new Sayre unit."

The article continued, "Married and father of three children, Morris was one of the most popular and considered by fellow officers to be one of the most conscientious troopers to serve in this part of the state since the highway patrol was organized in 1937. He was a tireless worker here in promoting safety on the highways and devoted countless hours to addressing school groups, directing driver safety projects and helping prepare newspaper publicity." (35)

The lieutenant of the Enid district was Dad's old friend from college, Otis Haltom. When asked if she thought their friendship had anything to do with Dad's promotion and new assignment, my mother replied, "No, I don't think there was any connection. They just gave it to him. It was a big territory and they needed help. He was one of their best drivers, and whenever they had an emergency run, like taking blood to a hospital, or an organ for transplant, they called on C.A. to do it." She did not remember that Dad had taken tests for promotion and had been involved in an extensive selection process.

The Enid territory, consisting of thirteen and one-half counties, with a total of 14,386 square miles, had one lieutenant and one supervisor. An additional supervisor position had been added to the Enid district bringing them into allignment with the other regions in the state. In the late summer of 1955, my parents prepared to move to Enid with Tom, who was in the tenth grade, and me, in the ninth. That fall, John would begin attending college on a football scholarship in Miami, Oklahoma.

Figure 5 — "Troopers Don McDaniel, Nat Taylor, and C.A. Morris in 1953."

Figure 6—"Trooper Nat Taylor; Pottawatomie Sheriff, LeRoy Flinchum; and trooper C.A. Morris, January 1, 1954."

Figure 7—"Trooper C.A. Morris in 1954."

Figure 8—"Trooper C.A. Morris beside his patrol car in 1955."

Figure 9—"Troopers C.A. Morris and George Moore investigate an accident in 1955."

CHAPTER 5

MORRIS' FIRST YEAR AS SUPERVISOR 1955-1956

DAD WAS VERY excited about his new position as supervisor. From what I can remember of our family discussions, he fully expected to have more responsibility for the work of others but believed that it would not be too much different from his previous assignments. He had been the oldest and most experienced trooper during many of the thirteen years he had been on the patrol and had prided himself on his ability to work with younger troopers and help them do a better job with the public as well as fulfill their responsibilities to patrol headquarters. Dad had provided leadership in developing safety education programs in the schools and the broader community while developing and maintaining close relationships with local and county officials and newspapers. Although he had worked in five different towns and unit assignments during his time on the patrol, all but one year of his experience had been in the Oklahoma City District. He thought that this district was run most closely to the way the higher officers wanted and believed his experience there would be an advantage when he went out to one of the other districts in the far reaches of the state. With the enthusiasm of an athletic coach, Dad thought he knew how things were supposed to be done and believed he could help those in the Enid district create the best district in the state.

However, as he traded his trooper's badge, # 64, for the new one designating him as a supervisor, # 27, Dad entered the world of middle-management. Here he would experience frustration as he tried to get the troopers for whom he was responsible to follow procedures and meet their responsibilities. He was no longer "one of them," now he was one of "the brass." Dad soon found that what he thought were hard and fast rules, tended to be bent a great deal — often for those troopers that he believed were the least deserving. He discovered that the squeaky wheels often did get the most grease. Although he would have opportunities to develop many safety education programs, Dad quickly realized that his new assignment was many times that of a delivery man, taking information, supplies, and equipment from headquarters out to the units in the field and relaying messages back. He was amazed to discover how much of his time would be taken up with paper work and clerical matters. His new responsibilities were broad in nature and for the most part fragmented. As he gained experience as a supervisor, Dad began to appreciate the saying that being a middle-manager was a lot like walking down the center line of the road; you get hit by trucks going both directions. The promotion to supervisor turned out to be a real learning experience for this somewhat idealistic trooper who, for the most part, had been left alone to do his previous job in the way he believed it should be done.

First Two Months as a Supervisor

Dad was not officially assigned to Enid until September 1, 1955; however, he began an orientation period on August 24, with Lieutenant Otis Haltom and Floyd Hayes, the other supervisor, who was preparing to retire. Although he had been friends with Haltom since their college days and he had called him "Oatie" most of the time, in his journal Dad referred to him as "Otis;" his badge number, "#13"; or "Lt. Haltom." As a supervisor, Dad was given a 1955 daily journal which had been supplied by the Dillingham Insurance and Bond Agency in Enid. It had both "Hayes" and "Haltom" written in the front, and the first pages from January 1 to May 30 were blank. There were twenty brief entries between May 31 and August 24, when Dad started his notes. Apparently the leadership of the Enid district had not been much on detailed daily record-keeping. Most of the existing entries in the journal noted problems troopers were having and what action had been taken; such as, "talked to [trooper] about [problem]."

Dad's first notes listed supplies needed by units or troopers and described things troopers were not doing correctly. In the six days before his official assignment he listed ten of their twenty troopers, which must have been the ones he would be responsible for, noting areas of their performances in need of improvement. Although he and Supervisor Hayes divided the district for the purpose of evaluating the troopers, they each worked with all of the troopers as they traveled around their area. Beginning September 1, Dad started accounting for how he spent his time as well as noting information about units and individual troopers. He seemed to be thorough in his record-keeping, listing numerous bits of information that he thought might be needed later.

At this same time in the larger arena of the state, controversy about the highway patrol continued. The Williamson case with the Raley allegations, reported earlier, and the wholesale shake-up of the highway patrol had resulted in a senate investigation of the Oklahoma Highway Patrol beginning in September of 1955. (1)

During the first week in September, Dad drove around his new area, meeting troopers, sheriffs, county attorneys, and some trooper's families. According to his journal, he discussed the following items with the troopers: Arrest reports; accident reports; department policies; and July breakdowns of their speeches, activities, and vehicle checks. He took supplies to the units and noted other supply and repair needs. He picked up some badges to be replated and recorded a request for the patrol airplane during an upcoming county fair. During these visits, Dad also returned some reports to troopers for corrections and made a small personal loan to a trooper, which he marked "Pd." Dad worked with two troopers, and on his own arrested two speeders and a drunk driver. During that busy first week in his new job he also attended the funeral of a county official, had lunch with the Alva Rotary Club, and attended a PTA meeting.

Dad stayed with my mother's aunt and uncle, Laurena and Clarence Dresser, in Enid until he could bring us on up there. Moving from Shawnee to Enid was more complicated for us than it had been in previous transfers. In addition to the house, we had to prepare two apartments, the out buildings, and pasture for sale. My parents sold or butchered what little livestock remained. With John in college, Mother had only Tom and me to help her, although Dad came back to Shawnee on his days off.

According to his journal, on September 13, 1955, Dad drove to Oklahoma City with Lt. Haltom and Trooper Patton. They picked up supplies and information. The other two went back to Enid together, and Dad drove a new unit. Since he was without his family, he often ate with troopers, either in a cafe or at the trooper's home. That evening, he noted that he ate dinner at the home of his old partner from Chandler, Joe Dobson, who was assigned to Enid. They played one game of Canasta, and Dad lost.

The next day, after Dad worked on the road from 8:00 a.m. until 8:30 p.m., he stayed in the office until 11:30 p.m. working on "questioneers[sic] reference moral[sic] and shake up". The outcomes of his questionnaires were not noted, but it is possible that they were part of a poll about trooper morale reported in a September 27, 1955, *Daily Oklahoman* article. The article stated, "Most of the answers seemed to agree that although troopers were not happy with their leadership, they were continuing to work diligently to serve the public. Many troopers acknowledged the role of politics in the patrol, but said they accepted this fact and would not allow it to interfere with their service." The controversy about allegations of corruption in the highway patrol and the subsequent legislative investigation continued to swirl across the state. (2) Dad had taken on his new and complex job during some very difficult times.

On September 16, 1955, our family was ready to move, and this time, because it was a promotion, the Department of Public Safety paid for the moving van. By 9:00 a.m. on Saturday, September 17, the van loaded with 6,870 pounds of Morris belongings started toward Enid. Tom rode along with John, who had come home from college to help, as he drove a borrowed pick-up truck loaded with additional items. Dad, Mother, and I followed in our car. Dad had rented a small house on East Maple Street in Enid with the hope of building a new house as soon as he and Mother selected the plans and location. We unloaded and sorted out the things we would need while waiting for the new house to be built.

By 5:00 that evening, Dad was back at work; he didn't return home until 1:00 a.m. His journal entry for that evening was similar to those that followed over the next few years. It stated in part, "Checked reports till 7:30 P.M. Otis and I went to 4 corners. Met 21. I worked with Boyd, Otis with McCoy. Boyd works good makes good contacts. Discussed getting along with partner and moving to Sayre."

To patrol the roads in the 14,386 square-mile-area located in thirteen counties which comprised the sixth district, there were twelve units with twenty patrolmen, two supervisors, and one lieutenant. Eight of the patrol units were located in towns scattered across the territory: Beaver,

Medford, Alva, Kingfisher, Woodward, Guymon, Watonga, and Fairview. All of the units had two men assigned with the exception of Guymon, where Trooper Cross patrolled alone. The five troopers assigned to Enid were divided into one two-man and one three-man units. Almost all of Dad's experience had been in the more populated part of Oklahoma where there were three-man units. Not only were the work schedules of two-man and three-man units different, but the dynamics between the troopers and their families were also different. Three men working together gave each man some time to be alone during day shifts and time to be in a team during night shifts. If two troopers in the unit didn't get along, they only had to work with one another one third of the time. There was also more flexibility for days off and vacation time. Two-man teams didn't give troopers much variety or flexibility, and many personal disagreements between two troopers developed and festered. To keep two men in the squad car at night, one trooper had to work split shift. On days off, the remaining trooper had to work alone trying to cover both shifts. At first Dad tried to coordinate his visits to troopers so he could be the second man at night. But with eleven two-man units, it became impossible to schedule, even with two supervisors. Two of the things Dad tried to focus on at this time were improving some of the troopers' interactions with the public and helping some of them get along better with their partners. From his viewpoint, both of these were just common sense and should be easy for any mature adult. On-going problems in these areas became a source of frustration for him over the next few years.

During his third official week in Enid, Dad continued to meet with troopers and become acquainted with their families when he had the opportunity. In addition to his supervisory responsibilities, he performed the role of a delivery service. His journal showed that he took a pistol that had been repaired to one trooper and a new pair of pants to another, with notes that one trooper needed a moving claim and another had a dirty cap cover. Items of discussion with all troopers during this time included: Football traffic, school bus inspections, methods of patrolling, amount of work done, and warning methods.

On September 24, 1955, Dad made his first trip to meet his troopers in the Panhandle. His discussion items for all troopers on this trip were making out reports, amount of work done, school bus checks, and results of contacts over holiday weekend. Some additional items listed for specific troopers included: Care and condition of vehicle, football assignments, and partners working together. After meeting with troopers along the way, he worked with Trooper Jim Cross around Guymon until 1:00 a.m. and stayed over night in the Dale Hotel in Guymon. The next day, after a morning meeting with Trooper Cross, he drove on out to Beaver where he worked with Trooper Hamilton. He started back to Enid at 6:00 p.m. stopping to meet with troopers on the way. He got back home at 11:10 p.m. This exhausting schedule became the norm for him about once a month. (The round trip from Enid to Guymon, with no other side trips was 424 miles.)

Diverse Responsibilities of Supervisor

The day after his September trip to the Panhandle, Dad went back west toward Woodward where he was scheduled to meet with members of the Red Cross who were organizing their Disaster Plan. He noted that he showed them his "Lost Kit." Earlier in 1955, the Civil Defense of Oklahoma had designated the patrol as the central coordinating agency for emergency relief because of its statewide radio system and its trained personnel. (3) Dad also helped with disaster plans in several other communities. On his way to Woodward, he had met with troopers in Medford and in Alva and discussed the same basic items he had mentioned to the other troopers earlier in the week. He noted that a liquor raid had occurred in Alva.

The illegal liquor problem that was raging in other parts of the state did not seem to be as big of a problem in the Enid District. By this time, the illegal liquor business was so lucrative in Oklahoma that gangland wars occasionally erupted, sometimes involving innocent citizens who happened to be in the area. Liquor dealers in Texas would sell whiskey to runners who would then transport the contraband to Oklahoma. The wholesaler in Texas, meanwhile, would send his own agents to hijack the runner, making a profit from sales plus retrieving the liquor. Since cars or trucks were common carriers, all this action took place on public highways. Occasionally innocent travelers were mistaken for runners and were caught in the fracas. When questioned about this problem, "O.K. Bivens, the State Crime Bureau chief whose duty it was to suppress such action, could only answer that he did not have enough men to patrol the highways, which was what was necessary to end the violence." (4)

Leonard Kelsoe, who was a trooper in district six at Fairview in 1955, stated, "We had bootleggers everywhere I worked. Actually an old school friend of mine was a wholesaler. He'd bring in whiskey from Texas and sell it to others to distribute. I never went looking for whiskey, but if I worked an accident or I had to stop him for some reason and it was there, I wouldn't overlook it." His remarks reflected the ambiguity with which many of Oklahoma's citizen's approached the liquor issue. "Actually, 95% of them [bootleggers] were the nicest people you'd find in a district. If anybody needed anything, they were there to help. I hated to catch one with whiskey," Kelsoe concluded.

On Thursday, September 29, 1955, Dad's first troop meeting as supervisor was held in Enid. They spent the morning at the pistol range where he shot 61.2 out of a possible 100 on his first round and improved to 84.8 on his final round. The group ate lunch at Failings, and had a meeting afterward.

Dad's part of the agenda was to talk about reports. His list of comments for the meeting included the following: Don't use carbon, check squares, get signatures on arrest summonses, and give more information on the backs of reports. In addition to checking trooper's reports for completeness and accuracy, the officers at the district headquarters summarized the information, looking for patterns or "hot spots" where accidents or certain offenses occurred. Dad, like most patrolmen, had learned to type using the old two-finger hunt-and-peck method. In the months and years ahead, he would spend many hours in front of the Royal upright typewriter, pecking out monthly and yearly reports for his district.

Not all of his job was spent on mundane duties and tasks. Dad was still able to get the OU football traffic assignments. His face got a little red on one occasion when he told us about getting into trouble while working football traffic as a trooper a few years earlier. He said that he had become sick and tired of stopping speeders and giving them a ticket, only to have them beat the charges somehow. He decided to dish out a little punishment of his own by delaying giving them the ticket, making the drivers sit along the road and wait a while. When someone complained, and his superiors heard about his playing "judge and jury," they told him not to do it again. And he didn't.

Some problems that may seem far removed from road safety came under the domaine of the Dapartment of Public Safety about this time. During the 1950s, cattle rustling had become a major problem in Oklahoma. The Oklahoma Statutes of 1951 (21 O.S. 1951, Section 1716) included one that dealt with larceny of domestic animals, listed as horse, jackass, jennet, mule, cow, or hog. In 1953 ten officers to deal with this problem had been authorized by the legislature to be under the command of the Oklahoma State

Crime Bureau, which was a part of the Department of Public Safety. (Title 47, Section 383.1 — 1953) The rustling problem increased, and in 1955 the total number of officers was increased to twenty. The House Bill authorizing the additional officers indicated that these officers "shall have no connection with the OHP but who shall at all times be subject to the orders and directions of the Commissioner; such special officers, however, shall not have authority to enforce any laws except . . . [that of larceny of domestic animals], with respect to which they shall have the same authority as any other peace officer." (5)

Nat Taylor, who was working in Size and Weights, remembered, "Ralph (Snake) Venom was in charge of the Crime Bureau for a while. There was so much cattle rustling that they'd check sale barns looking at brands. At one time every trooper was to stop every truck with cattle. They were to record the truck's tag number, list the type and number of cattle in the truck, and the owner's name. It was a real bad problem."

The controversies about the patrol itself continued across the state. An article in the *Daily Oklahoman* dated October 6, 1955, reported that during the legislative investigation of the Department of Public Safety, mentioned earlier, more allegations of cover ups of corruption emerged, again involving demotions for officers who tried to investigate irregularities in the enforcement of Prohibition. As the senate investigators gathered the facts about these cases, Assistant Commissioner H.G. Harmon and Patrol Chief Jack Rollins changed their decision on the innocence of Trooper Williamson in the Lawton case. When asked about this change of heart, both replied that new testimony had revealed Williamson's guilt. (6) On his trips to "the City" Dad heard a lot of talk about the mess. But he had all he could do to establish himself in the Enid district and get his family settled in their new home town. For the most part he left the gossip where he heard it.

The first week in October Dad was subpoenaed for three days to Pottawatomie County Court in Shawnee. While he was there he stayed in one of the furnished apartments on the North Harrison property he and Mother still owned. According to his journal, the first evening he attended the moving picture show, "To Hell and Back." After the show, he rode with Shawnee city police car #2. The next evening he rode with his former partner, Johnny Edwards. They were called to a Signal 82 accident in Tecumseh where four boys in a 1939 Ford had hit a telephone pole. Seventeen-year-old James Kieffer died that rainy night, and Dad wrote, "John and I saw him die." By the time he returned to Enid, he had driven 280 miles and was suffering from pleurisy.

The fatality Dad and Johnny Edwards had witnessed near Tecumseh was only one of many in Oklahoma during the month of October 1955. An article in the *Daily Oklahoman* on October 11, stated that because of twenty-seven traffic deaths during the first nine days of the month, the governor and commissioner ordered the patrol to intensify its traffic enforcement. Troopers were to pay particularly close attention to speeders, reckless drivers, and drinking drivers. To aid the patrolmen in this crackdown, the commissioner overcame the objections of the legislature to once again order radar used. With radar readings as proof, the article said that troopers were ordered to issue tickets, not warnings, in an effort to end slaughter on the highways. (7)

When this article was published, Dad was on his second trip to the Panhandle, where much of his time was spent with one trooper who was having trouble. Dad worked with him and discussed the breakdown of his time spent for daily reports, warnings, and accident reports. He emphasized the importance of completing a report for every accident worked. Dad bought their supper for $3.60 and noted an improvement in the trooper's and his car's appearances from those on his previous visit. The following day they discussed methods of arrests and warnings, morale, and up-keep of equipment. Since he spent so much time with the one trooper, Dad was not able to complete this trip in three days. He stayed the first night in Beaver, the second night in Guymon, and the third night in Woodward. He arrived in Enid at noon on the fourth day and found that he had to face another problem. After he went home for a few hours, he wrote "Mama mad at me—cause I didn't call from Woodward." My mother was used to his coming home in the wee hours of the morning, but was not at all happy that he had decided to spend the previous night in Woodward and hadn't called her. Dad worked on reports at the office from 6:30 until 10:00 that night.

As he continued to learn about his new job and responsibilities in District 6, Dad attended his second OU football game on October 15. This time he went with the other supervisor, Floyd "Tarzan" Hayes, who had been one of the original troopers and the only supervisor in the district until my dad had been promoted. Dad noted that they worked traffic at the overpass south of Moore on U.S. 77 before the game. The score was OU-44 and Kansas-6. After the game, they "cruised highway 74" back to Oklahoma City. They arrested one drunk who "vomited all over Unit 66." However, after they got rid of the drunk and most of the mess at the sheriff's office, they stopped to eat at Oklahoma City Hickory Pit, and got home about 9:00 p.m.

The first reference in Dad's journal to the use of radar to apprehend speeders was on October 21, 1955, when he and Lt. Haltom went to Fairview and worked radar on U.S. 60 west of town. The next reference was on October 28. This time he and Lt. Haltom worked with Unit #12 using radar east of Enid on U.S. 60. There were no references in his journal about encouraging troopers to increase the number of arrests as stated in the October 6 newspaper article cited earlier. According to his journal, most of his discussions with troopers continued to focus on completing their reports correctly, taking better care of their vehicles, and resolving personal problems.

Toward the end of October 1955, Dad was able to get one worry off of his mind; he and Mother signed the papers for the sale of the Shawnee property. They had been looking at new houses around Enid and were ready to have a contractor start building a house on West Maple Street. After twenty-three years of marriage, this was an exciting time for my parents as they planned for their first new house. A subpoena for a civil trial in Shawnee on October 25, gave Dad the opportunity to take Mother in a borrowed pick-up truck to get the last of our belongings from the place on North Harrison. He noted that he made $75.00 for the two days in court.

After they arrived back in Enid the next day at 7:00 p.m., Dad drove on out to Guymon so that he could attend the Five State Peace Officer's Convention. He listed the names of people he met from Texas and Kansas and stated that he joined the organization. Trooper Leonard Kelsoe rode back to Fairview with him; they stopped and ate supper in Woodward; and Dad arrived in Enid at 8:00 p.m. That same night, he took Unit 116 to Kingfisher to trade cars with Trooper Parks. On the way back to Enid, Unit 29 died, and he had to radio for Lt. Haltom to come and pick him up. Aging squad cars were becoming more and more of a problem for the patrol, and additional funds for new ones were not available. He got home at midnight.

During his first two months as a supervisor in Enid, Dad worked a total of 715.75 hours or an average of 14.9 hours per day. He was used to 12-to 14-hour days but not every day over an extended period of time, and he was not used to the problems that came from working with so many different people.

1955 Holiday Season

On November 1, Dad noted for the first time that one of the troopers had gone over his head and complained to the lieutenant. He had suggested to two troopers who were having trouble getting along, that they might want to change drivers after each contact, to alleviate some of the concerns of one about the driving of the other. The complaint indicated that Dad had ordered them to change drivers after every contact. The next time he saw one of the troopers, he confronted him about the complaint. The trooper said that he had known it had been a suggestion, not an order. He blamed the "squawk to the Lt." on his partner, stating that he "talked too much." Dad didn't like being caught in the middle, especially when he had been trying to help some troopers with a problem that he thought they should have been able to solve themselves. But there was very little he could do about it.

During the week before Thanksgiving 1955, Dad talked with troopers about holiday traffic and the road blocks they would be conducting the following week to check driver licenses. He recorded a suggestion from a trooper that a badge be made showing the dates served for all retired troopers or widows. Another trooper told him that he was so unhappy with the job he was going to quit. Dad listed these pieces of information so he could relay them to Lt. Haltom and Hayes. He continued on, delivering supplies, returning reports that needed to be corrected, and reminding troopers about the driver license check program. On Sunday, November 20, Dad worked radar with Hayes in Unit 103 four miles east of Cleo Springs on U.S. 60. They gave twenty-two warnings and made two arrests that evening. At this point, he began documenting in his journal each time he worked radar, with whom he worked, and the resulting number of warnings and arrests each session. It is interesting to note, over a month after the October 11,

Daily Oklahoman article reported that troopers were to increase arrests by using radar, evidence of the documentation of numbers of arrests and warnings first appeared in Dad's journal. Apparently it had taken over a month for this directive to make it through the chain of command.

For the next three days he worked on road blocks for driver license checks with troopers around Enid. Again, he listed the troopers' badge numbers, the location, and the results. On November 21, they made 253 contacts and four arrests; November 22, there were 413 contacts and five arrests; and November 23, they made 53 contacts and one arrest. He took Thanksgiving off and drove our family out to Chester to have dinner with the Louthans, my mother's sister and her family. Dad, Uncle Art, John, and Tom went hunting in the morning and watched the football game, Texas vs Texas A&M, in the afternoon. On Friday Dad continued with the driver license checks.

The next morning he and Lt. Haltom checked licenses at Waukomis and made sixty contacts with no arrests. That afternoon and evening he worked at Medford with Troopers Byrnes and McCoy making fifty contacts with no arrests. They changed to radar for one hour and gave six warnings. That evening Dad began giving a series of budget cutting messages to troopers. In these discussions which lasted well into December, he emphasized the following: Reducing mileage, doing more spot checking, cutting corners on expenses, taking care of their unit, and keeping accurate cost sheets.

During the trip to the football game at OU the following Saturday, Dad told Trooper Summers about the cost-cutting measures. In addition, his notes indicate that he talked to Summers, who was stationed in Enid, about driver license checks in "the Negro settlements." They stopped by headquarters in Oklahoma City on their way to the game so that they could report the "story of McCoy's coat."

Troopers were responsible for their uniforms, and winter coats were expensive. There was no record of what had actually happened with the coat, but it must have been a special case for him to document that he had reported the "story" to headquarters. Dad also noted that day, "Stogner had a heart attack."

December 1, 1955, was a busy day working with the public. That morning he had a television show on Channel 5 in Enid; then he did a radio show. That evening he went to the Richmond PTA meeting where he showed the film, "U Bet Your Life." Since Richmond was not far from Chester, he stopped by the Louthan's for supper. Dad always enjoyed meeting with community groups, and he also liked the opportunity to spend time with the Louthans and get a good home-cooked meal for no cost.

Later in the week, Dad worked with a three-way transfer of troopers to try to solve some problems one trooper was having in one of the district communities. The trooper who had been having difficulty was transferred out of the Enid District, and one of the troopers from close to Enid, who had been wanting a transfer, was moved into that position. A trooper from another district was brought in to fill the newly vacated spot. He talked to each of the men involved, including the partners of each. He hoped things would work out well for all of them. He emphasized that troopers needed to be responsible for doing their jobs which also included getting along with their partners and community members.

As the year was drawing to a close, more troopers began asking about the possibility of transfers. Since troopers' assignments were made by the higher ranking officers, all Dad could do was make a note of their requests and mention it to the lieutenant. Although district lieutenants made recommendations about trooper assignments, the final decision-making and paper-work were done in Oklahoma City by the "high brass."

Trooper Leonard Kelsoe, in Fairview, was having more and more difficulty with pain in his back, which he had injured in the patrol car accident cited earlier. In addition to his back problem, he had some other physical problems connected with his job. Kelsoe said, "I found out after I worked for a while that I didn't like to arrest people. I had ulcers for years until I went off of the patrol. If I arrested someone, I slept with it. It was on my mind all night. I kept wondering, 'Should I have arrested him or let him go?' I took a handful of Gelusel tablets during every night shift." Kelsoe and his doctors wanted him to be considered for another assignment within the patrol, so he wouldn't have to ride in a car as much. On December 14, 1955, Trooper Kelsoe accompanied Dad as he took their district's reports to headquarters in Oklahoma City. When they returned to Enid, Kelsoe was so distraught by the lack of understanding from the "brass," that he left his briefcase with the papers supporting his request in the car. Dad returned it to him two days later as he took supplies and other requested items around to the units.

As a supervisor, Dad continued to perform law enforcement duties as he drove from unit to unit making observations and taking information and supplies. Along the way he made arrests for drunk driving and speeding fairly regularly. With each arrest he had to file the cases in the corresponding county and be available if called to court. Many upper level officers avoided making arrests as they traveled around the state because it was difficult for them to be involved with the necessary follow-up.

In preparation for Christmas 1955, Dad discussed plans for holiday traffic control as well as cost-cutting strategies with troopers as he made his rounds. On December 13, he addressed Christmas cards in the office, and on December 22, he played Santa Claus for the OHP Christmas party in the Enid office.

On Christmas evening, he and Lt. Haltom met with a

trooper cited earlier, who had the new partner from another district. They had learned that "someone" was spreading rumors about the new trooper near four corners. Dad was discovering that personnel problems were not easily solved; they just seemed to change.

On Christmas morning, Dad's photograph, with his "Lost Kit" and some members of Enid Scout Troop 11, had been featured in the Enid *Morning News*. The accompanying article by Bob Mullins stated that there were 45 pieces of equipment in his little box. "Morris, while stationed at Shawnee as a trooper 1951-1955, packed and unpacked this tiny box of equipment before scores of groups of Boy Scouts, college students, civil defense officials, Girl Scouts, and Brownies, women's club members and other persons in meetings over the south half of Oklahoma." Mullins commented, "Although each item is large enough to fulfill its purpose, Morris is ribbed about the small size of the objects." Dad liked talking to the public and also enjoyed having a gimmick to catch their attention and imagination. He was always on the look-out for items that he could incorporate into his "Lost Kit."

Dad ended the year of 1955 on a trip to the Panhandle where he went over a progress report with each trooper and had him sign it. Lt. Haltom had already reviewed and signed each report as one of the evaluating officers. On his way back from the Panhandle, Dad worked with Troopers Holland and Young in Woodward from 7:00 p.m. until 2:00 a.m. He noted, "both men proud of progress report ratings."

While my dad was adjusting to his new job as supervisor in the fall of 1955, Nat Taylor, who now lived in Stillwater, had been busy establishing himself as a trooper in the Size and Weights Division. When the division was established in 1949, federal funds were available to help enforce truck load limits to keep from tearing up the state's roads. Also, by law, out of state trucks were not allowed to transport goods or materials from place to place within the state. The ten Size and Weights troopers, in addition to working traffic, were to enforce truck weight limits, truck size limits, and verify the legality of truck's license tags. Every loaded truck had to have a certified bill of laden which listed what the truck contained and its weight. Taylor commented that during the first few years of the division's operation there had been some concern that "some of the original troopers liked to play poker and get drunk when they had a chance to get together. On duty, a few of them just drove around, visited their friends, and killed time," he added.

After Red Etheridge, who had been one of the original Size and Weights troopers, took over as lieutenant in 1955, he made some changes to hold his troopers more accountable. Fifteen permit offices were placed around the state with a clerk who would sell special permits for trucks that were oversized. If a truck were too heavy for the guidelines, it would have to have extra axles in addition to the permit. Trucks that were too tall, too wide, or too long had to have a permit that restricted its travel to certain times on particular roads. Bridges and underpasses had to be considered when the route was approved. These permits generated a sizable amount of money for the state. Size and Weights troopers were responsible for supervising the clerks and checked in with them regularly.

Taylor commented, "Oklahoma did not develop a port of entry system like many states did. There were too many roads coming into the state. They went with the roving troopers to enforce the laws regarding trucks. We kept out-of-state trucks out of here that were illegally tagged, hauling overweight loads, or had no permission from the corporation commission to be here."

Starting a New Year

A new organizational structure was implemented beginning in 1956 when the number of Oklahoma Highway Patrol divisions was increased from two to six. Each was commanded by a captain, and Enid was assigned to Captain Shackelford. It was believed that "[b]y decreasing the size of each division, field captains were made more aware of specific needs in their divisions. Problems were aired at regular staff meetings where the Chief heard reports on each division and formulated plans for the entire Patrol." (8) There were concerns, as cited earlier, that the captain's role had been diluted with this structure. For Dad, this new organization model gave one more person for him to inform and receive directions from. Not only did he have to coordinate his activities with the other supervisor and the lieutenant in his district, but now he had to include the captain. He also had to be careful that he did not go over the head of Lt. Haltom or give the impression that he did.

The daily journal he used for 1956 was supplied by the Fred F. Fox Company. Although it was basically the same as the one he had used the year before, every day had been marked with a stamp designed to organize information for troopers. The patrol continued to suffer from lack of funds and each trooper was to make a decided effort to cut costs. Apparently it was believed that troopers would be more conscious of the tight budget efforts and keep better records if they only had to fill in the blanks for those things that they would have to include in their reports. The stamp gave a place to insert the time for "on duty and off duty; mileage start, end, and total; numbers of warnings; assists; and arrests." Another section, titled "How Time Spent & Hours," was designed to help troopers keep better records of how they spent their 54-hour work week. Categories listed were "patrol, spec. patrol, court duty, veh. check, veh. repair, road block, accident inv., other, and no acc." In the small space at the bottom of the stamp was a place for remarks. They hoped that the stamp would give them more structure and help troopers improve their record keeping, but it left my dad very little space to record the kind of lengthy notes he had kept during 1955.

On January 3, 1956, one of Dad's troopers resigned and turned in some of his uniforms the following day. He was sorry to lose a trooper, but knew it was better for him to do something else rather than stay on the patrol and be unhappy, like too many other troopers were. That didn't do anybody any good. After inventorying the clothing the trooper turned in, they found that many items were missing. Dad and Lt. Haltom first met with Captain Shackelford and then went to the trooper's house to get the missing uniforms.

Dad's trip to Oklahoma City on January 11, 1956, combined the annual Department of Public Safety Credit Union meeting with his monthly trip to take in District 6's reports and pick up needed supplies. At the meeting Dad was elected to the Credit Union Board of Directors. This meant that he would have to attend a monthly meeting in Oklahoma City, but he was happy to be involved in the board that made decisions to help Department employees, especially highway patrolmen. He tried to coordinate this meeting with his delivering of their district's monthly reports to headquarters.

The following day he went to Clinton to a lieutenant's meeting with Otis Haltom and Floyd Hayes. The meeting was for supervisors, or second lieutenants, and first lieutenants from the Lawton, Clinton, and Enid Districts. He noted, "Butch and Shack were there. Saw Mose, Awtrey, Burkes, Peek, Musson." Dad always found it energizing to be able to spend time with some of his old buddies and be able to share "war stories" about their work. In the past as troopers, they had talked about wrecks and car chases; now they talked mostly about being in the middle of personnel issues, trying to implement the cost cutting measures, and dealing with the on-going problems of making the roads safer.

New highway patrol hip jackets had been dispensed when Dad had attended the credit union meeting. He and

Hayes began to take them out to the field to issue them to troopers who worked too far away to easily drive into Enid.

My brother John returned to college in late January after three days of ice on the roads. Just as he approached Miami, his car slid on a patch of ice and ran into the back of a truck. John was only slightly injured; the truck wasn't damaged at all; but John's car, our old '47 Chevy, needed a lot of repair work. Dad drove to Miami to talk to John and the officer who had investigated the accident. Since he was concerned that there might be a lawsuit brought against our family, Dad drove on down to Seminole to see his old friend, attorney Frank Seay, about the accident. He needed some expert advice about his son's wreck. After meeting with Mr. Seay, Dad called John and told him to get some photographs of his bruised face. This would provide some documentation of his injuries, if they needed it. On his way back to Enid that evening, he stopped to spend some time with his old patrol unit in Shawnee and get information about their adult driver education course which he planned to start in Enid. He was determined to bring some of the special programs he had helped start in the Oklahoma City District to the one in Enid. It was another very long day; he returned home at 2:00 a.m.

At 10:00 a.m. that same morning, Dad and Lt. Haltom met with one of their troopers who complained that his partner was having extramarital affairs. According to the patrol manual and to department expectations, troopers were to be good examples in their communities. This trooper was very unhappy about his partner's behavior and what he thought it was doing to the reputation of the Oklahoma Highway Patrol. Dad knew that many troopers had affairs, but most of them didn't get caught. If it didn't interfere with his work and no one complained about it, usually nothing official was done. The next day, Dad and Lt. Haltom met with Captain Shackelford to plan a strategy to deal with the trooper. They apparently decided to take a low-key approach. The following day, Dad met with both troopers and discussed the following items: Reporting special happenings and injury accidents, more activity, vehicle checks, activities unbecoming to officers, and adult drivers' clinic. Evidently, this round-about method was not effective in solving the problem. Three days later Dad and Lt. Haltom had to meet with the first trooper again, and this time the word recorded was "adultery." District 6 officers had many other responsibilities to fulfill, and it seems they kept hoping this problem would get solved without their direct involvement.

Other problems related to lack of adequate funding for the patrol were becoming acute. In the early part of 1956 rising gas prices, increased highway mileage, and worn equipment caused Governor Gary to make a supplemental appropriation to the highway patrol of $150,000. Even this action was not enough, however, for more men and equipment were urgently needed. (9) Out in the field, Dad as supervisor continued to carry the message for troopers to observe cost-cutting measures.

From February 5 through 9, 1956, Dad was in court in Seminole. He sat in the witness room for four days before finally being called to the witness stand on the fifth day. He testified for forty-five minutes and was released by 10:30 a.m. While he was in the area, he went to Shawnee to "finish up some old cases," and have dinner with his former partner, Bryce Wilde, and his family. Wilde told him about a project he was working on to help troopers determine how fast a car had been going by measuring the skid marks at the scene of an accident. Dad was always interested in creative ideas and was particularly interested in something that would help troopers do a better job. He encouraged Trooper Wilde to continue working on the project with Professor Halley of the Physics Department of Oklahoma Baptist University in Shawnee.

The morning after he returned from Seminole, Dad went

with Lt. Haltom on a three-day trip to the Panhandle. In addition to making observations of troopers at work, they spent time socializing with some troopers in their homes. After returning to Enid on day three, Dad was sent to check on the trooper who had been accused of adultery. He called it "Bird dogging" and noted that he had "no luck." He did not like this part of his job at all, but he knew that a supervisor was often sent out to do the "dirty work" of a district and that was part of the job he had accepted. When he talked to supervisors in other districts, they described similar tasks.

Captain Shackelford met with Lt. Haltom, Supervisor Hayes, and Dad about once a month. After their Valentine's Day meeting, Dad took this information out to troopers: Captain's breakdown of their reports, a directive regarding vehicle care, mileage rates, disaster plans, white accident report sheets, civilians and family members in units, contacting local newspapers, activities in District 6 as compared to other districts, and the new pension plan. Regarding the vehicle care directive, Dad wrote in the back of his journal, "Get authorization on purchases & repair jobs over $10.00." He noted at one stop a trooper "didn't like it at all!" During another one of his information delivering sessions troopers gave him information regarding "riot in Negro town, whisky pay off of sheriff, relations with county attorney." At another stop during his February meetings, a trooper told him he was having family problems, and still another trooper asked about a transfer. He recorded these pieces of information and requests and brought them back to Enid to share with Lt. Haltom.

On the morning of February 27, 1956, our family moved into the brand new house at 2121 West Maple Street in Enid. It was a three-bedroom frame home that cost $12,500 including the lot; my parents got a government mortgage through the G.I. Bill. As was his usual pattern, Dad went back to work that afternoon as soon as we were moved in. During the evening he and Lt. Haltom again met with the two troopers who were having problems regarding the alleged infidelity of one of them. Two days later, Lt. Haltom and Dad met with them again. This problem just did not seem to want to go away, and Dad began to appreciate the adage that eighty percent of a supervisor's time was usually spent with twenty percent of the troopers.

At the end of February 1956, Dad recorded the following figures:

417.00	Salary
23.80	Tax
20.85	Retirement
8.83	Ins.
363.52	Check

This was $111.77 more per month than he had made four years before as a trooper in Shawnee. But with one son in college and two more children of high school age, a new house with mortgage payments of around $70.00 per month, and his own retirement not too many years down the road, Dad continued to be concerned about money.

According to his journal, March 6, 1956, was not a very good day. He had been subpoenaed to Shawnee to criminal court, and on his way, one tire on the patrol car "went 10-7," meaning out of service or flat. Sometime while he was changing the tire or waiting in the courthouse, he lost his "Lost Kit." "Boo Hoo," he wrote in his journal.

As days passed, troopers were using more and more radar, and Dad recorded that he worked with them frequently. He also continued giving speeches in a variety of community settings and was busy putting together another "Lost Kit." Late March and April brought the usual spring storms to northwest Oklahoma and officers as well as troopers helped with traffic.

Safety Education Efforts

Just as he had done around Chandler and Shawnee in previous years, that spring of 1956 Dad helped organize a regional Driver Education Contest in Guymon. Lt. Haltom went along to the Panhandle to help him give the written tests.

Dad had worked hard to plan for adult driver education courses to be held in various communities in his new district. He got the cooperation of the patrol and the Enid Police Department and then sought sponsors for the courses within each community. On April 10, 1956, the first adult driver education course began at Enid. It was sponsored by the Enid Business and Professional Women's Club and met for six Tuesday nights at Convention Hall. The structure of this course became the model for those that followed. In the first two-hour class Dad introduced the course and one of the license examiners discussed laws and driver improvement. Two sessions were devoted to the Oklahoma Uniform Traffic Code. Trooper Soucek worked with Dad and Trooper Summers worked with Supervisor Hayes for these sessions. Captain Walt Stewart from the Enid Police Department assisted with pedestrian safety, radar, and Safety Responsibility Law topics. Lt. Otis Haltom conducted the class on accidents and accident reporting. The final session included Trooper Patton explaining driver evaluation tests and Dad giving a final examination. After showing the film, "A Day in Court," there were graduation exercises.

Another course was held at Gate from May 7 to June 10. Lt. Haltom and Supervisor Hayes assisted along with Troopers Likes and Bogle, and license examiner, Harry Jones. Capt. Stewart and Sgt. Hopkins from the Enid Police Department made the trip to Gate High School to assist with a "drunkometer demonstration" and a discussion of pedestrian safety. Dad gave the final examination and awarded certificates of completion.

At the conclusion of the course in Enid, Mrs. Wilma Dean wrote a letter dated June 6, 1956, to "the State Highway Department" complimenting "Mr. Morris" on the course. A letter from Jack Rollins, chief of the Oklahoma Highway Patrol, responding to Mrs. Dean was placed in Dad's personnel file. The letter said in part, "It is always gratifying to receive letters, such as yours, and to hear that our troopers are rendering to the public the highest type of service. Supervisor Morris is one of our best troopers."

Arranging and conducting the courses took a lot of his time, but Dad believed that these classes would make a difference by educating drivers about safety on the roads. He sincerely believed that education was the key to making roads safer. After all, if people understood why accidents took place and learned how to avoid those problems, the rate of accidents and resulting fatalities would have to go down. He had received the encouragement he needed from the department to continue planning additional driver education courses. As with many other things in his life, once he focused on this project, he pursued it with tenacity. As Dad met with his troopers throughout the district, he tried to get them to make a commitment to coordinating and teaching an adult driver education course in their towns. He was willing to talk to community groups himself to get sponsorship. In fact, he and Captain Shackelford attended a meeting of the Lions Club in Alva on May 17, where Dad "Talked about Drivers Ed. school, what it was and does."

Two articles in the *Daily Oklahoman* on April 27, 1956, brought the Williamson case in Lawton back into the public's consciousness. They reported that the senate committee investigating the case found that Williamson had been guilty of the charges of allowing the driver transporting illegal liquor to leave the scene of the accident. The senate committee report added that "the case had been badly bungled and might have gone unheeded except for efforts by the press and citizens to achieve justice. After months of investigating the activities of the DPS [Department of Public Safety], the senate committee recommended a complete change in the patrol's policies governing promotion and demotion. The committee report also advised the governor to establish a non-political commission to oversee the DPS in order to halt abuses and take the patrol out of politics. The report criticized the leadership of the patrol, but ended by praising the worth and service that troopers provided." (10) Although the committee had made recommendations for immediate change, all indications are that work went along as usual for those out in the patrol districts around the state.

On the national level, the Federal Aid Highway Act of 1956 was enacted. This act had resulted from President Eisenhower's experiences with the Allied Forces on the German autobahn during the war. In 1954, he had established a President's Advisory Committee on a National Highway Program. The final report of this committee led to this act which spelled out guidelines for a 42,500-mile national interstate highway system. In Oklahoma, plans for Interstate 35 were from north to south, paralleling US 77 from Kansas through Oklahoma City to Texas. Interstate 40 was to cut across the state from east to west roughly following along US 64 from Arkansas to Warner; US 266 on to Henryetta; and US 62 to Oklahoma City, from where it followed US 66 west to Texas. Although it would take many years to complete these super highways and neither of them were to be located in District 6, the announcement of the routes and beginning of construction had an impact on communities all along the paths and created a ripple effect that extended to parts of Enid's district.

On May 14, Dad taught six classes of Driver Education at Enid High School. He discussed traffic courts, showed slides of accidents, and told the students about the reports that officers made out. He recorded that there was a total of two hundred pupils in the classes.

He had continued to meet with the trooper who had complained about his partner's infidelity and also with the partner. Finally, in early June 1956, the complaining trooper was transferred to another unit out of Enid's district, and a new trooper was brought in. Although he had spent many hours working with the previous trooper and his partner on personal matters, Dad's notes from the first meeting with the new trooper did not reflect any personal issues—they focused on "report making."

On June 6, 1956, Dad went to Oklahoma City to get a radar unit repaired. He wrote that he went to the new headquarters located just west of Lincoln Boulevard at 4th and Walnut. The patrol headquarters had been at the previous location on N.E. 23rd since 1945.

Later in the month, Dad attended the funeral of one trooper's grandmother and escorted the funeral procession to another town for burial. It was a tradition for troopers to pay their respects to a grieving patrolman and his family in this manner. Unless there was an accident to work or other emergency, as many patrol units in the area as possible attended the funeral of a trooper's family member.

During his June meetings with troopers, in addition to reminding them about the importance of filling out reports completely and correctly, Dad began to record how many total arrests they made and warnings they gave out each time he was working with them. Acccording to his journal, he also talked to individual troopers about outside work, going 10-10 (out of service-subject to call), and a complaint that had been filed against one trooper. Since he believed that most of the troopers were hard working, he tried to focus on the positive instead of the negative. Although the notes he kept in his journal were about the things that needed to be worked on and improved, he remembered how he and his fellow troopers had felt in Chandler and Shawnee when they didn't get much praise. He made an effort to tell troopers when he thought they were doing a good job, and he tried to implement the leadership skills that he had learned from being a teacher and a coach.

At the beginning of July 1956, Dad worked on trooper progress reports. Since this was the second time he had completed them, it was a little easier. He used his detailed notes and the impressions he drew from observations made while working with troopers, comments from Lt. Haltom and Supervisor Hayes, as well as summaries from the trooper's reports to complete the evaluation of each patrolman assigned to him. He then reviewed the reports with Lt. Haltom, adding, changing, or eliminating items as directed.

On July 3, 1956, Dad had to take Mother to the hospital for some blood transfusions. She was forty-six years old and had become weaker and weaker during the time we had been in Enid. The doctors said that my mother was very ill and would need to be built up quickly before they could even consider any surgery that might be need to be done. After asking for the name of the best internal medicine doctor in Enid, my dad and mother chose Dr. Evan Chambers. When they heard about Mother's emergency, several Enid troopers immediately went to the blood bank and donated blood to offset the five units she needed. This event shook our family's world to its very foundation. Mother had never been sick before, and the possibility that she might have stomach cancer, which had caused the deaths of her mother and grandmother, was our worst nightmare. Our family rallied around and began to prepare for whatever might come.

It was during this same time that Dad received a formal evaluation of his first year's work as a supervisor. The report was in the form of a memorandum from Capt. W.E. Shackelford to Chief Jack Rollins and was dated July 10,

1956. The progress report, as it was called, stated that "Supervisor Morris is making a good supervisor for the following reasons: . . ." There were nine positive points listed covering the topics of loyalty, appearance, decision-making, dependability, being liked by troopers and the public, public relations, suggestions and constructive criticism, courtesy, and fairness. The report concluded with two suggestions for improving: "(1) Analyzing the records available and using the results for future planning. (2) Assuming more responsibility as he gains experience." Chief Rollins had signed Dad's copy and dated it 7/11/56.

Dad's vacation time was scheduled to begin on July 10. In spite of Mother's poor health, they decided to continue with our plans to once again go fishing with the Louthans in Minnesota. There our families could spend time having fun together as we waited for Mother's body to become stronger for whatever might follow. After two weeks away, Dad returned to work on July 25, and worked ten-to eleven-hour days until his next day off on July 30, when Mother had surgery. He took one extra day off to be with her in the hospital. On August 4, my parents were told that the growth in her stomach had been malignant, but Dr. Chambers felt sure he had been able to remove all of the diseased tissue.

This was a very dark time for us. I tried to take over the household chores, but there were many things I didn't know how to do. Dad spent as much time as he could at the hospital while trying to keep up with his work responsibilities. He had always been our strong rock, and it was very disconcerting for Tom and me to see how shaken he was by Mother's illness. We were aware that our dad had an emotional side and sometimes teared up during a sad television program. But it broke our hearts to hear him sobbing in dispair when he finally had the opportunity to shut himself in their bedroom to get some rest. Fortunately, Mother began to show improvement, and she returned home on August 8. Then her long recuperation period began.

Dad's first year as a supervisor on the Oklahoma Highway Patrol had been a very busy one, personally and professionally. He had learned about most of the various aspects of his new role and was developing new skills. During that year he had also been able to make an important impact on the district's safety education programs. However, in many ways the serious illness of my mother overshadowed the joys of our new home and the excitement of his new job as Dad began his second year.

CHAPTER 6

THE LIFE OF A SUPERVISOR
1956-1964

IN AUGUST OF 1956, as my mother recuperated from cancer surgery at home, my dad helped distract himself from worrying about her by working on a slightly different approach to safety education which he hoped would help raise public awareness. He had designed a newspaper article called "Traffic Lifesavers," which consisted of a weekly quiz about traffic safety with the answers provided by "Your Local Highway Patrol Trooper." He wanted this column to be carried by every local newspaper in the district to inform the public about traffic safety issues and also help build better relations with local troopers. Dad went out to sell the idea to the editors himself. His journal documented twenty-eight newspaper contacts in six days during August and noted that the responses were positive.

He continued his usual responsibilities of making observations of troopers and carrying information as well as supplies and equipment during this same time period. Sometimes routine visits to troopers were interrupted by some unexpected happenings. On Sunday, September 2, four boys escaped from the juvenile detention center in Helena. Dad joined the manhunt east of Pond Creek where the boys were caught.

September 7, 1956, was Dad's first notation of Lt. Art Hamilton bringing the highway patrol airplane to work in the Enid district. That Friday morning, he and Enid Trooper Don Patton worked in one car and Trooper Stephens from Fairview in the other. They stopped speeding vehicles that had been spotted and timed by Lt. Hamilton in the airplane.

Later in September he expanded his safe driving speeches to include Vance Air Force Base in Enid. He spoke and showed a film to four groups in two days with both morning and afternoon sessions.

With the beginning of football season, Dad again attended as many home games at OU as he could. He took reports to and picked up supplies from Oklahoma City once a month and usually coordinated this with his monthly credit union meetings. Many months he had to make a second trip to get additional supplies or to pick up cars that had been repaired. Most of his trips to the Panhandle took the better part of three days, and he continued to make this trip once a month.

The Oklahoma Highway Patrol consisted of only 257 troopers in October 1956. Of these, fourteen were assigned to the turnpikes, ten were in the Size and Weight Division, and twenty-five were so sick or disabled as to keep them off of the roads, leaving only 208 troopers to patrol the highways. Besides its shortage of troopers, the patrol was using eighty-three cars with more than 100,000 miles of use, and most radio equipment was more than ten years old. (1) To deal with these issues, Dad's journal reflected activities related to taking better care of vehicles and equipment and making the most of the troopers' time on the roads. On his routine visits, he took repairs for cars and radios and sometimes traded cars, so the troopers' units could be repaired. He continued to encourage some troopers to show evidence of more activity through their reports and to get others to make their reports more accurate.

Dad continued to perform trooper duties in addition to his supervisory responsibilities. On his way back to Enid after attending a credit union meeting in Oklahoma City on October 18, he recorded that he and Supervisor Hayes apprehended a burglary suspect in Kingfisher.

From November 8 through December 20, 1956, an adult driver education course was held in Alva. This time Supervisor Hayes took charge of the course assisted by Troopers Brown and Beierschmitt, License Examiner Jones, Enid Police Department Capt. Stewart, and Lt. Haltom. Dad attended the last class and gave out the certificates.

He and Lt. Haltom went to Alfalfa county on November 26, once again hunting escapees from Helena. This time "Hayes made the catch." For the next three days, Dad gave safety speeches at Vance Air Force Base where he focused on the actions of lower courts.

Beginning in December 1956, Dad noted that he talked to his troopers about the state-wide effort to decrease traffic accidents and fatalities called "Back the Attack." There had been a lot of publicity regarding this effort, and district supervisors had the responsibility to approve and document each unit's plan to address traffic safety concerns for their territory. When he contacted the second unit, the trooper said that he had never heard of "Back the Attack" himself. He told Dad that his partner had looked at some of the materials and informed him "it didn't amount to anything." Dad was aggravated with the attitude of the trooper and even more distressed that his partner had not been at the meeting. He wrote in his journal that the partner had been late getting back from Guthrie and that was why he wasn't there for the meeting. Later that evening, Dad met with another trooper to speak to him about "Back the Attack" and also had to scold him about missing the call on the escapees from Helena.

As the year was drawing to an end, Dad had trouble fitting his notes into the space provided. He was very busy with speeches and meetings of his own. He documented more supplies being taken to each unit, more problems with troopers, and more comments or complaints from troopers.

For example, on December 4, two troopers complained about the quality of tires they had on their patrol car. They said that they had been told to drive only 65 miles per hour on 65 mile-per-hour tires. They asked how could they keep driving 65 miles per hour when the people they were supposed to stop drove much faster? Usually Dad tried to make suggestions to try to help solve problems or concerns in the field. But, in this case, he didn't have any answers or the power to make the needed changes; he could only take the comments back to his lieutenant.

In mid-December, Lt. Haltom, Supervisor Hayes, and Dad met in Oklahoma City where they heard about the new pension plan being proposed. Upon retirement, it would provide one-fortieth of a patrolman's base salary for each year served. They were asked to get their troopers to work on public support for this proposal. Beginning on December 17, as he went out to deliver supplies and repairs, Dad told the troopers about the new pension plan and suggested that they talk with influential citizens to get their state legislators to vote for the bill. This was a tight-wire act, since troopers were supposed to stay out of politics.

Some Highs and Lows of 1956

Looking back through the journal for the year 1956, it appears that Dad had begun to establish himself in Enid. He had worked closely with the newspapers in Enid and other towns in his district. He had given six radio speeches and one television speech and had made over thirty-five talks to community organizations from PTA groups to the Hot Rod Club. He started adult driver education courses that were spreading to many more communities in his district.

Lt. Otis Haltom completed a formal progress report regarding his evaluation of Dad's work as supervisor for the period ending December 31, 1956. The report consisted of information in these categories: Personal Appearance and

Care of Equipment, Initiative, Relations With Other People (All), Judgment and Common Sense, and Quality of Work. There were positive remarks in all categories. The only criticism was in the first one, which said, "Believe he has improved in driving. Does not drive quite so hard." Apparently, the hard and fast driving that had been one of Dad's trademarks as a trooper was not the model they wanted him to display as a supervisor. The final remark from Lt. Haltom was "This man is doing a good job in the capacity of a supervisor. He is a willing worker and is always thinking of some way to improve the efficiency of the department especially in this district." The report was signed by J. Rollins, the chief, on 1-21-57. 1956 had been a good professional year for Dad.

However, out on Oklahoma highways, 1956 had not been a good year. It was the deadliest since the patrol had started in 1937. There were 572 fatal accidents with 683 persons killed during 1956. There had also been 13,460 persons injured during this same time. In 1955 the number of fatal accidents had been 487, with 595 persons killed and 12,720 injured.

To try to stop this killing on the roads, the leadership of the Department of Public Safety knew that they needed additional appropriations from the legislature. However, they had not been successful in convincing Oklahoma lawmakers to allocate more money to the highway patrol. Hoping that the legislature would heed the recommendations of national experts, on January 28, 1957, Commissioner Lookabaugh contacted the International Association of Chiefs of Police (Inc.), Traffic Division located in Evanston, Illinois, and requested "a study of the traffic accident problem in Oklahoma with particular reference to the Highway Patrol." (2) This study was begun in 1957.

That winter of 1956-1957 was a difficult one in other aspects of life in Oklahoma. There was a terrible drought in western Oklahoma and the surrounding area. The U.S.

Government paid for hay to be shipped in by rail so that farmers and ranchers could buy it for a nominal cost to feed their cattle. On January 14, 1957, President Dwight Eisenhower flew into Woodward for a drought inspection. Dad wrote that he went to Woodward to help with security and traffic control. Units 116 from Seiling, 103 from Fairview, and 66 from Enid also assisted the Woodward troopers, Young and Holland. Later he worked two accidents as the large crowd dispersed. His only reference to another disaster, the big snowstorm that occurred in March of 1957, was on Friday, March 8. He wrote "snowed" in his journal. Either he was too busy to write details of the effects of the storm, or it didn't cause enough problems to record.

1957 Legislative Actions

In his message to the legislature in 1957, Governor Raymond Gary addressed the growing death rate on Oklahoma highways as well as needed changes in the Department of Public Safety and the Highway Patrol. Governor Gary agreed with the recommendation from the senate investigation committee of the Lawton incident that there should be a non-political commission directing the Department of Public Safety. He asked the legislature to create a Public Safety Commission consisting of three men and give it authority to draft rules and regulations for the department's operations. He also recommended merit testing for promotions in rank, which would remove much of the personal factor in promotion to levels of leadership. According to this new merit system, a trooper seeking promotion would be judged on this basis: Fifty percent written examination, ten percent interview, thirty percent work record, and ten percent length of service. (3) To address the need for additional highway patrolmen, the legislature authorized and allocated funds for a patrol school to be held that spring, the first since 1953.

The legislature made a number of other changes in the operation of the department which affected patrolmen directly or indirectly. The State Crime Bureau was removed from the Department of Public Safety and renamed the Oklahoma State Bureau of Investigation (OSBI). To pay for the operation of OSBI, $190,000 was removed from the departments' appropriation leaving only $2,160,000, which was $50,000 less than the department had received the previous year, when it could hardly make ends meet. In fact, Commissioner Lookabaugh feared that the patrol would have to junk many of the patrol cars because there was no money for replacement of worn parts. To meet this need, he had asked for $441,419 in January of 1957. (4)

There was great concern that illegal trucks were not only tearing up Oklahoma highways but that they were also contributing to the growing death rate. To address this concern, Senate Bill No. 146 was passed authorizing fourteen troopers and one captain for the Size and Weights Division. The bill also authorized the hiring of 18 permit clerks and one supervisor of permit clerks, with fees collected going to the Oklahoma Tax Commission. The act called for fourteen Oklahoma Tax Commission revenue enforcement officers to work with the Oklahoma Highway Patrol in a different uniform. Also included in this act was a notation that retirement benefits for Oklahoma Highway Patrolmen would be one-fortieth of their base salary for each year they served. (5) The retirement plan the troopers had hoped for had passed.

With fourteen troopers assigned to him, the newly promoted Captain Red Etheridge reorganized the Size and Weight Division and added several permit clerks to OHP district offices. The size of a trooper's territory depended on the amount of truck traffic that was on the roads. Nat Taylor recalled, "My territory was fourteen counties in north-central Oklahoma. They also sent me to help the trooper at Enid with the Panhandle. I set up a system when

I started helping with the northwest area. I got to know all of the sheriffs and big trucking companies. There was still a lot of oil drilling going on, and some of the trucks didn't get the required permits. If there was an illegal bunch of trucks working an area, one of the trucking companies would call and ask me to check it out."

Taylor continued, "Size and Weights had all of the duties of a regular highway patrolman, if needed, but their specialty was trucks. I'd work an accident if I ran on to one. If it was a real bad one, I'd call in and ask if they wanted me to go ahead and work it. However, insurance people would want to talk to the trooper later, and I'd be gone. Oatie [Lt. Haltom] always appreciated my help and told me so." He added, "I worked a lot more accidents than many of the traffic troopers did."

Taylor believed that his work indirectly promoted automobile traffic safety even though non-truck traffic was not his primary responsibility. "I'd have my lights on checking trucks. If there wasn't a shoulder, I'd stop the truck right in the road and put out a flare. People would have to slow down and go around us. Nothing slows down traffic like a flashing red light does."

He explained, "We carried our own scales. We could weigh a truck of 115,000-120,000 pounds and get within 2,000 pounds of it's true weight right there on the road." Regarding the money that was generated from the sale of permits, Taylor explained that the money from oversized vehicles went to the Oklahoma Tax Commission and that from overweight vehicles to the Highway Department. Even with the regulations and checking by Size and Weights troopers, truck traffic continued to be a problem in Oklahoma.

From 1943, the highway patrol had been responsible for providing security for the State Capitol Building with its surrounding buildings and grounds, as well as providing transportation and security for the governor and lieutenant governor. In 1957 the legislature transferred the responsibility for these buildings and grounds to the State Board of Public Affairs. The Department of Public Safety continued to provide personal security for the Governor. (6) This change allowed for more highway patrol troopers to get back on the roads and focus their attention on preventing traffic accidents.

Implementing Plans in the Field

To try to decrease the number of fatalities and injuries on their roads, the Enid district was preparing for "Back the Attack" programs in each community. For most of January 1957, Dad noted meetings regarding this effort. He and Lt. Haltom held "Back the Attack" meetings in their headquarters; they met in the field with troopers to discuss their plans; and they attended "Back the Attack" meetings in communities throughout their district.

Trooper evaluations which had been previously called Progress Reports were termed Efficiency Reports in 1957. This reflected a change in emphasis from the personal focus on improving a trooper's performance to that of streamlining the operation and becoming more efficient. As usual, Dad and Supervisor Hayes completed the evaluations, had them approved by Lt. Haltom, and took them out to review with each trooper they supervised.

Dad listed various automobile parts and the prices of each in the back of his 1957 Journal to deal with the emerging needs for patrol car repairs in the field. The list had been amended with additional items and revised prices. His original list was: Tires $14.75; Tubes 1.78; Purolators .78; Peri—Filters 1.26; AFB 5 Air Cleaner 1.46; Spark Plugs 3.96; Fan belt 1.20; Voltage Reg. 1.50; Condenser .40; and Points .80. Later he added: Batteries 60 $12.24 & 120 $17.24; Alternator 3.50; Fire Extinguisher 2.60; Prestone 1.80; Pellets .34; and Tire Chains 7.20. The price revisions he made for four items indicated that the price had dropped from one to four cents except for tires where the price increased to $15.50 each. Troopers were authorized to charge the items for the listed prices at local gas stations.

There were several personnel changes in Dad's district at the beginning of 1957. The two-man unit that had been assigned to Enid was moved to Seiling. Two of Enid's troopers left the district, and two troopers new to the district were moved to the new Seiling unit. At long last, the trooper who had been accused of adultery was moved to another district, and a new man was brought in. An additional new trooper was assigned to Guymon forming a two-man unit there. All four of the newly assigned troopers had been working in other districts before, but Dad spent quite a bit of time with each of them discussing how they were expected to do things in District 6. At patrol headquarters in Oklahoma City, Jack Rollins left, and Lyle M. Baker was appointed chief.

As soon as it was official that there would be a patrol school in 1957, each district was asked to help with the screening of applicants. In addition to his other responsibilities, Dad began to interview individuals who had applied for the patrol school. Between February 8 and March 24, he was involved in fourteen meetings to interview patrol school applicants.

In addition, Dad continued working with adult driver courses in his district. An article in the Enid *Morning News* on May 15, 1957, described the final evening of one of the courses. "111 students received certificates . . . The course was instructed by Highway Patrol Lt. C.A. Morris, with sponsorship of the Enid Safety Council. Phillips University provided the facilities for the course. Speaking at the final session, Lt. Otis Haltom stated he felt this was one of the best such classes ever held in the state. The class, incidentally, was originated by Lt. Morris." The article continued, "As a result of the example set by Enid's class, other similar schools are scheduled at Medford and Okeene and others may be scheduled later." (Figure 10) Dad's adult driver education courses were gaining momentum.

McDaniel Returns to Patrol

On Sunday, March 17, 1957, Dad wrote that he had gone to Medford to work radar with Unit 21. Don McDaniel, one of his old partners from Shawnee, went along with Lt. Haltom and him. Don had quit the patrol in 1953 to work for the Reed Bit Company. "I knew right away that it wasn't what I wanted to do, but I stuck it out three years," McDaniel said.

He explained, "I discovered that there was a three-and-a-half year time limit for returning to the patrol, so I immediately applied. They called me up and told me I was to go before a board of officers and fifteen troopers. I decided to list all of the questions I would ask if I were on the board to find out why in the world this trooper wanted to come back."

McDaniel continued, "At the beginning of the meeting Chief Baker asked if I had anything to say to the board before they started. I talked for forty-five minutes, going over all of the answers to the questions I had made up. They just sat there dumbfounded. When I got through, he said that he hadn't intended for me to talk so long. Then he asked the board if anyone had a question. The only one was from a guy who was about to retire. He asked how he could apply for my job at Reed Bit." He concluded, "At the time I was the only guy who applied for reinstatement who got every vote. That made me feel real good."

Trooper McDaniel was assigned to Medford where there had previously been problems with troopers and the community. On March 30, Dad went to Medford and followed the same format he used with every other new trooper to his district. "Worked with McDaniel 3 hours, discussed report writing, Drivers Education Classes & speeches in schools."

McDaniel said, "I never worked with anyone who was more dedicated and honest than C.A. was. He really was. C.A. wanted to do a day's work, and he wanted you to do one too." Dad was happy to have Don McDaniel as a trooper, and McDaniel was happy to be there.

Dad continued to write and deliver "Traffic Lifesavers" to local newspapers in District 6. His journal notes regarding personnel issues began to show less patience, especially with those troopers he had to talk to many times. One interchange included the following: "Fire Chief cussed [Trooper X] bad, said he wishes we'd move him away. Told [Trooper X] to get with it, he was hurting the wrong people by shirking. [His partner] says he wants to get out of [town]. Told him to write a letter." After a later session with the partner Dad wrote, "Blue and depressed. Said he was going to Fuck up to see if he could get what he wanted." This was strong language for my dad to record, and, in fact, this was the only time his journals contained profanity.

The twelfth patrol school was held at the University of Oklahoma in May 1957. There had not been a school since 1953, and K.O. Rayburn, who continued as lieutenant in the Public Education Office, was responsible for much of the training that was provided. On May 18, thirty-five graduates from the 1957 patrol school joined the ranks of the seriously understaffed highway patrol. The Will Rogers Turnpike, an 88.5-mile-stretch north from Tulsa to the Oklahoma/Kansas border, was scheduled to open in June. The new troopers would scarcely begin to meet the personnel needs of the patrol. (7)

Back in Enid, Lt. Haltom, Supervisor Hayes, and Dad worked with troopers and other law enforcement officers to provide assistance to Dover, a small town south of Enid. On May 16, the Cimarron River overflowed and a terrible flood washed through the town closing US 81 for the better part of four days. Their district office continued to field calls regarding the flood for several days afterward.

In June 1957, the department began to look for troopers to promote to supervisors' positions. On June 24, Dad recorded, "Took men in for supervisor's test." He also wrote, "Talked to hi brass" while he was in Oklahoma City. Trooper Otto Rauch, who was stationed at Okmulgee at this time, was one of those who took the the test for promotion.

Trooper Kelsoe no longer hoped for another job within the patrol by 1957; now he was trying to get approval for early retirement. With the lack of funds, this was not a good time to apply for something that looked like it would cost the department a lot of money over the following years. However, Kelsoe had not been able to work without pain and discomfort for several years. He recalled, "Assistant Commissioner Butch Harmon got mad at me and tried every way in the world to get me out at a lower amount. He wouldn't even sign my retirement. Jim Lookabaugh, the commissioner, helped me get full retirement, even though I lacked two months having my 15 years in." Kelsoe continued, "After I retired I finally started making a living for my family. I was an independent insurance adjustor." For Dad, Kelsoe's retirement meant a new patrolman would be assigned to Fairview to join Trooper Stephens.

There seemed to be continued unrest among the patrolmen on the roads in the first part of 1957. As he took supplies, repairs and equipment, and new clothes to the troopers in the field, Dad listened to a lot of general complaining. He noted, "listened to bitches ref. pay, expenses, retirement . . ."

New Supervisor Assigned to Enid

There were a number of new personnel assignments to address when Dad returned to work after his vacation that summer. Supervisor Floyd Hayes had retired, and Otto

Rauch was brought in as a new supervisor to work with him and Lt. Haltom. Rauch had taken the test for supervisor in 1955, but said he had decided not to take a promotion at that time. The summer of 1957 was a good time to move for his family, and Otto, Catherine, and tweve-year-old Mary moved to Enid. "C.A. was a man who had both knowledge and judgment," Rauch said about his first impression of the other supervisor in the Enid District. They did not spend much time working together since they alternated schedules. One month Dad would work mostly in the field while Rauch stayed close to the office, and the next month they would do the opposite. With their large district, there was always plenty of work to keep both men very busy.

In addition to the change in the supervisor position, Trooper Dvorak moved to Alva to join Beierschmitt; Sturgeon moved to Kingfisher with Tucker; and Hensley and Burgess moved to Guymon. By July 24, 1957, eleven of the twenty-one troopers in the Enid district had come in since the beginning of that year. For the two supervisors, this meant a lot of work with new troopers needed to be done to orient them to their district's practices and expectations.

Troopers in new territories were encouraged to get acquainted with members of the community as soon as they could. Don McDaniel remembered, "One of the first things I always did when I went to a new place was to make a point of getting to know the district attorney and the judges. You need to get their backing if law enforcement was going to work. If a district attorney got it in for you, he could make it tough. The district attorneys were elected."

Nat Taylor thought it was also very important to also get to know the people who lived in the territory. As he was traveling with his Size and Weights job, he said he could tell which troopers had good working relations with the public and which ones did not. He recalled one example.

"I was driving out around Woodward and ran onto an accident. The first farmer to come along sent his son to call an ambulance. First thing I knew I had ten farmers there helping me. They did it just because they wanted to. The trooper there expected it of 'em, and they did it." He added, "If they hadn't of liked him, they wouldn't have done it."

According to his journal, Dad made his rounds, taking supplies in late July 1957, and discussed driver license checks, report making, and care of unit. At Seiling, he noted that newly assigned Troopers Barnes and Davis "sure did like Seiling and the people."

At another stop, Dad told a trooper about a complaint from the sheriff's office that he was allowing family members to ride in the patrol car. This message calls to attention a practice that had been held over from the days of the Auxiliary Patrol during the Second World War. Troopers had been encouraged to have two men in the patrol cars at night, and sometimes the second person was an adult male who had not been officially authorized to do so. Troopers continued to have male friends and family members "ride with them" at night to promote public relations and a certain level of camaraderie. However, troopers were not supposed to use the patrol car to transport women and children unless it was an emergency situation. They certainly were not to use it as their family car. As he was making his rounds, Dad often picked up my mother's father, John Hussman, and took him to one of his children's homes. (Laurena Shimek lived in Okarche right on the route from Enid to Oklahoma City. Ernie Hussman lived in Seiling, and Donna Louthan in Chester, both in Dad's district.) It is possible that the trooper being chastised for allowing his family members to ride in the patrol car could have seen this message as a double standard from Dad; however, Dad continued transporting my grandpa.

Personal problems between and among troopers continued to take up a lot of time. At one of his units where there had been trouble before, he noted, "Discussed no. of warnings contacts. Asked to increase them. Said they would. Talked about [previous trooper] and how he had told everything to everyone in [the] county."

On August 8, 1957, Dad worked on reports in the office with Supervisor Rauch. Later he and Lt. Haltom went to Waynoka where they met Trooper Beierschmitt from Alva. His notes continued, "told him about new expense claim $15.—went to rodeo—Otis & I caught 2 car thieves who had ridden freight train into Waynoka, had stolen car at Okarche—turned them in to S.O.[sheriff's office] Woodward."

Although he never said anything to us about it, two years after being promoted to supervisor, Dad was considering another step up the leadership ladder on the highway patrol. He wrote that he went to Oklahoma City for supplies on August 22, 1957, and while he was there, he took the test for promotion to lieutenant.

By the end of August, summer vacations were over and communities were getting ready for the beginning of school. Dad drove a '37 Ford in a parade at Woodward and attended the rodeo. He was in the Beaver parade several days later. As football games began to be held in local communities, Friday night usually found him working traffic near by. School bus inspections began in late September, and, according to his journal, he started to remind troopers to schedule safety talks in schools.

Problems with patrol cars continued throughout this time. There were generator troubles, and four notations about trading units for repairs to be done. Five wrecks involving troopers in patrol units were also listed. Two of these occurred on the same day, September 28, 1957, when both of the units stationed in Enid were in accidents. Fortunately, there were no serious injuries.

Dad continued to work radar with his troopers often. Although they did not have as much traffic as some other areas of the state, the Enid district participated with the patrol plane surveillance. On September 12, units from Medford and Enid worked with Dad and Lt. Art Hamilton in the airplane to check speeders near Pond Creek. On October 15, he again worked with the patrol plane and with troopers from Beaver. He did not record the numbers of arrests or warnings during these sessions. However, for Art Hamilton this was a very busy time. It was reported that in October of 1957, Lt. Hamilton identified fifty-seven traffic violators in one day, a record for any trooper. In one three-hour period flying over the Stillwater area, Lt. Hamilton documented twenty-one violators. (8)

Dad began an adult driver education course at Phillips University on September 30, 1957. He taught four of the six sessions and worked on the road in place of Troopers Freeney, Patton, and Summers so they could teach the class on one of the other nights. Lt. Haltom covered the class on the remaining night.

Another adult driver course was held in Beaver City from November 19, 1957, through February 4, 1958. Retired supervisor Floyd Hayes covered most of these classes for Dad. Troopers Likes and Bogle and EPD Capt. Stewart also assisted. By this time, Dad had gathered information from many sources to augment the adult drivers courses. He had a copy of the course that was taught in Chandler, materials from the Kansas Highway Patrol, and information from a trooper in Mississippi. Dad always prided himself in doing a thorough job.

As the year of 1957 went on, Dad's notes in his journal became more brief, usually stating the hours he worked, who he worked with, and one or two words about what he did. Apparently, most of his activities were becoming routine, and he only recorded the information he needed to complete his reports.

He worked radar with his troopers at least three to four times per week. Much of his time was taken up with completing or checking reports or other office work. Another large portion of his time was spent making speeches or teaching classes. By the end of the year, Dad had made speeches to twenty-one community groups plus twenty-four at Vance Air Force Base, and five on the radio. He had taught the adult driver education classes, as well as a session at a criminology class at Northwestern State College and a session at an FBI school that were held in Alva.

I took driver education in high school in the fall of 1957 as one of my scheduled classes. I can still remember how embarrassed I became when my Dad came to speak to our class. During his talk, much to my chagrin, Dad used his middle finger to point to things and several times whistled through his false teeth as he spoke. From the second grader who had been so proud to be a part of the Safety Junior Program with my father a few years before, I had become a typical adolescent who was concerned about what the other kids would think of him and, more importantly, of me. Struggling in my own teenage world, I had little appreciation for the great efforts he was making toward educating Oklahoma drivers to make the roads safer for all of us. Although I still had pride in my dad's position as a supervisor on the Okahoma Highway Patrol, I just wished he wouldn't show up where I was with my friends.

By the end of 1957, highway patrol troopers state wide had issued 59,678 tickets and 188,716 warnings. The number of fatal accidents was 571, one less than the previous year, but the number of fatalities had increased to 703, the highest number in Oklahoma's history. The number of persons injured was also a record, 14,194. (9)

1958 Brings Major Changes to OHP

In an effort to get more patrolmen on the roads and encourage better care of the patrol cars they had, Commissioner Lookabaugh, in January of 1958, began to implement a policy of using only one officer in a unit. (10) Don McDaniel remembered, "At some point they decided that they were short of equipment, and it was just as safe for one man to work alone. They never could convince me it was just as safe for one man as for two. But the decision was made — probably based on economics rather than safety."

K.O. Rayburn, who by this time had been working at OHP headquarters in Oklahoma City for almost seven years, viewed this decision from another perspective. "The legislature was concerned about the cost of keeping up the cars. With three men using them, no one really felt responsible. The cars were being used almost twenty-four hours a day many times. I lobbied to get more money so we could assign a car to each man and hold him responsible."

Funds were not available immediately for enough new cars to assign one to each trooper, so the work schedules of two-man units were changed to have each of them working in the same car alone on two different shifts. This would allow for patrol units to be on the roads sixteen to eighteen hours a day. The training programs had to be changed somewhat to address the new policy of working alone. Although new troopers were not usually assigned to a one-man car at first, they needed to be even more ready to face emergencies and solve problems when they did work by themselves. They couldn't rely on a veteran trooper to be there to help.

Although Nat Taylor had worked alone since he went on Size and Weights in 1954, he still believed that two men should be in a car at night, especially in areas like the Panhandle where troopers could not easily get a back-up unit. "You could be out fifty miles from town, out of radio range and by yourself. If you ran on to a carload of drunks, you'd have to think twice before stopping 'em. You'd be crazy to put 'em in your car all alone. If there was another trooper with you, you could stack 'em in your car and have the other trooper keep an eye on 'em and threaten to hit 'em with a blackjack." He laughed and continued, "A few times when I stopped a bunch of drunks, by the time I got through fightin' all of 'em I'd have one by the neck and the others would all be gone down the bar ditch. I'd never see 'em again." Taylor concluded that as a lone trooper "I could only take the one in, handcuffed and all."

All but one of the units in the Enid district were already two-man units, therefore there were few new cars allotted to their troopers. (The only new car noted in Dad's journal was received on March 28, 1958, and kept in Enid for a breaking-in period before he and Lt. Haltom delivered it the 274 miles to Boise City three days later.) To keep cars on the road as much as possible, they changed each trooper's fifty-four hour a week work schedule to have troopers working either day or night shifts. The troopers in the two-man units already worked alone when their partners had days off and during vacation times. The change to one man in a car at night did not have as much of an impact on troopers in this district as it did in other areas of the state were three-man units had been the norm. However, this increase in use of the patrol cars only seemed to exacerbate the problems with the aging vehicles.

The District 6 office consisted of one lieutenant, two supervisors, twenty-one regular traffic troopers, two Size and Weight troopers, four permit clerks, and two dispatchers in early 1958. By then, Dad had settled into the role of a supervisor. His journal entries became brief and to the point. It appears that he knew what was expected of him and for the most part, what he could expect to deal with.

Tests were given again for promoting troopers to supervisors in February of 1958. Dad took Trooper Beierschmitt in to take the test on the 11th, when he had a credit union meeting. Funds for another patrol school had been allocated and plans were underway for recruiting candidates. Between April 22 and May 1, Dad participated in six interviews of prospective troopers. On May 2, he participated on an Interview Board held at Convention Hall in Enid.

A new avenue of safety education opened to Dad when on Saturday, February 22, 1958, he began participating in weekly radio programs. The first one was over WKY Radio in Oklahoma City. The scripts, prepared and distributed by the Public Information Office, consisted of a fourteen minute dialogue between the announcer and a trooper. Each script focused on some timely topic about safety on the highways. In the following weeks, Dad participated with announcers at KGWA and KCRC radio stations in Enid. By the end of 1958, he had participated in sixty-four radio programs, covering topics such as, "So You Think You are a Good Driver," "Back to School and Labor Day," "Defensive Driving," "Winter Driving," and "Little Mistakes that Cause Big Accidents."

1958 Newspaper Releases from Jerry Marx in the Department of Public Safety's Information Office included "Traffic Lifesavers" which were now being used all across the state in Thursday's newspapers. (There was no indication that my dad had been credited with originating the idea.) For Wednesday's publications Marx provided articles stressing different aspects of highway safety, and Dad often submitted suggestions to his old friend. (11) The "Safety Signal," a weekly newsletter that went out to all Department of Public Safety Employees, also came out of Marx's office. Dad did not actively seek personal recognition for his work although he thoroughly enjoyed working with the public, especially in front of groups. His journal reflected that interest; he had made twenty-nine speeches to community groups by July of 1958.

Although DPS Commissioner Lookabaugh had begun implementing many of its suggestions earlier in the year, in May of 1958, the report from the International Association of Chiefs of Police was presented to the state legislature. The report was titled, "A Report to the Oklahoma Highway Patrol on the Development of a Traffic Law Enforcement Program," and was designed as a blueprint for improvement over a four-year period. One of the major findings of the study, based on the review of troopers' accident reports, was that in a total of 10,855.3 miles of highway, forty-five percent of the accidents had occurred on 2,704 miles of the roads. Thus they concluded, "The accident problem, particularly where accidents of a serious nature are involved, is essentially a rural one." They further deduced, "The major part of the rural accident problem occurs each year on the state trunk system, which is a comparatively small part of the total rural highway network." (12)

To address these findings, the report recommended that "a total of 564 uniformed personnel [an increase of 303] and sixty-five civilians are needed for effective operation of the Division of the Highway Patrol." It recommended three major responsibilities for the Oklahoma Highway Patrol:

1. The reduction of accidents through enforced supervision of driving behavior on the rural highways of the state.
2. Provide service to the community which includes such activities as the investigation of accidents, serving of warrants and revocation notices, answering complaints, and providing general patrol coverage for a given area.
3. Enforcement of laws relating to the weight and size of commercial vehicles.

Another major recommendation addressing accidents on rural roads dealt with the number of vehicles needed by the patrol. The report recommended "291 cars in the motor pool [an addition of 160] plus nine station wagons and five trucks." It noted that there were thirty-two vehicles at headquarters at that time and recommended that this number be reduced.

The report noted that troopers had fifty-two days off plus six holidays and fifteen vacation days per year, and recommended further that the patrol "continue 2-man detachments and create more 1-man detachments with a 24 hour car." (13)

In the lengthy report there was a total of forty-four recommendations in the following categories: Personnel, Equipment, Organization, Management, and Legislative Requirements. With gubernatorial and legislative elections coming in the fall of 1958, Commissioner Lookabaugh scrambled to try to get as many of the recommendations addressed by the sitting legislature as soon as possible. A patrol school held in 1958 added thirty-five new troopers to the force.

To address their traffic accident problems, District 6 had already added a new one-man unit to Boise City, and discussions had begun about decreasing the size of the mammoth Enid District. It was impossible for one lieutenant and two supervisors to give the close communication and supervision recommended for effective operations. According to Mother, Dad was told that there would be a new district formed with headquarters at Guymon, and he was asked if he would be interested in becoming the lieutenant there. This proposal was a complex and difficult one for him to consider. On one hand he could see many possibilities for starting new public safety efforts and had forged many community relationships upon which he could build. However, he did not like the political overtones that tended to rule the operations of the Department and was not sure he wanted to deal with the often ambiguous and conflicting demands from above. His children were almost grown, but Mother was still not really well. For the first time in their married life he and Mother had a home they had built and the opportunity to live the way they wanted in Enid. It was not an easy decision for him to make.

In Oklahoma City, additional plans for reorganizing operations to follow recommendations of the International Association of Chief's of Police report were being discussed. One of the surprises that year was that Captain Bob Lester left the patrol to become the Chief of Police in Norman. Eugene "Chick" Clark retired from the patrol on July 16, 1958, and after three months, went to work for the Oklahoma County Sheriff's Office.

Professional and Personal Issues for Morris

Lt. Otis Haltom completed the mid-year Progress Report for Dad on June 30, 1958. The contents of that report follow:

Appearance and care of equipment: "Takes good care of unit and equipment. Personal appearance very good."

Initiative: "This man is making an exceptionally good supervisor. He sees things that need to be done and does them without being told. He accepts responsibility and makes decisions on the spot in the field without consulting the lieutenant. Is a pusher of safety education and is very active in that field."

Relations with other people (all): "He gets along very well with the troopers of this district. Is plain spoken but not discourteous. Is well liked by other law enforcement officers of this district. Is well known and liked by the public also."

Judgment and common sense: "Has good common sense and makes good decisions. Is a good thinker and usually comes up with the right solution for any type of a situation."

Quality of work: "Quality and quantity both very good. He is fair and impartial. Is technical in his work and likes things to be done in detail. He is exceptionally good in the field of safety education and devotes lots of time to it."

Remarks: "This man is making a very good supervisor. He is always thinking of some way to improve the efficiency of our troop. He is loyal to the department and is a clean liver. It is my opinion that he is material for a district commander." Clearly, Dad's supervising officer believed that he should be promoted to lieutenant. The new district at Guymon would enable them to work together as more atonomy and greater leadership responsibilities were given to the smaller districts.

However, on July 23, 1958, Dad went to Oklahoma City and made the following notation: "Took my last test." With my mother's fragile health and my entering the senior year in high school, he had decided that he did not want to move to Guymon. In the Enid supervisor position, he had been able to focus on areas of the job that interested him the most. Nearing his fifty-second birthday, he did not want to take on the responsibility for an entire district so late in his career. Although Dad took the test, it appears that he had already decided he would not pursue a promotion to lieutenant.

Mother had not been feeling at all well when she and Dad returned home from Minnesota that summer. On July 31, she went to the hospital and had major surgery on August 8. Fortunately the cancer still had not returned, but Dad knew that his decision not to seek a promotion was a good one.

His enthusiasm for his supervisor's job continued even though he didn't want added responsibility. On August 23, his third day out in the Panhandle, he wrote in his journal, "Worked in Unit 24N My first time to fly and operate an airplane! Worked Bryant's Corner. Radar SW Guymon P.M." In addition to his usual activities, he began to list the highways that he "cruised." As he met with troopers he encouraged them to make more moving violation contacts. At some meetings he recommended that the trooper make at least two a day.

Two more adult driver education courses were held in the fall of 1958, one at Lambert and one at Cleo Springs.

Another film called "Miracle of Paradise Valley" had joined "A Day in Court" on the program in these courses.

Dad continued to take equipment for the aging patrol cars and work with troopers to get necessary repairs. Problems with individual troopers continued, and he recorded times that he worked with county attorneys, sheriffs, and a commissioner to try to resolve trooper related issues. The fall school bus inspections and speeches were listed in his journal along with the regular contacts with troopers.

On December 3, 1958, Dad went with Lt. Haltom, Supervisor Rauch, and Troopers Reed and Butler to a meeting at Clinton to be trained on the new trooper rating sheet. At the end of December, he was evaluated on the new form which had ten service factors listed. They were: interest, quantity of work, quality of work, judgment, dependability, social adaptability, temperament, job knowledge, potentialities, and loyalty. Each factor had five descriptors that were to be rated as Unsatisfactory, Improvement Desired, Satisfactory, Excellent, or Outstanding. Most of Dad's ratings were satisfactory or above; however, there were three areas identified as improvement desired. Two of them focused on needed efforts to get the troopers to do something and one focused on a personal issue.

Quantity of work—Warnings. "Has not stressed with troopers sufficiently the importance of warnings as a must in our accident prevention program."

Dependability—Punctual in answering radio calls—'Needs to discuss with troopers more the importance of radio contact such as 10-7 & 10-8 with their base station. We need closer contact with them."

Loyalty—Care of departmental property—"He is a little rough on the unit and needs to be a little more prompt in having minor repairs and adjustments made." (It seems strange that care of a patrol car appeared under the category of "loyalty.")

There is no indication of this, but it is possible that an activity during the training session on the new rating sheet may have included the opportunity for officers to identify areas in which they believed they needed to improve. Dad had continued to document his suggestions to troopers that they make more moving violation contacts. Keeping track of troopers had always been a problem, one which had been cited in the state's political arena as a new commissioner was named. And the concern about aging patrol cars along with Dad's aversion to keeping his car serviced, which had been commented on by his former partners, made this area a natural target for improvement. Dad was realistic, and I'm sure he knew that there were areas in which he needed to improve.

Although there were the three areas identified for improvement in his evaluation, there were thirty-seven areas identified as satisfactory, seven as excellent and three outstanding. One of the areas of outstanding performance was that of safety education; Dad had made fifty-two speeches at community organization meetings and fifteen adult driver education classes, as well as twelve programs at Vance Air Force Base and his sixty-four radio programs in 1958.

Prohibition Issues in Oklahoma

During the gubernatorial campaign in 1958, prohibition had become an important issue. J. Howard Edmondson ran not as an advocate for repeal, but on a platform calling for a special election to allow people to decide for themselves whether or not they wanted legal liquor. Before this time all governors had supported prohibition but had failed to enforce the law strictly. (14) At thirty-three years old, Edmondson was elected the state's youngest governor and appointed his old friend, Joe Cannon, commissioner of public safety. Before the year's end members of the highway patrol began to feel the pressure that was to only intensify after Cannon took office.

In early November, Trooper Don McDaniel was transferred from Medford. "They activated a new unit at Prague. Chief Leo White called and asked if I would move. He said that the people at Prague had been asking for a unit, and they were going to put one there. He asked me how soon I could move, and I told him I'd be ready in the morning."

When he and his family arrived in Prague, McDaniel recalled, "We were treated like a king! School was going on, and the first day the girls made some friends. One of our daughters came home and said she had met a real nice girl who wanted her to come and spend the night at her house. We thought it would be fine, so we sent both of our girls. About two days later I was working down town and a guy hollered at me. He suggested we get a cup of coffee. He was one of the fathers at the school. He said, 'Don, I thought you ought to know this, they are wonderful kids, but their dad is the king bootlegger in this county.'"

McDaniel continued, "I said, 'Good Lord, that does make a difference.' Everybody in town really liked the kids, but people didn't like for the dad to sell illegal whiskey. People liked him too, except for the bootlegging. I couldn't start out in a community with my kids staying at a bootlegger's house."

Commissioner Joe Cannon began reorganizing the department and the highway patrol as soon as he took office in 1959. This shake-up kept only one previous captain in the new reorganization. Four new captains were brought in, which meant that four old captains lost their positions at the top. While Governor Edmondson disclaimed any knowledge of the changes, Cannon reportedly said he initiated these in order to "put the highway patrol back to work." Claiming that too many troopers were sitting in coffee shops watching traffic pass, Cannon said he wanted a new leadership which would push the patrol to more active enforcement of traffic laws even if it required working extra shifts.

Commissioner Cannon reorganized the officer level of the patrol and changed the nature of some of the positions. The assistant commissioner position was to be held by someone outside of the uniformed patrol. Thus the chief of patrol became the top uniformed official with the rank of colonel. This marked a return to the tradition that all rank was held exclusively by uniformed members of the patrol, while assistant commissioner and commissioner were held by civilians appointed by the governor. This began a change in the commissioner's role, which increasingly emphasized personnel administration rather than actual law enforcement. Several senators became concerned about the shake-up, and Senator Fred Harris of Lawton recommended a complete senate investigation. (15)

While Cannon was reorganizing the patrol, Gov. Edmondson continued pushing for strict enforcement of liquor laws. It was contended that two factors were behind the governor's policy of strict enforcement of Prohibition. One was his aversion to half-hearted enforcement of the law. If Prohibition was the law, then it would be strictly enforced. The other reason was to force a special election for repeal. As long as the state's drinkers could get tax free liquor with ease, they would tolerate official Prohibition. However, if that source of illegal whiskey dried up due to stricter law enforcement, drinkers would encourage their legislators to put repeal to a vote. (16) Will Rogers was alleged to have remarked that historically Oklahomans continued to "stagger to the poles and vote dry." (17) Edmondson was forcing the voters to make a stand that they would have to live by.

Commissioner Joe Cannon was a colorful individual

who drew much attention from the press. He was a year younger than the new governor and went about his new duties so enthusiastically that the press called him "the crew-cut commando." Threatening to usurp county sheriff's authority statewide if they didn't cooperate and enlisting the highway patrol to his cause, "Cannon organized a deafening symphony of roadblocks, raids, searches and mass arrests. The only thing more deafening were the wails of protest and the gnashing of teeth from all echelons of the vice world, the money barons of the business world and the halls of the government." (18)

Commissioner Cannon used the highway patrol in these raids, although this raised the ire of many citizens and lawmakers. The chairman of the Senate Committee on Public Safety, Everett Collins, claimed that using troopers as liquor agents would take them away from their main duty of enforcing traffic laws. "In response, Cannon said he was not sacrificing the safety of the highways because he used only captains, lieutenants, and off-duty personnel in the raids . . ." (19) This assertion was to be challenged.

Bootleggers and law enforcement officials meanwhile, responded to the crackdowns with ingenious measures. Bootleggers learned to equip their vehicles with radios fixed on police frequencies to evade highway blockades, while state troopers and involved agencies responded with revised code signals or radio silence. "The climax came two days before the state wide balloting on repeal. Cannon and his men conducted on April 5, 1959, thirty-nine highway roadblocks, examined 3,253 vehicles for liquor, made 128 arrests, and closed numerous cafes." (20)

Although Commissioner Cannon continued to insist that he was using only supervisory personnel in the raids, Assistant Commissioner Ray Page told a senate investigating committee that approximately fifty non-supervisory troopers had been used in four major whiskey raids. For four months Commissioner Cannon used the patrol successfully to enforce Prohibition in Oklahoma. As liquor sources disappeared, legislator's mail increasingly favored repeal. (21) In April of 1959, with a special election for repeal on the calendar and a senate investigation of his tactics underway, Joe Cannon resigned as commissioner of public safety. The special election was held on April 7, 1959, and passed by a vote of 396,845 to 314,380. Prohibition that had been on the books since Oklahoma became a state in 1907, was no longer the law.

Ray Page, who had been an agent for criminal investigation in the army and a detective for the State Crime Bureau and the the Tulsa Police Department, became the new commissioner after Cannon resigned. The assistant commissioner, Norman Hunter, also had a background in criminology. During the next three and one-half years, while they ran the department, there became an increased emphasis on patrol investigations. (22)

Before he left office in early 1959, Commissioner Cannon had announced the creation of a Special Detail and Rescue Division of the patrol. Ex-trooper R.E. Frusher became the leader of a six-member rescue squad trained to deal with such disasters as riots, prison breaks, floods, tornadoes, marine disasters, major fires, and manhunts. Four-wheeled vehicles with rescue and medical supplies were provided in the unit. (23) By 1970 one segment of this unit evolved into the Lake Patrol.

Supervisor Job Continues As Usual

Out in the field, Dad began New Year's Day 1959 by spending from midnight to 6:00 a.m. hunting for A positive blood for an Arnett boy. Later that day he went to Cleo Springs for the last night of the adult driver education class which was held on the holiday. According to his journal, Dad continued with his usual routines: Working with troopers, transporting supplies, reviewing and completing reports, making speeches, visiting driver education classes, and dealing with problems and issues as they came up. On January 23, he wrote that Trooper John Barter had been shot and killed by a cab driver three miles west of Altus. Official reports stated that Trooper Barter, a five-and-one-half year veteran of the patrol, had been shot and killed by a parolee, whom he knew, and a woman friend on January 12, 1959. The pair had earlier shot at two other persons, and Trooper Barter had been called to deal with the disturbance. The two fugitives were arrested at a Highway Patrol roadblock near Randlett some three hours later. (The man was executed for the crime in 1960, and the woman was sentenced to a prison term and paroled in 1975.) Trooper Barter had been the fifth trooper to die in the line of duty since the patrol began. Dad attended the funeral at Altus and Frederick on January 26, 1959.

There were four adult driver education courses scheduled during the early part of 1959, at Fairview, Deer Creek, Shattuck, and Dover. Although other officers had taken responsibility for teaching the various classes included in each course, Dad made sure he was present for the first and last sessions at each town. He enjoyed welcoming the new class members, giving an overview of the course, and then congratulating those who had successfully completed it at the end.

With the new year came a new captain, Clyde Awtrey, who was assigned to supervise the Enid district. Dad wrote that Capt. Awtrey had accompanied him to Woodward in heavy snow on January 31. They met Unit 103 with Trooper Stephens, Unit 24 with Trooper Dvorak, Unit 31 with Trooper Young, and Unit 29 with Trooper Sturgeon. During one of the meetings he noted that a unit from another district had let Unit 103 down on a Signal 89, or hit and run, when they went out to a basketball game instead of helping.

On February 5, from 1:00 a.m. to 9:00 a.m. he recorded that he was "On Roadblock 1/2 mile So. Tonkawa at River

Bridge 'Cannon Whiskey' with Guy Parks in Unit 306." This entry indicates that contrary to his claims, Commissioner Cannon had used non-supervisory personnel in this action, for Trooper Parks was stationed in Fairview at the time. However, the only notation about the commissioner himself found in Dad's journal was when he noted that he had met Joe Cannon at a troop meeting on February 19.

To deal with the important issue of taking better care of the units and monitoring their condition, Dad began to record the mileage and any problems with patrol cars as he met with troopers. Unit 77 had 53,868 miles; Unit 24 – 39,552 miles, Unit 103-49,458 miles; Unit 29-6,687 miles; Unit 116-5,278 miles; Unit 37-71,313 miles with window problem/ air problem; Unit 310-45,860 miles with no tail light or license light, emergency brake gives out, and radiator leaks; Unit 18-9,246 miles with emergency brake and voltage regulator problems; Unit 112-25,648 miles with emergency brake problems and wheels out of balance; Unit 31-15,314 miles with window problems, radio doesn't work, and dirty motor. Twenty-one days after recording information about Unit 24, he noted that the mileage went from 39,552 to 43,620 and the motor was beginning to heat up.

In April, in an effort to decrease the number of traffic violators, the patrol started a state-wide program called, "selective enforcement." This program identified certain points along highways which had proven dangerous and then assigned extra units to patrol that specific area. Often one county with a high accident rate would be chosen for selective enforcement, and as many as eight units would patrol all areas of that county which normally would have been patrolled by one unit. They hoped that the number of accidents caused by violators would be decreased by this intensive patrolling and enforcement of traffic laws. (24) On June 20, 1959, Dad wrote that he worked on a "selective enforcement" program in Blaine county. (This was the only time he used this term.)

In order to tighten the budget, Governor Edmondson was successful in getting the legislature to pass a measure authorizing a central purchasing system for the state. The legislature at first opposed it, but passed it on June 30. The measure was expanded in 1960. (25) Although this would save the state money, it meant that even more of the supplies and equipment needed by troopers in the field would have to be transported from Oklahoma City, typically by supervisors.

Another project for Governor Edmondson was a merit system for state employees. Governor Phillips had previously instituted one in agencies that received federal funds. This was designed to eliminate the patronage system which had been in place since statehood. The Oklahoma Personnel Board, plus one interagency board for DHS-type commissions and a separate one for the Oklahoma Highway Patrol were established. As might be expected, there was much opposition from some legislators who continued to enjoy the patronage system. The bill passed on July 3, 1959, but many senators thought the new system gave Governor Edmondson too much power. (26)

Dad received another performance evaluation from Lt. Haltom in early July of 1959. This time he received three outstanding, six excellent, and forty satisfactory ratings. The only area still identified as improvement desired was that of "care of department property." This comment had been underlined in red: "This man has on a few occasions neglected to have minor repairs done on unit. However, believe he has improved from last report." Apparently closer monitoring of the condition of each patrol car and Dad's reluctance to take his in for minor repairs continued to be something that he needed to work on. Old patterns of behavior seemed difficult to change.

On July 14, Dad reported that he had gone to Oklahoma

City for a credit union meeting and also to attend an "intoxometer school". The rest of the month his job continued as usual, working with troopers, making speeches, and dealing with problems. He was also involved with a drowning at Salt Plains Lake and a "boy hunt" near Bouse Junction. There were no details about either incident in his journal.

Captain Awtrey, Lt. L.W. White, Charles Hughes, and Dad went to Guymon to plan for the new headquarters on August 25. It was a very quick trip, for they left Enid at 7:30 a.m. and Dad had time to make a Boy Scout meeting on the way back to Enid that evening. On September 1, he returned west to check on land for the Guymon headquarters. Although he had told his superiors that he was not interested in the lieutenant job at Guymon, it seems they still hoped that he would change his mind. Dad continued to be very involved in the preparation for the new district, and his judgment and opinions were apparently valued.

In early November 1959, Dad worked with Trooper Bryce Wilde, from Shawnee, and the "Talking Bicycle Program." On November 2, they visited Cherokee, Lambert, Carmen, and Aline grade schools, involving 430 children and twenty-two adults. The next day they went to Goltry, Helena, Byron, and Burlington where they talked to 310 children and twenty-six adults. Trooper Wilde's Accident Speed Determiner had been produced the previous year by Science-Safety Products at Shawnee. The measuring instrument and an instruction manual were distributed free to law enforcement officers by Oklahoma Farm Bureau Mutual Insurance Company in Oklahoma City.

Dad received a letter of commendation from Lyle M. Baker, Chief, dated November 10, 1959. A sergeant from Camp Pendleton, California, was passing through Enid in October and stopped at the patrol headquarters to ask for information. He was so pleased with the assistance my dad had given that he wrote a letter to the head of the highway patrol, even though he did not know Dad's name. Copies of the letters were placed in Dad's personnel file, and he kept copies in his scrapbook. Compliments from the public and the department were rare, and he valued them greatly.

From November 29 to December 4, 1959, Dad was in Norman attending a course called "Supervisory Development Workshop, Department of Public Safety." By this time, K.O. Rayburn had been appointed the first director of the Plans and Training Unit. Part of his new role was to organize and supervise all training programs for the Department of Public Safety, including trooper and examiner schools, and in-service training. (27) The short course Dad had participated in was one of the first in-service training programs Rayburn had developed in cooperation with the University of Oklahoma.

K.O. Rayburn explained the circumstances around his appointment to the new position. "One Christmas [several years before] there was a long box under the tree with tuition to law school inside. While I worked days, I went to law school at night and got my *juris doctorate* from Oklahoma City University in 1959. I was promoted to captain when I was appointed head of Plans and Training as well as Insurance and Retirement for the department."

Rayburn commented that since he had been involved in almost all of the patrol schools, he knew every one of the 290 troopers in the state. One of Rayburn's first acts after he was appointed head of his division was to select a secretary. He selected Mary Haning who began to specialize in the areas of insurance and retirement. She became so proficient in those areas that she remained in that office until her retirement in 1999. Rayburn commented proudly, "Hiring Mary Haning was one of the best professional decisions I ever made."

During the year of 1959, Dad had managed to continue spending a great deal of time on the aspect of his work that he enjoyed the most, that of safety education. By the end of the year, he had been on eighty Saturday radio programs, taught eleven adult drivers education classes, talked twenty-four times in schools, spoken to twenty-five community groups, and made thirteen speeches at Vance AFB. In addition, he had represented the Oklahoma Highway Patrol at the following events: International Pancake Race in Liberal, Kansas; Elks Rodeo; Okeene Snake Hunt; Tri-State Festival Parade; Boy Scout Show Safety Trailer; and eight funerals.

On his Performance Evaluation for the period ending December 31, 1959, Dad received all satisfactory or above ratings, with six excellent and three outstanding. This time there was no mention of the earlier criticism regarding care of his patrol unit. The final general remark Lt. Haltom made was "Never bitches or belly aches. Accepts orders and carries them out cheerfully. It has been a pleasure to have a man like this as a supervisor. In my opinion he is definitely Lieutenant material, and I do not hesitate to recommend him." It appears that Lieutenant Haltom continued to lobby for Dad to take the leadership position in Guymon.

By the end of 1959, the number of fatal accidents in Oklahoma dropped from 539 the previous year to 523; the number killed also dropped from 670 to 642. However, the number of persons injured continued to climb from 14,788 to 15,976. The new year began once again with a statewide increased emphasis on traffic safety. Troopers were expected to devote as much time as they could to the prevention of accidents.

The year 1960 had an unusual beginning for Dad with a bank robbery in Cleo Springs on January 11. On January 19, he attended the funeral of Trooper Pop Snelson who had lived in Edmond. Dad continued with his regular activities including trips to the panhandle as well as to other meeting places with his troopers, trips to Oklahoma City for supplies and credit union meetings, speeches in schools and the adult community, and solving problems as they arose. On May 10 through 12, he taught a class on "Hit and Run Accidents" at F.B.I. schools being held at Enid, Alva, and Woodward.

Personnel Changes and Issues in 1960

From April 8 until June 17, Dad interviewed candidates for the next patrol school. K.O. Rayburn reminisced about the 1960 school. "Vernon Sisney [a former trooper] was back at the V.A. in Oklahoma City as chief psychologist. We decided that we should weed out applicants who would not make good troopers before the patrol school started. Well, he came by one day while the recruits were doing calisthenics. He said that the next rainy day he would come back and give some psychological tests. He did, and he identified a couple that he thought were questionable. I watched them, and sure enough, in a short time they were both in trouble." Captain Rayburn worked with Dr. Vernon Sisney and Dr. Robert Phillips, a former psychologist for the St. Louis police department who was in private practice in Oklahoma City, to develop a selection process which included psychological testing. They got authorization to use the tests to eliminate candidates in future schools. Rayburn recalled, "One governor was very upset when we weeded out one of his friends." But Rayburn gave credibility to the tests, "One time Sisney identified one, and I decided to keep him. But sure enough Sisney was right; the guy got in trouble right away." According to his journal, on August 8, Dad taught a class at the 1960 patrol school.

Dad's July 1960 Performance Evaluation again showed all satisfactory and above ratings. The comments emphasized his attention to improving his work and helping the district improve. However, this time there was no reference to his moving to a higher position. Either Lt. Haltom understood that Dad planned to end his career as a supervisor at Enid, or the position at Guymon had been filled and there was no longer a pressing need for him to become a lieutenant at this time. Before he left on vacation on August 14, Dad made his last official trip out to the Panhandle. On the journal page where he listed the troopers for whom he was responsible, he crossed out ten names; eleven names remained. By the time he returned from vacation the span of control for District 6 was cut virtually in half.

Don McDaniel had a memorable vacation time that year. "The night before I left on vacation the supervisor came to ride with me at Prague. He had to have known what was going on. The next morning my family and I went to Arkansas City to spend the night with my cousin before we went on to Colorado. I got a long distance call from the chief. He asked how soon I could get back to Prague because things had changed. He said they needed me to come back and take vacation later. He told me I was going to be promoted to supervisor at Durant."

McDaniel continued, "We had to go home. Jerry [his wife] was upset, and I was upset. Jerry asked, 'Where in the world is Durant?' The next morning we went to the chief's office, and Jerry sat in the car. I came out and she asked, 'How soon do we have to report to Durant?'

I said, 'We don't go to Durant, we go to Tulsa!' Well, all hell broke loose; the cost of living was terrible in Tulsa."

McDaniel explained, "The supervisor at Tulsa moved to Durant so he could retire there. So the opening was at Tulsa." Supervisor McDaniel moved to Tulsa to enter the world of middle management, where he, like many other troopers before him, would learn new skills and face new problems.

Although the patrol had apparently tried to implement the new promotion policies, troopers in the field were not convinced they were impartial. Nat Taylor explained how many troopers felt about Don McDaniel's promotion, "They let Mac come back on the patrol after he quit for three and a half years. In less than a year he was a second lieutenant. All the other guys who had stayed with it night and day and night and day, were upset. They all liked Mac, but they didn't like how it was done. Mac had been a dispatcher for Bob Lester for three years before he went on the patrol. Bob and his friends just took care of him, that's what happened. I liked them both, but it didn't seem fair."

Taylor described his own feelings about being promoted, "I had every confidence in myself in the job I had. I didn't want to leave it to go to another job I didn't know. My kids were in school, my wife had a good job, and I didn't want to move. I turned down supervisor once and turned it down again two years later. You had to go to Oklahoma City to take the test each time. I would go take the tests because I wanted to play poker with the other guys over there. We didn't have a chance to see one another very often, and some of them were like brothers to me. We'd enjoy ourselves; some of them drank. And we'd play poker and whoop and holler around."

Taylor continued, "I took the test so many times over the years that I was first on the list. They'd call me up and say, 'Are you going to take the promotion this time?'

And I'd say, 'No, I really don't want to change.'" He concluded, "Most good troopers didn't really want to change. They liked where they were, people liked them, and they enjoyed what they were doing." Taylor continued working with Size and Weights.

Governor Edmondson received a study from the National Safety Council in October of 1960. The study echoed the one by the Chiefs of Police in calling for the enlargement of the highway patrol, recommending that it be doubled. The report also suggested that each trooper's working time be shortened from the 54 hours six days per week which had been in effect since 1937. (28) The Department of Public Safety had received appropriations of $2,550,000 for 1960 and 1961. This was an increase of $150,000 from the previous year. However, this was not enough to address the patrol's personnel and equipment problems. The troopers and their aging equipment continued to be asked to do more and more.

Under Captain K.O. Rayburn's leadership, the Plans and Training Division conducted another school for patrol supervisors in December at the University of Oklahoma. Dad attended the five day course called Police Administrative Management, beginning on December 5, 1960. At the conclusion, he received another Short Course Certificate for satisfactorily completing the course.

Back in their districts, supervisors continued applying their administrative skills as they tried to resolve issues with a few of their troopers. Don McDaniel recounted, "One new trooper shouldn't have been hired in the first place. He had a history of woman troubles. One night he arrested a young lady and made advances toward her. He told her that as long as she went along with it, he'd hold the ticket up and wouldn't file it. He thought he was in the best deal he ever had; he had a uniform and power over women." McDaniel concluded, "He was fired."

Dad began documenting some problems involving a few troopers not being where they were supposed to be. One evening he tried to contact a trooper to find out his location so they could meet. The trooper did not respond to his radio calls, and he had not checked out (gone 10-10 or 10-7) with headquarters. Dad finally found him at a cafe sitting with the local policemen. He recorded, "Said he didn't go 10-10 [out of service, subject to call] because he thought he would only be there a few minutes, and he was there 15 min. or more." Dad knew it had been longer than that because he had been trying to reach him for over an hour.

Another trooper was more difficult to deal with. Dad went to his house one day and recorded the mileage on his car before the trooper went on duty. He went back the following day without the trooper knowing about it and again recorded the mileage. The car had been driven only twenty-five miles. Nat Taylor explained more about the situation. "I hated to work in an area where one or two troopers were about to hurt the whole bunch. There was one trooper in C.A.'s district who would step so far over the line he was hurting all the troopers. It was hard to prove and no one would stand up and tell on him. C.A. really liked the guy, but he was a crook. He would park his car and have his partner go over to the car and go 10-8 (in service) for him. Then he would go on a bowling tour to Chicago. He'd fly up there and fly back. He was a great bowler, I guess . . . . He'd get back from his trip in time to go 10-7 (out of service), and he hadn't worked a lick all day." Regardless of what Dad had documented, the trooper continued to work in his district for the next several years.

Other districts within the state were also having problems with troopers not staying where they were supposed to. In Chandler one trooper was an avid hunter, keeping his bird dogs penned up near a small trailer where he lived by himself. His wife had chosen to stay in their home at another town. On more than one occasion this trooper would haul his dogs in the patrol car and go hunting while he was supposed to be on duty. Some other hunters came upon the patrol car one rainy day and there was only a young boy in it. When they asked what he was doing, he replied that he was supposed to listen to the radio and go get the trooper if he had a call. The backseat was covered with mud from the hunting dogs. Although there was an attempt to transfer him, this trooper stayed at Chandler until he retired. (29) Although most troopers were putting their lives on the line and doing what they were supposed to, there were a few who did not uphold their responsibilities. These exceptions often made a stain on the reputation of the whole force.

The Department of Public Safety published a summary

of information from the department called *Annual Report 1960*. During that year, the actual number of fatal accidents had decreased from 577 in 1937 to 543 in 1960. However, there was an increase in number of persons killed from 639 in 1937 to 659 in 1960. Putting these numbers in a positive perspective, the department reported the information in the following way:

"Not only had the numerical death toll showed a decline but the death rate per miles traveled has dropped steadfastly from 14.2 in 1937 to an all-time low of 5.9 in 1960. If the death rate had remained constant, the toll in 1960 would have been 1576 instead of 657."

The report included this paragraph in its Foreword:

"Enforcement begins with the people and the laws enacted by their representatives. It continues through the actions of the enforcement officer and through prosecution and adjudication in the courts. Such prosecution and adjudication is only as strong as the people will allow it to be." Thus the department wanted the public to realize the highway patrol could not do the job alone. More understanding and cooperation from other segments of government and the citizens themselves were needed to bring about the desired changes and safer roads.

Dad's performance evaluation for the last six months of 1960 showed the highest ratings ever. All ten indicators in the areas of interest and job knowledge were in the excellent category, with thirteen additional excellent and three outstanding ratings. The brief comments this time focused on his devotion to his work and his family.

Beginning a New Year 1961

Dad used a different type of journal for this year. Provided by Oklahoma Farm Bureau Mutual Insurance Company in Oklahoma City, it was smaller and had three days to each page. There was an alphabetical address book in the back. He listed those with whom he worked. (This was the last year he listed names in his journal.) The names of officers and office personnel were:

Bill Beierschmitt #287 — Alva
Royce Baker — Enid
George Baker #106 — Medford
Dave Dvorak #237 — Seiling
A.H. (Tubb) Freeny #274 — Enid
Otis Haltom #13 — Enid
Lloyd Hurd — Enid
Harry Jones — Enid
Don Patton #286 — Enid
Otto Rauch #44 — Enid
H.F. (Pappy) Summers #153 — Enid
G.W. Stephens #194 — Fairview
W.P. Tucker #224 — Kingfisher
Bill Young #117 — Woodward

Jim Baker — Enid
John Balisle #98 — Enid
Dan Combs #102 — Enid
Sherman Dotson #166 — Seiling
Claude Griffin — Enid
Jim Holland #114 — Woodward
Johnnie Jones #214 — Alva
Ed.G. Knowles — Enid
Guy Parkes #216 — Fairview
B.W. Reed #211 — Watonga
Calvin (Skipper) Smith #296 — Medford
Bob Sturgeon #137 — Woodward
Harve D. Washmon #292 — Watonga

A variety of efforts were underway to try to help citizens focus on safety in 1961. Each unit was encouraged to develop plans that would be effective with the people who lived there, and these plans were not limited to traffic safety. Dad met with the troopers at Fairview in January to help with their plans. On February 4, he worked in Fairview with Dan Combs, a trooper from Clinton, to make a presentation at a gun program. And the following day, Dad was involved with "Safety Stamp" in Enid.

Two communities used the adult driver education courses to expand into broader areas of safety education. In Watonga, the Civil Defense committee increased the number of sessions from six to ten and included a film called, "Bombing of Hiroshima and Nagasaki" along with firearm safety demonstrations by Troopers Dale Petty from Oklahoma City and Dan Combs from Clinton. The Enid Civil Defense System joined the police department and highway patrol to sponsor the adult driver education course held at Phillips University. The Community College at Phillips and the Safety Committee of the Garfield County

Farm Bureau Women's Auxiliary were listed as co-sponsors. Troopers Petty and Combs came to make presentations on firearm use and safety. Dad was the ranking officer from the patrol who attended both of these courses.

An extremely important and lengthy piece of legislation passed by the twenty-eighth Legislature was approved on July 28, 1961, to take effect on September 1, 1961. It amended a 1951 law by including driver license examiners and radio operators in the Department of Public Safety pension plan. This had been a hotly contested subject as highway patrolmen who were laying their lives on the line every day didn't think other employees who had office jobs should be given equal retirement considerations. Since one legislator's son was in the disputed group and he had been one of those who had drafted the bill, there were serious political overtones. On the practical side, the increase in number of contributors to the system would provide a broader base for funding the plan, which was becoming shaky as many troopers retired early on disability, others approached mandatory retirement age, and other retirement provisions were added. This somewhat generous law authorized full retirement payments to a retired trooper's widow as long as she remained unmarried; for surviving dependent, under 18, child or children of deceased widow; or dependent parent or parents for life. Although this seems like a paltry sum at this time, the law provided $10 per month per child of a deceased retired member until the child reached 18.

Across the state, there continued to be a struggle between those who wanted to maintain local control and those who believed there must be consistency in laws statewide. To make sure it was clear that the state laws took precedence over local laws, Chapter 15 stated, "The provisions of Chapters 10,11,12,13 and 14 of this act shall be applicable and uniform throughout the state and in all political subdivisions and municipalities and no local authority shall enact or enforce any ordinance, rule or regulation in conflict with the provisions of such chapters unless expressly authorized herein." Those chapters related to Accidents and Accident Reports; Rules of the Road (14 articles); Equipment of Vehicles; Inspection of Vehicle; and Size, Weight, and Load.

The newly passed Uniform Traffic Code of 1961, revised the one from 1949, clarifying old laws, adding many new ones, and giving more power and flexibility to the patrol in dealing with violators. The patrol leadership distributed extracts from the code to troopers in the field so that they might understand the changes and fully utilize the benefits of the new laws. (30)

Another of the important provisions of the law was one which clarified that Oklahoma Highway Patrolmen were not subordinate to the sheriffs of the state. K.O. Rayburn stated, "I was instrumental in rewriting the State Statute taking the highway patrol out from under the control of the county sheriffs." This comprehensive law was a major step in legitimizing the position the highway patrol had obtained in its twenty-four-year history in the state and providing financial security for dependents as troopers worked on the dangerous roads.

An additional boost was given to highway patrolmen as the legislature gave a three percent longevity raise to all troopers until they reached $400 per month, in addition to the other $2,550,000 allocated to the department. (This positive action by the legislature may have improved the morale of the patrolmen because Dad's journal for 1961 had only one entry dealing with a problem with a trooper.)

Among the new law's many sections, was one that stated that the purchase of a vehicle for the governor as chief officer of the Department of Public Safety would not be limited to the cost limits of other vehicles for the department. The law also raised the salary of the commissioner to $12,000 per year with a bond of $25,000.

Lt. Haltom completed another Performance Evaluation Report on Dad for the period ending June 30, 1961. This time he received nineteen satisfactory, twenty-six excellent, and five outstanding ratings. The comments on the back, which were very similar to the comments on the previous report, were related to the outstanding ratings. Lt. Haltom wrote,

> -In my opinion this man is one of the best troopers in the state in the field of safety education. He is constantly scheduling appearances for safety work. He is also interested in that field which makes the task easy for him.
> -When this man is told something you can forget about it and feel assured that the order will be carried out as given. He carries on without being told, and can see things that need to be done.
> -In the absence of the lieutenant this man carries on without being advised. Accepts responsibility and acts on his own.
> -This man is interested in Scouting and is very active in this work. He also participates in church work. Is an outstanding worker with young people.
> -This man sets a very high moral standard for one to live by and strives to set an example for others. Is a devoted family man, and in my opinion is qualified for advancement.

Although his friend and lieutenant, Otis Haltom, once again recommended him for promotion, at fifty-four years of age, Dad was beginning to think more and more of retirement, certainly not of taking on additional responsibilities.

On October 4, Dad's photograph appeared in the Enid *Morning News*. The event was a school bus inspection at the Garfield County fairgrounds. Buses from the west part of the county were inspected that day, and those from the eastern half were inspected the following day.

From October 9 to October 13, 1961, he attended another short course at OU. This one was called "Advanced Police Administration" and was part of the on-going training program developed by K.O. Rayburn. One of the tasks officers worked on as a part of this course was the development of a new evaluation instrument for troopers and officers.

Dad's photograph with Lee Teague, FBI agent in charge of the Oklahoma City office appeared in the *Morning News* on November 16. They were attending a school for bankers and law enforcement officers which was held "to familiarize bankers and lawmen on ways of preventing bank robberies and ways to help officers in case one occurs." Dad had not been involved with a bank robbery except the one in Cleo Springs in January the previous year. However, there had been several others in the region during recent months, and bank robberies were becoming more of a problem in other areas of the state.

Capt. Rayburn had revised and formalized the selection procedures for candidates for the patrol school to be held in 1962. There had been no school during 1961, and additional troopers were desperately needed. The *Department of Public Safety Annual Report 1961* explained that there had been 366 troopers in 1954 and only 367 in 1961, when the needs were much greater. (It is difficult to compare the numbers of troopers from year to year due to a discrepancy in reporting. The number of officers above the trooper level was sometimes included and at other times not included in the figure for troopers.) The report stated that the legislature had authorized 400 troopers but had not appropriated enough money to pay for them. It reported that Governor Edmondson stated one hundred new troopers would be added to combat "fantastic" death increases. The new patrol candidate selection procedures consisted of the following steps:

Field Investigation — Including visits to home and family
Field Oral and Physical Interview — Panel of 5 local officers at District Hqts.
Written Examination — Training Division & Psychologists
Psychiatric Screening — The services of a psychologist with a police background have proven to be very useful.
Medical Evaluation
Driving Test
Final Screening & Oral Interview
Training — Six weeks — University of Oklahoma Campus

On December 4, 1961, Dad had gone to Dacoma, Alva, and Buffalo investigating patrol applicants, and the following day he went to Cherokee. Field interviews were held at the office in Enid on December 8. On the 20th he went to Alva and Freedom for field investigations, and on December 21, interviews were again held at the Enid office. On January 12, 1962, he went to Medford to investigate another candidate, and a field interview for one candidate was held at Enid on February 22.

The psychological consultants, Doctors Sisney and Phillips sat on the final selection board as well as promotions boards. K.O. Rayburn vividly recalled one candidate's interview. "Sisney asked the candidate why he wanted to become a highway patrolman. The candidate responded with a vague answer, and Vernon pressed him. The candidate finally said that he wanted to carry a gun. When Vernon asked him why he wanted to carry a gun, the guy said that he thought he would stand out in a crowd if he were carrying a gun." Rayburn stated, "We didn't keep that man on the list for our patrol school." Dad was asked to teach a class on Civil Rights at the patrol school. Although the school was not held until late April, according to his journal, he began his outline for the class on February 18. Dad taught the class on April 25, and returned to help at the school again on May 12.

The year of 1961 had been an eventful one for Dad and for other members of the Oklahoma Highway Patrol. The *Department of Public Safety Annual Report 1961* highlighted accomplishments of the department during that year. It reported several items from the new law that had been passed by the legislature, as well as stating that driver examiners would attend the first four weeks of OHP Recruit School. It noted that a "new performance evaluation process had been developed by the OHP supervisory personnel while attending in-service training program at the University of Oklahoma under the guidance of Professor M.L. Powers."

The report also listed coordinated activities from 1961:

- DPS coordinates activities with the State Fire Departments & Civil Defense
- OHP, FBI, State and municipal officers meet with state bankers in order to coordinate their efforts reference bank robbery problems.
- Members of DPS contribute to the development of the Southwest Center for Police Training located at the University of Oklahoma.
- The OHP participates in the regional meeting for national emergency and local disaster plan.
- DPS officers & 27 other organizations cosponsor community vehicle safety checks.

Problems Grow in the 1960s

In February of 1962, Dad was involved in the next step to prepare for possible bank robberies. They held practice implementations of small communities' Bank Robbery

Plans. On February 5, he participated in a roadblock plan for Drummond, Okeene, Canton, Vici, Taloga, Camargo. The following day the roadblock was for Hennessey, Kingfisher, Okarche, Watonga, Geary, and Seiling banks. He followed up later in the month with meetings at banks in Medford and Watonga.

Dad taught all six sessions of the adult driver education course held from March 5, through April 9, 1962, at the Community College of Phillips University in Enid. Claude Griffin, license examiner, and Capt. Clyde Hopkins from the Enid Police Department assisted. He showed the films, "A Day in Court" and "Signal 30." This was the last course description in his file and according to his journal, was the last he conducted.

Governor Edmondson asked the legislature for a $600,000 increase in the allocation for the patrol in 1962. He also requested authorization for new patrol schools to expand the number of troopers from 227 to 339 (authorized by statute). To pay for this large increase, Edmondson proposed a one-percent sales tax. This proposal practically guaranteed opposition from the senate which continued to look at any increase in the patrol's size with suspicion. "To the rural senators, Edmondson not only was trying to gain the power to police rural governments, but also he was attempting to get the rural population to pay for that increase."(31)

My dad's father, Aubrey Morris, died on April 13, 1962, in Independence, Kansas. Since this was located very close to the Oklahoma border, Oklahoma Highway Patrol troopers treated the funeral as they would have if it had been held in Oklahoma. A long line of Oklahoma highway patrol cars followed the group of Kansas squad cars which led the funeral procession. Dad had remained an active member of the Northern Oklahoma and Southern Kansas Peace Officer's Organization, and the Kansas troopers also came to the funeral to show their respects. The death of his father and the feeling of responsibility for his mother, in addition to concern about my mother's health, helped move Dad even more quickly into a different phase of his life. He began to think more and more about retiring from the patrol and planning what he would do next.

At the end of March, Dad was rated on the new patrol evaluation instrument, which he had helped develop. It was called "Oklahoma Highway Patrol Personnel Comparison of Performance" and the ratings were based on comparisons with others on the patrol. The rating categories were: Low 5%, Below Average 25%, Average 40%, Above Average 25%, Excellent 5%. The factors to be evaluated were essentially the same as the instrument used before. Dad received four average ratings, four above average ratings and two excellent ratings. The remarks on the back highlighted his performance in the areas in which he received the average ratings: judgment, social adaptability, temperament, and job knowledge. The only comment that indicated an area of weakness was, "He is not a high activity man in such [areas] as warnings and arrests, however supplements this laxity by an extra effort in the field of safety education." Perhaps the great amount of time Dad was devoting to safety education interfered with the time he could have been using to intervene directly with traffic law violators.

The 1960s brought some new problems to the forefront in Oklahoma, and the patrol had to change with the times. Don McDaniel, who was a supervisor at Tulsa at the time, stated, "In the early '60s we started training some of our troops for riot squads. Each district was doing some training. We used them down at OU several times, and they were very effective."

He continued, "We were training our riot squad at the National Guard Armory—getting it set up. We had always worked with the news media and had tried to give them information. But one day they busted in there with cameras. I took them to the side and told them this was going on all over the state, and we were trying to keep it quiet. It was for the public's benefit and for the school's. I asked them, 'For Pete's sake, give us time to get out a little information first. Don't make it look like this is Nazi Germany, and we are planning to take over the country.' They held up on the story."

McDaniel explained, "They called them 'Panty Raids.' They were burning mattresses, and boys were invading girls' dorms. The Enid squad went to OSU at least once. The squads really put a stop to them."

"To try to prevent them, the patrol checked with universities about professors who might lead rebellions. Most universities had done back-ground checks, but some of them claimed they hadn't checked on people at all before hiring them," McDaniel concluded incredulously.

In Dad's journal, he wrote on May 25, 1962, "1:30 a.m.-5:30 a.m. Stillwater panty raid." In North Murray Hall, one of the girls' dormitories, I was looking down at the end of the year disturbance from a window on the top floor. I never dreamed that my dad was one of the officers working in the melee I was watching below.

It was about this time that Dad for the first and, presumably, the only time, refused to follow a direction given by one of his superior officers. He was told to go out to see one of the troopers in his district and chastise him because his unmarried daughter was pregnant. I was about the same age, and Dad knew that the girl's father was undoubtedly heartsick. He also knew that a daughter of one of his superiors had been in similar circumstances not long before, and the story had been hushed up. Dad went home to discuss his dilemma with Mother. He told her what he had been directed to do and said he was told in the small town this unfortunate happening would make the whole patrol organization look bad. My mother, who was known to have a bit of a temper, told him in no uncertain terms that he should not confront the trooper about his daughter, especially in light of what had happened with the higher officer's daughter. Dad went back to the office and refused to go. Mother said that he had not told her what had transpired at the office; he just assured her that he had not confronted the trooper.

Dad began to investigate new trooper applicants in July 1962. During the same time period he explained District 6's bank robbery plans to some cadet troopers who had just completed the previous patrol school. On August 5, Dad met with John Eddleman, who had moved into our rental house in Chandler when he was transferred from Shawnee in 1951. Trooper Eddleman had now been transferred to Watonga.

The following day, August 6, 1962, Dad was admitted to the hospital where he remained for thirteen days while he was treated for pneumonia. The long hours and heavy work load of a patrol supervisor was taking its toll on his health. He returned to work but stayed in the office doing clerical tasks until September 7.

During the time he was in the hospital, a large photograph of Dad appeared on the second page of the August 19, 1962, *Daily Oklahoman* Sunday magazine section called "Oklahoma's Orbit." It pictured him with his new "Lost Kit." A short article by David Tull stated, "In an emergency, the problem of survival can loom like a giant — as big as life itself! Yet you may be able to pack your 'survival' in a box about half the size of a package of gum. A 'Lost Kit' developed by C.A. Morris, Enid, contains 60 easily obtained items calculated to simplify survival for anyone stranded far from civilization. Perhaps the smallest kit of its kind in the world, it can also come in handy for lesser emergencies closer to home."

Tull continued, "Here's What Is Inside the Tiny Kit

Aluminum foil (2"x3")	Safety pin; compass
2 pieces paper	11 fish hooks
Pencil stub	Line coiled on hook
2 bandages; tape	Sinker, swivels
100-ft. fine wire	Dry fly; button
Piece heavier wire	3 rubber bands
Needle & thread	Miniature pliers
Tacks & nails	Matches & striker
4 pins; razor blade	Water purity pills"

Dad got a lot of pleasure from his "Lost Kit" and from presenting his stories of survival and preparedness to a wide variety of people. It allowed him to use his active imagination in a way that also complimented his interest in performing before groups. He truly enjoyed this part of his job.

When Dad returned to work on the roads on September 8, he began to keep track of his mileage in addition to the hours he worked. The notes he had always kept about what he did as a supervisor became increasingly brief. As aspects of his job had become routine and his interests were focusing more on things outside of his work, Dad's journal began to resemble the one he had inherited when he first went to Enid as a supervisor. Though he did not leave any blank pages, his notes were often only one or two words.

Nat Taylor had some vivid memories of 1962. He explained, "I got into trouble [in Size and Weights] stopping trucks on weight violations that were directly connected to the commissioner. And they put me back into traffic at Cushing." Taylor's family continued to live in Stillwater while he worked as a regular trooper at Cushing.

Working as a traffic patrolman again, Taylor was reminded of the importance of a trooper's reputation. "At the first accident I got called out on, there were three or four truck drivers working traffic for me. Now, I had arrested every one of them at some time or another. They knew the other troopers in the district and knew they were good guys. If they hadn't respected me, they would have left me on my own."

During the gubernatorial campaign in the fall of 1962, Henry Louis Bellman, a farmer from Billings, won the support of the *Daily Oklahoman* and *Oklahoma City Times* editor, E.K. Gaylord. This was the first time Gaylord had supported a Republican. Bellman had a reputation for being hard-working and frugal and was elected the first Republican governor in Oklahoma's history. However, Democrats won in other state administrative and judicial offices and in both houses of the legislature. (32)

During the presidential campaign, candidate John F. Kennedy came to Oklahoma. Highway patrol troopers formed an honor guard at Kennedy's arrival. Nat Taylor was one of the troopers assigned to provide security and work traffic at the campaign stops. He recalled, "Kennedy flew into Fort Smith and went to the Kerr Ranch. Then he flew every place, and we had to drive. We were driving through there at about 100 miles per hour, trying to get to the next stop ahead of him." Kennedy made no stops in the northwestern part of the state which had been historically Republican.

Some sections of Oklahoma had a white Christmas in 1962. Snow, ice, and stalled cars were all over the roads in Major county. On the highways across the state that year, 709 people died in 575 accidents, and 18,930 persons were injured. Once again, all of the numbers were increasing. The Department of Public Safety continued to report the "death rate" which was calculated by dividing the number of persons killed by the number of miles traveled. Looking at things from this prospective indicated that the problem was not as discouraging for troopers and the public as they might at first think. In fact, the roads were becoming somewhat safer when one considered the number of miles people were driving. The death rate per thousand miles driven decreased from 6.0 in 1961 to 5.8 in 1962. (The actual numbers of deaths increased from 706 in 1961 to 709 in 1962.)

Shortly before Governor-elect Bellman was to take office, US Senator Robert S. Kerr died unexpectedly. Sitting Governor Edmondson appointed himself successor to Kerr's senate seat, leaving Lt. Governor George Patterson Nigh to serve as Oklahoma's governor for the nine days remaining of his term. (33)

Governor Bellman Institutes Changes

According to Blackburn, "A few weeks after he stepped into the governor's chair, Bellman established a Council on Highway Safety to study the DPS and report on what it found. Martin Garber of Enid chaired the council which conducted a thorough examination of the department, the patrol, and the leadership of both. Most of its findings dealt with administration, reporting that previous commissioner appointments had been politics instead of qualifications. According to the report, this political influence in the selection of commissioner almost always brought drastic turnover in top personnel, resulting in a worsened morale in the highway patrol."

He continues, "The council recommended that the commissioner be selected on a basis of administrative abilities inasmuch as he would be handling a department of more than 500 employees and a biennial budget of more than $7,000,000. According to the report the qualifications for commissioner should be: knowledge of personnel organization and administration, budgetary procedures and control, business administration, and public relations." (34)

From the eighteen candidates who submitted their applications for the position, the council selected four to send to the governor for final selection. By February, Governor Bellman chose Bob Lester, who had left the patrol to be police chief in Norman in 1958. Commissioner Lester was the first to move up the ranks from trooper to commissioner. Contrary to what had happened in the past when a new commissioner was appointed, Lester did not make any major changes in the organization of the highway patrol and made very few personnel changes. He appointed Byron McFall as assistant commissioner, kept the patrol chief, Lyle Baker, in the job, and promoted Captain K.O. Rayburn to assistant chief.

One of Commissioner Lester's first actions was to target the growing fatality rate by intensifying traffic safety enforcement. He planned to establish a state-wide system of cooperation between the patrol, municipal police officers, sheriffs, and constables. He believed that he would supplement the number of troopers available if he could coordinate all law enforcement officers in the state. (35)

K.O. Rayburn reported that he had lobbied a bill through the legislature which mandated training for all law enforcement officers in the state. The bill signed on June 19, 1963, created a Council on Law Enforcement Education and Training that was composed of five members. One peace officer selected by the Court of Criminal Appeals, one peace officer selected by the Commissioner of Public Safety, one peace officer selected by he Board of Directors of the Oklahoma Sheriff and Peace Officers Association, one peace officer selected by the Board of Directors of the order of police, and a fifth (5th) member who would be the Director of the Southwest Center for Law Enforcement Education. To upgrade Oklahoma law enforcement to a professional status, $27,000 was allocated for 1964 and $20,000 for 1965. (36)

Rayburn said the law gave responsibility for the center

to the University of Oklahoma. "When we were writing the law," he recalled, "I had a person from Texas in mind to be the director, but he didn't want to move up here. So they asked me to help develop the program. I told them I would stay for one year, and I stayed on for twenty." K.O. Rayburn retired from the Oklahoma Highway Patrol in 1963, but continued working on the University of Oklahoma campus with the training of troopers as well as other law enforcement officers in the state.

Commissioner Bob Lester immediately started working with the patrol to build morale and support for the statewide law enforcement officer effort. Dad's journal listed three patrol meetings involving the new commissioner, his old friend, that were held that spring. On March 29, 1963, a troop meeting was held at the capitol building. A troop meeting for District 6 was held in Enid on April 5, and a photograph of Commissioner Lester and my dad appeared in the Enid *Morning News*, with the explanation that troopers from nine Northwest Oklahoma counties were on hand for the inspection and introduction to the new commissioner. On May 22, the Governor's Safety Conference was held at the state capitol. Dad took Trooper Dan Combs to the conference with him. Since Bob Lester had come up through the ranks, he knew many of the patrolmen well and built on these relationships to get them to cooperate with the new efforts.

Governor Bellman enjoyed the general support of both legislative bodies and was able to get an emergency appropriation of $153,631.04 for the Department of Public Safety for 1963. However, with the prospect of new turnpikes opening and expensive advancements in technology for crime detection and law enforcement, Bellman and Lester knew that this appropriation was only a drop in the bucket compared to what they really needed. To meet the need for more men on the patrol, the legislature approved five patrol schools to be held between 1963 and

1967. The first of the series was held in 1964. These schools would be held at the new Southwest Center for Law Enforcement Education at Norman under the direction of K.O. Rayburn, who was now a civilian state employee.

Rayburn said that he had always tried to adjust the training to reflect needs at the time. For example, the law enforcement training program began to address the problem of witchcraft and satanism during one period, and later, domestic violence and child abuse, which continues to be a severe problem. He related a personal experience that led to another addition to the patrol school program. Trooper Charlie Dawson had a heart attack and died after rescuing a driver from a wreck. Rayburn had the responsibility to deliver a check for over $5,000 to Trooper Dawson's widow. The check was a result of the $25.00 donation from each trooper that had been a tradition of the patrol. Rayburn learned that Mrs. Dawson was not aware she would receive that check and knew very little about the benefits she was entitled to. Rayburn went home and discussed this situation with his wife, Gerri. They decided that there should be a way to inform new troopers' wives of these matters. Beginning with the next school, on the day of graduation the session about insurance and retirement was presented so that the wives could attend with their husbands and be informed about their benefits. Through this program, he hoped that some of the personal needs of the troopers and their families were being directly addressed.

Morris Prepares to Retire

My dad had made the decision that he would retire from the Oklahoma Highway Patrol in February of 1964, so during the fall of 1963 he began to phase out of the major role he had played in safety education. He tried to get individual troopers, county sheriff's deputies, and local police officers to take over the responsibility of providing leadership in this area. Several years before this Dad had been appointed to the Board of the Great Plains Council of the Boy Scouts and began to limit his scout involvement to those meetings. He no longer did the Saturday radio shows nor did he speak to the Vance airmen. However, during 1963, he still made eighteen speeches to community groups and met with the Enid Safety Council four times.

During the last full year of his work on the highway patrol, Dad worked an average of nine hours a day for six days a week. For the most part, he worked one of these three schedules: 9 a.m. to 6 p.m., 12 p.m. to 8 p.m., or 3 p.m. to 12 a.m. He continued to prefer the night shift, so he worked more of the three to midnight schedule than any other. During his last year, the troopers in District 6 were: Alva—Bill Beierschmitt and Barney Girdner; Cherokee—Sherman Datson; Enid—Dan Combs, A.H. Freeney, Claude Griffin, Don Patton, and H.F. Summers; Fairview—Guy Parks and John Pruitt; Kingfisher—Don Hadlock and W.P. Tucker; Medford—George Baker and Skipper Smith; Seiling—Doyle Boyd and David Dvorak; Watonga—John Eddleman and B.W. Reed; and Woodward—Bill Young and B.A. McCurley.

Nat Taylor had been placed back in Size and Weights after Bob Lester took office. Taylor said that while he was on the patrol he had never dreaded going to work, regardless of his assignment. He saw every work day as a challenge with the responsibility of making the roads a safer place. However, Trooper Taylor continued to be frustrated by some of the actions of "the brass." "They were always jumping me about something I did or didn't do, and one time I added up my hours. That year I worked 300 days, 3,005 hours. I never griped about the number of hours I worked."

Taylor continued, "They owned me. One year they canceled my vacation at 7:00 a.m. when I was supposed to leave at 5:00 p.m. I was gone a month to Vinita. There was an anthrax quarantine for cattle coming into that area." He concluded, "They asked so much and offered very little." Many other troopers felt as Taylor did and became so frustrated that they quit the patrol.

During my dad's last full year on the patrol, he dealt with two bank robberies. On May 15, 1963, there was an armed robbery at Hennessey, and the extensive Bank Robbery Plan was put into action. Dad worked with Unit 29, Trooper 224 on the robbery. On August 16, a bank was robbed in Covington. He worked with Unit 693 from Ponca City on that robbery. The aging patrol cars and the nature of the job continued to cause problems for the patrol. During the last part of 1963, Dad had to relay replacement patrol cars four times for major mishaps such as cars catching fire and cars being wrecked.

He continued to make traffic stops when he encountered drivers who were breaking the law. While he and Lt. Haltom were in the western part of their district on October 13, Dad documented information to support a charge of drunk driving: "Observed entering US 281 from city street. [Driver] crossed from one side of the road to the other, driving 1952 Chevy — dark green over light green. WD4982 — 63 O.K. Said he worked for some pipeline Co. in Seiling. Said he had been drinking only beer. Unsteady, eyes swollen, odor of alcohol. Leaned against car and dropped billfold. 10-5 to 24. 13 & 27 5:15 pm." Dad turned the drunk driver over to a local trooper to complete the tests and the paper work before taking him on to jail.

Commissioner Lester created a new patrol task force to try to lower the death toll on the highways. It was reminiscent of the old "Flying Squadron" of motorcycles in 1937, consisting of ten new, unmarked patrol cars capable of speeds in excess of 125 miles per hour. Lester activated this task force in December 1963, moving it to areas where extra enforcement seemed necessary to ensure traffic safety. The cars were various colors with only the Oklahoma

Highway Patrol emblem on the sides. (37) On December 17, a lieutenant's meeting was held at the capitol in room 510, where other new strategies to reduce traffic accidents were introduced. In spite of all of the efforts to prevent traffic accidents, at the end of 1963, the story from the roads of Oklahoma was the worst it had ever been. There were 629 fatal accidents with 765 persons killed and 20,389 injured. The death rate had also climbed from 5.8 in 1962 to 5.9 in 1963. This was very discouraging to those who had worked so hard to try to reduce these numbers.

My dad did not retain his journal for 1964. He apparently passed it on to his successor as supervisor for District 6. During his years on the patrol, he had seen many changes. He had joined the Oklahoma Highway Patrol in 1942 as he and others in the state were struggling to deal with the economic issues of the Great Depression and the ravages of the Dust Bowl and a World War. Dad served his early years during a time of severe patrol manpower shortage due to the war while at the same time some of the problems on the roads included gangsters and bootleggers as well as drivers who often were drunk, wreckless, and/or speeding. In those early years he worked with some of the rough-and-tumble patrolman legends and was at times involved in physical encounters of his own. My dad was known as a fast and hard driver, whose partners shot out tires to stop fleeing drivers on a regular basis. Later, his experiences paralleled the inclusion of more technology as use of airplanes and radar assisted troopers in their work. I believe that my dad always gave 100 percent to his job and over the years chose to focus his attention more on prevention of accidents rather than apprehension of law breakers. During the later part of his career, he tried to make a difference in the area of safety education by establishing a number of programs that continued on under the leadership of others. I know that the reality of ever-increasing highway death tolls frustrated and saddened him. During his career, the patrol continually faced difficulties recruiting and keeping quality patrolmen and adequate equipment to meet the challenges of the job. After over twenty years working on the Oklahoma Highway Patrol, Dad was ready to turn his responsibilities over to a younger man. On February 4, 1964, my dad, C.A. Morris, wrote the following letter to Lt. Otis Haltom:

> Dear Sir:
>
> Please accept my resignation from the Oklahoma Highway Patrol effective February 22, 1964, at the end of the working day.
> I wish to express my deepest appreciation for these wonderful 21 plus years that I have been privileged to serve the people of the Oklahoma as a trooper in this fine organization. It has been a most wonderful experience.
>
> Very truly,
C.A. Morris
Trooper #27

His resignation was accepted, and he retired at the age of fifty-seven with full benefits beginning February 23, 1964.

Figure 10—"Supervisor C.A. Morris with members of the adult divers education class in 1957."

Figure 11—"Supervisor Morris in a patrol car passing District 6 Headquarters in Enid in 1961."

POST SCRIPT

DAD WORKED AS a relief permit clerk for the Size and Weights Division during the spring and summer after he retired from the patrol in 1964. That fall, he entered the world of politics by running for the position of sheriff of Garfield county. He, my mother, and some of their friends spent many hours campaigning door to door around Enid. However, Dad would not allow anyone campaigning for him to say anything negative about the incumbent—he just wanted them to stress that he would do a better job. Dad did not win the election, and that brought a swift end to his political career. He wanted to qualify for Social Security benefits in addition to his patrol retirement, so he and Mother closed their house in Enid and moved to Bartlesville where he worked for a funeral home for several years. During the early 1960s, Dad had expanded his hobby of collecting pennies to include coins, stamps, and, finally, antique postcards. Once he qualified for Social Security, he and Mother devoted their lives to helping their children; enjoying their two grandsons, Wade and Doug; and traveling across the country to postcard shows. Dad and Uncle Art Louthan continued fishing together at Canton Lake. My dad died of heart failure at the age of seventy-eight in March of 1985, as he was in the process of getting ready to go fishing with Uncle Art. As this is written in 2002, my mother, who is ninety-two years old, lives in her own little cottage in an Edmond retirement village where she tends her garden and still loves to cook for others.

After retiring from the patrol in 1958, Eugene "Chick" Clark worked for the Oklahoma county sheriff's office for seventeen years. He was twice widowed, and moved to a retirement village in Oklahoma City where he died in 1999. Jack Smith had a seven-year break in service and retired from the patrol in 1967. He then worked for the Tulsa county sheriff's office. He lived in Tulsa with his wife, Jane, until his death in 2000. Both Eugene Clark and Jack Smith were honored at the 60th Anniversary Gala of the Oklahoma Department of Public Safety held on October 18, 1997. Floyd "Tarzan" Hayes, who retired as a supervisor in Enid in 1957, was unable to attend the Gala. He resided in a nursing home in Clinton until his death in1998.

After serving as commissioner of public safety, Robert R. "Bob" Lester was appointed as director of a number of state agencies. His career in law enforcement spanned nearly fifty years. He lived in Norman until his death in 1996.

Although Vernon Sisney officially left the patrol in 1946, he worked as a consultant in selecting troopers until 1975. After leaving the Veterans' Administration, he went into private practice in Oklahoma City. Dr. Sisney said, "Nothing could replace the experiences I had on the Oklahoma Highway Patrol. It taught me a great deal about people and how to deal with them. It set a framework for my future." He lives in Oklahoma City and continues to work as a clinical psychologist.

Otis "Oatie" Haltom worked for the patrol for over forty years. He retired as the lieutenant at Enid in 1979. (1) Haltom lived in a nursing home in Enid until his death in 1999.

Otto Rauch retired from the patrol in September of 1964. He taught on Navajo Indian reservation in Arizona for two years and then was with the Division of Probation and Parole for eight years. Since that time he devoted his efforts to political issues and game hunting, including a big game hunt in Africa. He lives in Enid with his wife, Catherine.

Kermit O. Rayburn continued to work as the director of the Southwest Center for Law Enforcement Education at the University of Oklahoma and later at the Bob Lester Training Center located near the new Department of Public Safety offices and patrol headquarters on Eastern Avenue in Oklahoma City. He retired in 1983, and lived in Durant with his wife, Gerri, until his death in 2000.

Leonard Kelsoe, who retired from the patrol in 1957, worked for many years in the insurance business. He lives in Oklahoma City with his wife.

Don McDaniel retired as the lieutenant of the Tulsa District in 1972. He worked for the Department of Corrections as a parole officer for several years before assuming the role of supervisor of security in a new state office building in Tulsa. Soon after he retired, his wife, Jerry, died, and he remarried. He and his wife, Bonnie, moved to Siloam Springs, Arkansas, where they lived on the edge of a golf course until his death of ALS (Lou Gehrig's Disease) in March of 1998.

Nat Taylor retired from the Size and Weights Division of the patrol in 1969. He worked for the Department of Corrections as a parole officer until 1984. He and his wife, Betty, live in Stillwater during the summer and bordering on a golf course in Mission, Texas, during the winter. Nat drives their motor home between their two residences, often taking time to explore new areas whenever he or Betty get the urge to see another part of the country.

Since 1937 when the Oklahoma Highway Patrol was established, there have been thousands of men and approximately twenty women who have served as troopers. Like the former troopers interviewed for this book, each one of them had unique experiences and different perspectives of what it was like to be a highway patrol officer. However, there are similarities among all of those who joined the patrol. Each of them sought to make a living for themselves and their families and was willing to lay down his or her life to make Oklahoma a safer place for everyone traveling on the state's roads. In 2002, there were

810 men and women serving as highway patrol officers. Although times have changed and technology has improved since the patrol was first established, the dangers are just as real.

As of this date, there have been twenty-eight Oklahoma Highway Patrol troopers and one Lake Patrol officer who have been killed in the line of duty. One of the worst tragedies for the Oklahoma Highway Patrol occurred in May of 1978, when two of the troopers with whom my dad worked in the Enid District were killed by fugitives. Houston (Pappy) Summers, age 62, and Billy Young, age 50, were killed along with Lieutenant Pat Grimes during a manhunt in southeastern Oklahoma. Citizens across the state and across the nation shared in the shock and sadness of this great loss. Law enforcement officers from as far away as New England came to Oklahoma to attend their funerals. A complete list of troopers killed in the line of duty appears in Appendix B.

It is my hope that this story built around the recollections of eight pioneer troopers and the journals and scrapbooks of my father will not only add to the rich history of the state of Oklahoma, but will serve as an important cornerstone for increasing the institutional memory of the Department of Public Safety and the highway patrol. The information presented here gives an idea of what it was like to be a trooper in the early years of the Oklahoma Highway Patrol when they served as Soldiers of the Law and established a proud tradition for others to follow. I also hope that this effort will encourage others to seek out other former troopers and scrapbooks in order to document additional aspects of the history of one of Oklahoma's finest organizations, the Oklahoma Highway Patrol.

NOTES

CHAPTER 1 EARLY OKLAHOMA AND THE ESTABLISHMENT OF THE OKLAHOMA HIGHWAY PATROL: 1889-1937

1. An overview of the history of the state of Oklahoma can be found in books such as *Progressive Oklahoma: The Making of a New Kind of State; Oklahoma, A History;* or *The History of Oklahoma.* For an indepth look at politics in Oklahoma, *Oklahoma Politics: A History* is highly recommended. A more complete history of the Oklahoma Highway Patrol can be found in Blackburn's Masters Thesis, "The Oklahoma Highway Patrol: Growth and Change" and in his Dissertation, "Oklahoma Law Enforcement Since 1803."
2. Wenner pp. 3-4; Morris, Goins, and McReynolds p. 62.
3. Edwards and Ottaway I, #30. *The Daily Oklahoman* was founded in 1889 in Oklahoma City by Samuel Small, an itinerant preacher. E.K. Gaylord acquired a substantial interest in the enterprise and in 1909, planned and oversaw the construction of a distinctive five-story building at 500 North Broadway. This became the home of the Oklahoma Publishing Company.
4. Shirley 1978 p. 3.
5. Ibid. p.3.
6. Gibson p. 34.
7. Buchanan and Dale p. 181; Shirley p. 5.
8. Lamar p. 18.

9. Gibson p. 97.
10. Shirley 1978 p. 5.
11. Lamar p. 18.
12. Shirley 1978 p. 6.
13. Wenner p. 9.
14. Shirley 1957 pp. 25-66. and Shirley 1978 pp. 29-30. More information about early law enforcement in this region can be found in Glen Shirley's books, *Law West of Fort Smith* and *West of Hell's Fringe: Crime, Criminals, and the Federal Peace Officer in Oklahoma Territory, 1889-1907.*
15. Wenner p. 28.
16. Green p. 18.
17. Blackburn 1979 pp. 162-176.
18. Morris, Goins, and McReynolds pp. 47-49, 57.
19. Morgan and Morgan p. 73.
20. Ibid. pp. 72-74.
21. Ibid. p. 73.
22. Goble p. 26.
23. Ibid. pp. 26-27.
24. Shirley 1978 p. 33.
25. Goble pp. 28-29.
26. Shirley 1978 p. 33.
27. Goble p. 88.
28. Shirley 1978 p. 28.
29. Gumprecht p. 146. "A Saloon on Every Corner, Whiskey Towns of Oklahoma Territory, 1889-1907," in *The Chronicles of Oklahoma*, Summer 1996, gives a good description of this part of the story of the settling of Oklahoma.
30. Ibid. pp. 153-158.
31. Shirley 1978 p. 138.
32. Ibid. p. 136. Some other deputy marshals were: Lafe Shadley, Ed Kelley, Joe Severn, Bob Hutchins, Andrew "Frank" Clark, and Tom Houston. Some Black Lawmen

of the period were: Bass Reeves, Ike Rogers, Eugene Walker, Bill Colbert, Zeke Miller, and Marzon Tucker.
33. Bill Edson, Staff writer for the *Enid News & Eagle*, Sunday, 1990.
34. Morgan & Morgan p. 150.
35. Ibid. p. 151.
36. Ibid p. 151.
37. Ibid. p. 153.
38. Ibid. pp. 158-159; Morris postcard collection contains several examples of oil towns in Indian Territory.
39. Franklin p. 33.
40. Morgan & Morgan p. 73.
41. Gibson p. 48.
42. Morgan & Morgan pp. 74-75.
43. Buchanan & Dale p. 278.
44. Morgan & Morgan p. 75.
45. Ibid. pp. 75-76.
46. Ibid. pp. 77-78.
47. Goble pp. 190-191.
48. Ibid. p. 191.
49. Ibid. p. 198.
50. Morris, Goins, & McReynolds p. 56.
51. Lamar p. 19.
52. Morgan & Morgan pp. 154-159.
53. Buchanan & Dale p. 278.
54. Morris, Goins, & McReynolds p. 75.
55. Gibson p. 117.
56. Morris, Goins, & McReynolds p. 58.
57. Goble pp. 203 & 205.
58. Morgan & Morgan p. 83.
59. Ibid. p. 93.
60. Franklin pp. 31 & 131.
61. Morgan & Morgan pp. 84-85.
62. Ibid. p. 86.
63. Goble p. 214.

64. Morgan & Morgan pp 88-89.
65. Ibid. pp. 86-87.
66. Morgan & Morgan pp. 87-88; Scales & Goble pp. 25-30.
67. Buchanan & Dale p. 284.
68. Morgan & Morgan pp. 87-88.
69. Goble p. 225.
70. Morgan & Morgan p. 90.
71. Edwards & Ottaway #120; Morris postcard collection.
72. Howard p. 4.
73. Morgan & Morgan p. 139.
74. Shirley 1978 p. 421.
75. Department of Public Safety 1990 p. 12.
76. Blackburn 1979 p. 177.
77. Morris, Goins, & McReynolds p. 60.
78. Edwards & Ottaway #20 & #38.
79. Department of Public Safety 1990 p. 12.
80. Hazell p. 81.
81. Wallis p. 5.
82. Morgan & Morgan p. 103.
83. Ibid. p. 115.
84. Ibid. p. 104.
85. Ibid. pp. 118-119.
86. Scales & Goble p. 66.
87. Ibid. p. 106.
88. Hazell p. 80; White p. 88.
89. White p. 88; Morgan & Morgan pp. 106-107.
90. Debo p.
91. Morgan & Morgan pp. 104-105.
92. Isern pp. 121-122; Morgan & Morgan pp. 108-110.
93. *Session Laws of Oklahoma 1925*.
94. Blackburn 1981 p. 140.
95. Ibid. p. 161.
96. Ibid. p. 140.
97. Tracy p. 177; Morgan & Morgan pp. 119-120.
98. *Session Laws 1927*. These ten Rules of the Road served

as Oklahoma's traffic laws until 1949, when the Uniform Traffic Code was passed.
99. Tracy p. 188; Morgan & Morgan pp. 119-121.
100. Hanson p. 38.
101. *House Journal Regular Session of the Twelfth Legislature of Oklahoma, January 8-March 6, 1929 and March 7-March 30, 1929.*
102. Morgan & Morgan pp. 123-125.
103. Bilger p. 59; Morgan & Morgan p. 126.
104. Morgan & Morgan p. 126.
105. Ibid. p. 161.
106. Ibid. pp. 164-168.
107. *Senate Journal Fourteenth Legislature Oklahoma Regular and First Extraordinary Sessions 1933.*
108. Bilger p. 63; Morgan & Morgan p. 127.
109. *Session Laws 1933.*
110. Morgan & Morgan p. 116.
111. Ibid. p. 130.
112. Scales & Goble pp. 184-187.
113. Buchanan & Dale p. 349.
114. "Brookings Institution Report" p. 106.
115. *Journal of the House of Representatives Fifteenth Legislature 1935.*
116. *Senate Journal 1st Extraordinarty and Regular Session: Sixteenth Legislature of Oklahoma 1936-1937; Journal of the House of Representatives Regular Session: Sixteenth Legislature of the State of Oklahoma 1937 Vol 1 and 2; Session Laws of Oklahoma 1936-1937.*

CHAPTER 2: THE FORMATIVE YEARS OF THE PATROL: 1937-1946

1. *Journal of the House of Representatives Regular Session: Sixteenth Legislature of the State of Oklahoma 1937 Vol 1 and 2.*
2. *Enid Daily Eagle* May 12, 1937.

3. *Daily Oklahoman* May 13, 1937, p. 13.
4. The patrol school in 1999 was for 18 weeks in contrast to the three-week schools in 1937. There were even shorter schools in the early 1940s. Ronnie Johnson was the first African American to work for the Oklahoma Highway Patrol until retirement. He was a trooper from January 1968 until he retired in August 1987.
5. Department of Public Safety 1977 p. 90.
6. Otto Rauch interview.
7. Blackburn 1976 pp. 12-13.
8. Department of Public Safety 1977 p. 90.
9. *The Oklahoma Hornet,* Waukomis Thursday Paper, July 29, 1937.
10. Blackburn 1976 p. 11.
11. Nat Taylor interview April 16, 1997.
12. Blackburn 1976 p. 12.
13. Ibid. p. 23.
14. Ibid. p. 13.
15. Ibid. p. 16.
16. Department of Public Safety 1977 p. 40.
17. Blackburn 1976 p. 24.
18. *Session Laws 1941*, allocations.
19. Ibid.
20. Department of Public Safety 1977 p. 95.
21. See D.M. Stephens' *One Room School Teaching in 1930s Western Oklahoma* for more information about the earlier life of C.A. and Helen Morris.
22. Undated clipping from Morris scrapbook.
23. Undated clipping from Morris scrapbook.
24. Information from Edwards & Ottaway II #299 & 300 and from Beverly's archives. Beverly's original Grill was located at 209 W. Grand and opened on May 19, 1921, serving 19-cent meals. Rubye and Beverly Osburne originated "Chicken in the Rough," the world's first franchise food dish in 1937. It grew to

be franchised at 350 locations throughout the nation and in two foreign countries. Beverly's Drive-In at 2417 North Lincoln opened in 1937.
25. Wallis pp. 20-21.
26. *Session Laws of Oklahoma 1943*.
27. Duden 1989.
28. John Morris and Dan Erwin, a childhood friend and a practicing attorney in Chandler, remembered hearing two different versions about Cactus Face Duggan and the German prisoners. Other than the location of the prison and the number injured, the stories were essentially the same.
29. Department of Public Safety 1977 p. 14.
30. Blackburn 1976 p. 11.
31. Department of Public Safety 1977 p. 40.
32. Morris letter dated March 31, 1944.
33. Letter from C.A. Morris to his parents dated July 15, 1945.
34. Undated clipping from Morris scrapbook.
35. Undated clipping from Morris scrapbook.

CHAPTER 3: THE POST-WAR YEARS: 1946-1951

1. *Session Laws 1946*, allocations.
2. Department of Public Safety 1982 p. 151.
3. Ibid p. 130.
4. Morgan & Morgan pp. 135-136.
5. Wallis pp. 20-21.
6. Ibid. pp. 21-23.
7. Ibid. pp. 21-23.
8. Blackburn 1976 p. 14.
9. Department of Public Safety 1977 p. 100.
10. Edwards & Ottaway II # 63. Earl Hull made the first broadcast from station WKY located in his garage in Oklahoma City in 1922. This was the first commercial

radio station west of the Mississippi. The station grew, moving to the Shrine Auditorium Building, the Huckins Hotel basement, Plaza Court, and then the Skirvin Tower Hotel. It eventually located at its own building on East Britton Road.

11. Department of Public Safety 1982 p. 151.
12. Unidentified clipping dated December 15, 1947 from Morris scrapbook.
13. *Session Laws of Oklahoma 1948, 1949.*
14. Department of Public Safety 1977 p. 96; Department of Public Safety 1982 p. 118.
15. Undated clipping from Morris scrapbook.
16. Undated clippings from Morris scrapbook.
17. Department of Public Safety 1977 p. 130.
18. Undated clippings from Morris scrapbook.
19. John Morris and Dan Erwin interview, April 15, 1999.
20. Duden p. 21.
21. *Session Laws 1949.*
22. Department of Public Safety 1977 p. 133.
23. Department of Public Safety 1982 p. 151.
24. Ibid. p. 156.
25. Ibid. p. 156.
26. Rayburn interview July 15, 1997.
27. Department of Public Safety 1977 p. 40.
28. Department of Public Safety 1982 p. 152.
29. Jerry Marx's Press Release, March 9, 1950.
30. Undated clipping from Morris scrapbook and interview with Tom Morris 1998.
31. Undated clippings from Morris scrapbook.
32. Interview with Helen Morris 1997.
33. Owens p. 152.
34. Interview with John Morris 1998.
35. Jerry Marx's Press Release, March 12, 1950.
36. Jerry Marx's Press Release, May 6, 1950.
37. Undated clipping from Morris scrapbook.
38. Undated clipping from Morris scrapbook.

39. Undated Press Release.
40. Jerry Marx's Press Release November 2, 1950.
41. Jerry Marx's Press Release November 22, 1950.
42. Department of Public Safety Accident and Enforcement Records Division Summary.
43. Jerry Marx's Press Release, December 20, 1950.
44. Undated clipping from Morris scrapbook.
45. It appears that C.A. Morris began to keep the journal to document the expenses he had while on duty so he could file for reimbursement from the Department of Public Safety.
46. Undated clipping from Morris scrapbook.

CHAPTER 4 THE THREE-MAN UNIT AT SHAWNEE, 1951-1955

1. Department of Public Safety 1977 p. 106.
2. Jerry Marx's Press Release December 1, 1950.
3. Department of Public Safety 1977 p. 130.
4. Ibid. p. 16.
5. Department of Public Safety 1982 p. 156.
6. Shawnee *News-Star* Tuesday, January 1, 1952.
7. Undated clipping from Morris scrapbook.
8. Undated clipping from Morris scrapbook.
9. Department of Public Safety 1977 p. 118.
10. Undated clipping from Morris scrapbook.
11. Undated clipping from Morris scrapbook.
12. Undated clipping from Morris scrapbook.
13. Owens p. 160.
14. Department of Public Safety 1990 pp 230 & 237.
15. Department of Public Safety 1977 p. 98.
16. Blackburn 1976 p. 18.
17. *The Daily Oklahoman* September 15, 1953.
18. Undated clipping from Morris scrapbook.
19. Undated clipping from Morris scrapbook.
20. Undated clipping from Morris scrapbook.

21. Undated clipping from Morris scrapbook.
22. Undated clipping from Morris scrapbook.
23. Department of Public Safety 1977 p. 98.
24. Undated clipping and certificate from Morris scrapbook.
25. Department of Public Safety 1982 p. 146.
26. Blackburn 1976 pp. 36-37.
27. Morgan & Morgan pp. 143-144.
28. Blackburn 1976 pp. 54-55.
29. Ibid. p. 38.
30. Ibid. pp. 38-40.
31. Undated clipping from Morris scrapbook.
32. Department of Public Safety 1982 p. 146.
33. Blackburn 1976 p. 55.
34. Undated clipping from Morris scrapbook.
35. Undated clipping from Morris scrapbook.

CHAPTER 5 FIRST YEAR AS A SUPERVISOR: 1955-1964

1. Blackburn 1976 p. 40.
2. Ibid p. 41.
3. Department of Public Safety 1977 p. 100.
4. Blackburn 1976 p. 64.
5. *Session Laws 1955*, House Bill No. 1058.
6. Blackburn 1976 p. 40.
7. Ibid. p. 56.
8. Department of Public Safety 1977 p. 98.
9. Blackburn 1976 p. 26.
10. Ibid. p. 41.

CHAPTER 5 THE LIFE OF A SUPERVISOR

1. Blackburn 1976 p. 26.
2. International Association of Chiefs of Police Report 1958.

3. Blackburn 1976 p. 42.
4. Ibid. p. 27.
5. *Session Laws of Oklahoma 1957.*
6. Department of Public Safety 1977 p. 120.
7. Department of Public Safety 1990 p. 237.
8. Blackburn 1976 p. 58.
9. Department of Public Safety Accident and Records Division Summary.
10. Blackburn 1976 p. 29.
11. Department of Public Safety Archives Box # 3.
12. International Association of Chiefs of Police Report p. 9.
13. Ibid. p. 35.
14. Blackburn 1976 p. 65.
15. Ibid. pp. 43-45.
16. Ibid p. 66.
17. Morgan & Morgan p 116.
18. Owens p. 172.
19. Blackburn 1976 pp. 66-67.
20. Hawkins p. 92.
21. Blackburn 1976 p. 68.
22. Ibid. p. 69.
23. Ibid. p. 70.
24. Ibid. p. 58.
25. Hawkins p. 96.
26. Ibid. p. 99.
27. Department of Public Safety 1982 p. 138.
28. Blackburn 1976 p. 30.
29. Dan Erwin interview April 15, 1999.
30. Blackburn 1976 p.60.
31. Ibid. p. 32.
32. Hanneman p. 103.
33. Hawkins p. 102.
34. Blackburn 1976 p. 46.
35. Ibid. p. 60.
36. *Oklahoma Session Laws 1963,* Chapter 311.
37. Blackburn 1976 p. 60.

POST SCRIPT

1. Garland Peek worked as a trooper for the Oklahoma Highway Patrol from July 1, 1941, until January of 1984. He was a dispatcher for the patrol before he became a trooper. According to Mary Haning at the Department of Public Safety Insurance and Retirement office, Peek currently holds the record for number of years served on the highway patrol.

REFERENCES

Books

Bilger, E.L. "William Henry Murray, 1931-1935," in *Oklahoma's Governors 1929-1955: Depression to Prosperity*, LeRoy H. Fischer, Editor. Oklahoma City, OK: Oklahoma Historical Society, 1983.

Blackburn, B.L. "Martin E. Trapp, 1923-1927," in *Oklahoma's Governors 1907-1929: Turbulent Politics*, LeRoy H. Fischer, Editor. Oklahoma City, OK: Oklahoma Historical Society, 1981.

Buchanan, J.S. & Dale, E.E. *A History of Oklahoma*. Evanston, IL: Row, Peterson and Company, 1924, 1929, 1935, & 1939.

Department of Public Safety, *Oklahoma Department of Public Safety 1937-1990: Continuing a Tradition*. Oklahoma City OK: DPS, 1990.

Department of Public Safety. *Oklahoma Department of Public Safety 1937-1982: Our 45th Year*. Oklahoma City, OK: DPS, 1982.

Department of Public Safety. *Oklahoma Department of Public Safety: The First Forty Years*. Oklahoma City, OK: DPS, 1977.

Debo, A. *Prairie City: The Story of an American Community*. Tulsa, OK: Council Oak Books, LTD. 1944, 1969, & 1985.

Edwards, J. & Ottaway, H. *The Vanished Splendor: Postcard Views of Oklahoma City*. Oklahoma City, OK: Abalache Book Shop Publishing Co., 1982.

Edwards, J. & Ottaway, H. *The Vanished Splendor II: A Postcard Album of Oklahoma City*. Oklahoma City, OK: Abalache Book Shop Publishing Company, 1983.

Franklin, J.L. *A History of Blacks in Oklahoma: Journey Toward Hope*. Norman, OK: University of Oklahoma Press, 1982.

Gibson, A.M. *The History of Oklahoma*. Norman, OK: University of Oklahoma Press, 1984.

Goble, D. *Progressive Oklahoma The Making of a New Kind of State*. Norman, OK: University of Oklahoma Press, 1980.

Green, D.E. *Panhandle Pioneer: Henry C. Hitch, His Ranch, and His Family*. Norman, OK: University of Oklahoma Press, 1979.

Gumprecht, B. "A Saloon on Every Corner, Whiskey Towns of Oklahoma Territory, 1889-1907," in *The Chronicles of Oklahoma*, Vol. 74 No. 2, Summer 1996, pp. 146-173.

Hanson, M.J. "William Judson Halloway, 1929-1931," in *Oklahoma Governors 1929-1955: Depression to Prosperity*, LeRoy Fischer, Editor. Oklahoma City, OK: Oklahoma Historical Society, 1983.

Hazell, T.A. "Robert Lee Williams, 1915-1919," in *Oklahoma's Governors 1907-1929: Turbulent Politics*, LeRoy Fischer, Editor. Oklahoma City, OK: Oklahoma Historical Society, 1981.

Howard, J.H. "Charles Nathaniel Haskell, 1907-1911," in *Oklahoma's Governors 1907-1929: Turbulent Politics*, LeRoy Fischer, Editor. Oklahoma City, OK: Oklahoma Historical Society, 1981.

Isern, T.D. "John Calloway Walton, 1923," in *Oklahoma's Governors 1907-1929: Turbulent Politics*, LeRoy Fischer, Editor. Oklahoma City, OK: Oklahoma Historical Society, 1981.

Lamar, H. "An Overview of Westward Expansion," in *The West as America: Reinterpreting images of the frontier*, William H. Truettner, Editor. Washington: the Smithsonian Institution Press, 1991.

Morgan H.W. & Morgan A.H. *Oklahoma, A History*. New York & London: W.W. Norton & Company, Inc., 1984.

Morris, J.W.; Goins, C.R.; & McReynolds, E.C. *Historical Atlas of Oklahoma*, Third Edition. Norman, OK: University of Oklahoma Press, 1986.

Owens, R. *Oklahoma Justice: The Oklahoma City Police. A Century of Gunfighters, Gangsters and Terrorists*. Peducah, KY: Turner Publishers, 1995.

Scales, J.R. & Goble, D. *Oklahoma Politics: A History*. Norman, OK: University of Oklahoma Press, 1982.

Shirley, G. *West of Hell's Fringe: Crime, Criminals, and the Federal Peace Officer in Oklahoma Territory, 1889-1907*. Norman, OK: University of Oklahoma Press, 1978.

Stephens, D.M. *One Room School: Teaching in 1930s Western Oklahoma*. Norman, OK: University of Oklahoma Press, 1990.

Tracy, K.L. "Henry Simpson Johnston, 1927-1929'" in *Oklahoma's Governors 1907-1929: Turbulent Politics*, LeRoy Fischer, Editor. Oklahoma City, OK: Oklahoma Historical Society.

Wallis, M. *Route 66: The Mother Road*. New York: St. Martin's Press, 1990.

Wenner, F.L. *The Story of Oklahoma and The Eighty-Niners*. Gutherie, OK: Co-Operative Publishing Company, 1939.

White, J.L. "James Brooks Ayers Robertson, 1919-1923," in *Oklahoma's Governors 1907-1929: Turbulent Politics*, Leroy Fisher, Editor. Oklahoma City, OK: Oklahoma Historical Society, 1981.

Unpublished Documents

Blackburn, B.L. "Oklahoma Law Enforcement Since 1803." Ph. D. dissertation, Oklahoma State University, 1979.

Blackburn, B.L. "The Oklahoma Highway Patrol: Growth and Change." Master's thesis, Oklahoma State University, 1976.

From Jan Eric Cartwright Memorial Library Oklahoma Department of Libraries Oklahoma State Capital Building

Brookings Institution, *Organization and Administration of Oklahoma*. Oklahoma Library Commission, Oklahoma City, OK: Harlow Publishing Corporation, 1935.
House Journal 1929.
House Journal 1933.
House Journal 1935.
*House Journal 1937,*Volumes 1 and 2.
House Journal 1963.
Senate Journal 1933.
Senate Journal 1936-1937 Parts 1 and 2.
Session Laws of Oklahoma 1925.
Session Laws of Oklahoma 1927.
Session Laws of Oklahoma 1933.
Session Laws of Oklahoma 1935.
Session Laws of Oklahoma 1936-1937.
Session Laws of Oklahoma 1941.
Session Laws of Oklahoma 1943.
Session Laws of Oklahoma 1946.
Session Laws of Oklahoma 1948.
Session Laws of Oklahoma 1949.
Session Laws of Oklahoma 1955.
Session Laws of Oklahoma 1957.
Session Laws of Oklahoma 1961.
Session Laws of Oklahoma 1963.

Archives of Oklahoma Department of Libraries

Department of Public Safety Box # 1.

1963 Annual Report, Safety Division of Oklahoma State Highway Commission.
Training Manual: Oklahoma Highway Patrol 1937.

Oklahoma State Laws and Rules Regulation Use of the Highways 1937.
Manual of Iniform Traffic Control Devices for State Streets and Highways, June 1941.
Oklahoma Highway Patrol Calamity Catalogue: A Story in Black that Reveals in Red What Took Place on Oklahoma Streets and Highways in 1946.
Oklahoma Disaster Relief Plan, April 1, 1948.
Oklahoma Highway Patrol Operations Manual 1954.
A report to the Oklahoma Highway Patrol on the development of A Traffic Law Enforcement Program, 1958.
Department of Public Safety Annual Report, 1960.
Department of Public Safety Annual Report, 1961.

Department of Public Safety Box #2

Marx, J. Department of Public Safety Newspaper Releases 1958-1963
Marx, J. Department of Public Safety Information Officer Press Releases, January-December 1950.

Newspapers

Daily Oklahoman
Enid Daily Eagle
Enid News & Eagle
Shawnee News-Star

Personal Interviews

Clark, Eugene	Oklahoma City	August 8, 1997 and July 14, 1998
Erwin, Dan	Chandler, OK	April 15, 1999
Haltom, Otis	Enid, OK	May 22, 1997
Kelsoe, Leonard	Oklahoma City	July 2, 1997
McDaniel, Don	Siloam Springs, AR	June 25, 1997
Morris, Helen	Edmond, OK	ongoing 1997-2002
Morris, John	Tuttle, OK	ongoing 1997-2002
Morris, Tom	Edmond, OK	ongoing 1997-2002

Rayburn, Kermit	Durant, OK	July 15, 1997; April 27, 1998; and June 12, 1998
Rauch, Otto	Enid, OK	May 22, 1997 and May 22, 1998
Sisney, Vernon	Oklahoma City	July 22, 1997 and July 16, 1998
Taylor, Nat	Stillwater, OK	April 16, 1997, September 26, 1997; and June 15, 1998

Other Materials

Morris Antique Postcard Collection, property of Donna Stephens.

C.A. Morris Scrapbooks, property of Helen Morris.

APPENDIX A

SESSION LAWS OF OKLAHOMA 1927 AMENDING SECTION 10164, COMPILED OKLAHOMA STATUTES OF 1921

Ten Rules of the Road

1. Vehicles keep to the right when meeting another.
2. Vehicles keep to the left when passing.
3. Vehicles turning right keep close to curb.
4. Vehicles turning left pass around the center of intersecting road.
5. Vehicles crossing from one side to another must turn left.
6. Vehicles preparing to pass must signal (honk), other vehicle must keep right to let pass.
7. At intersection, vehicle on right has right-of-way. Mail, fire, ambulance, police, physicians shall have right-of-way.
8. No person shall operate vehicle with cut-out open or exhaust pipe disconnected.
9. No person shall operate vehicle with spot light.
10. Vehicle must be on right side of road when stopped on hard surfaced road.

Speed limit 45 miles per hour.
Fines from $5.00-$25.00

APPENDIX B

OKLAHOMA HIGHWAY PATROL TROOPERS KILLED IN THE LINE OF DUTY FROM 1937-2002

Trooper Robert Eugene Ake	September 18, 1972
Trooper Rondal Ray Alexander	July 3, 1978
Trooper John R. Barter	January 12, 1959
Trooper Travis Leon Bench	October 5, 1982
Trooper Theo Cobb	July 24, 1951
Trooper Larry V. Crabtree	April 4, 1977
Trooper Howard M. Crumley	June 28, 1970
Trooper David (Rocky) Eales	September 24, 1999
Trooper Edward A. Elliott	August 23, 1980
Trooper Matthew Scott Evans	August 31, 2000
Second Lieutenant James Pat Grimes	May 26, 1978
Trooper Duane L. Grundy	April 11, 1990
Trooper Sam R. Henderson	May 7, 1941
First Lieutenant Cell C. Howell	April 27, 1977
Trooper Thomas F. Isbell	December 20, 1972
Trooper Randy J. Littlefield	January 15, 1990
Trooper James A. Long	July 12, 1942
Trooper J.C. Magar	June 29, 1975
Trooper Guy David Nalley	September 27, 1984
Trooper Joseph E. Nicolle	July 26, 1990
Trooper Richard D. Oldaker	July 3, 1978

Trooper Kenny Lee Osborn	July 13, 1978
Trooper Larry B. Smith	January 29, 1971
Second Lieutenant Kenneth D. Strang	March 1, 1980
Trooper Houston F. "Pappy" Summers	May 26, 1978
Trooper Willie James Walker	February 17, 1971
Trooper Johnnie Whittle	September 14, 1953
Trooper Billy G. Young	May 26, 1978

APPENDIX C

Untitled Poem
Author Unknown
[Hand written copy by Helen Morris]

When the hours seem long and the going rough
When the pay seems small and the criminals tough
Just square your shoulders and call their bluff.
Let them be the ones to cry "enough."
        You're a Patrolman.

When the public scoffs and the papers rave,
And blame you alone, for a new crime wave
They will change quick enough, when there are lives to save.
For deep in their hearts, they count you brave.
        You're a Patrolman.

When politics step in and tie your hands,
With word heeler tactics and raw demands
Do the best you can, despite these bands.
They will go their way, while the force still stands.
        You're a Patrolman.

When you bid your loved ones good-bye each day,
Don't be too sure you've the harder way,
You shoot it out with the crooks at bay.
They're the ones who sit at home and pray.
        You're a Patrolman

When you get back home dog tired at night,
And wonder if life is really worth the fight,
Your cares will vanish and your burdens seem light,
If you've done your best and your conscience's right.
        You're a Patrolman.

When promotion comes, as it surely will,
If you do your job and are loyal still,
Don't forget soon in your new found thrill
Those others, who are plodding up the hill.
        You're a Patrolman

When you leave at last this worldly din,
And seek, like mortals, Paradise to win.
Saint Peter, I trust, will o'erlook every sin
And say, "Well done, my boy. Come right in.
        You're a Patrolman."

INDEX

Adult driver education, 250, 254, 255, 263, 264, 271, 277, 278, 285, 287, 291, 292, 304, 311.
Air Patrol, 135.
Auxiliary Highway Patrol, 107, 108, 275.

"Back the Attack," 263, 269.
Baker, Lyle M., 225, (chief), 270, 271, 295, 318.
Bellman, Henry L. (governor), 316-319.
Bellati, Lawrence (commissioner), 212, 220.
Beverly's (restaurant), 104, 141, 189, 336, 337.
Blackburn, Bob (trooper), 124, 220.
Blackburn, Bob L., 13, 220, 317, 331.
Bootlegger, 18, 34, 60, 64, 222, 236, 288, 290, 323.

Cannon, Joe (commissioner), 288-291, 293.
Chaplain's Corps, 182, 183.
Clark, Eugene ("Chick"), 14, 70-72, 75, 76, 80, 81, 83, 84, 86, 87, 89, 90, 96, 110, 112-114, 120, 121, 128, 134-136, 140, 161, 284, 327, 328, 347.

Dobson, Joe, 136, 137, 232.
Driver education classes (Driver training classes), 119, 137, 138, 256, 278, 292.
Driver Education Contest (Driver Training Contest), 138, 167, 186, 254.
Driver Examiners Division, 118, 132, 146.
Driver Improvement Division, 224.

Drunk driver, 64, 66, 71, 90, 91, 102, 105, 106, 121, 126, 132, 148, 164, 178, 181, 183, 203, 206, 208, 216, 232, 240, 245, 247, 279, 280, 322, 323.
Duggan, Guilford ("Cactus Face"), 98, 102, 109, 110, 198, 337.

Edmondson, J. Howard (governor), 287-289, 294, 300, 308, 311, 317.
Eisenhower, Dwight D. (president), 256, 266.

"Flying Squadron," 79, 87, 90, 322.

Gambill, Coble (chief), 159, 212.
Gary, Raymond (governor), 219, 220, 223, 251, 266.
Gentry, J.M. (state safety director), 69, (commissioner), 69, 71-73, 76, 78, 80, 89, 100, 111, 112, 118, 119.
Gilmer, Dixie (commissioner), 159, 161, 197, 212.

Halloway, William Judson (governor), 59.
Haltom, Otis ("Oatie"), 77, 81, 87, 90, 97, 98, 102, 112, 139, 225, 230-232, 240-243, 245, 246, 248-254, 258, 263-265, 268-272, 274, 276, 277, 280, 284, 286, 294, 297, 298, 304, 307, 322, 324, 328, 347.
Hamilton, Art. M., 135, 197, 200, 201, 261, 262, 277.
Harrison, William H. (president), 28, 31.
Hayes, Floyd ("Tarzan"), 230, 231, 240, 242, 249, 250, 252, 254, 258, 263, 264, 269, 272, 273, 277, 328.
Haskell, Charles, 42, 47, (governor), 48, 49.
Hitch, R. J. ("Jack") (chief), 71, 80.

Johnston, Henry Simpson (governor), 58, 59.
Johnson, Walter B. (commissioner), 91.

Kelsoe, Leonard, 103, 106, 108, 111, 115, 123, 124, 127, 131, 133, 141, 142, 151, 205, 236, 241, 245, 273, 329, 347.

Kennedy, John F. (president), 316.
Kerr, Robert S. (governor), 100, 111, 113, 128, 316.
Ku Klux Klan (Klan), 54, 56-58.

Lake Patrol, 291, 330.
Lester, Robert R. ("Bob"), 83, 139, 150, 172, 189, 284, 300, (commissioner), 318, 319, 321, 322, 328.
License examiner (Driver license examiner), 87, 91, 118, 132, 133, 146, 148, 149, 156-158, 192, 254, 263, 296, 305, 310, 311.
Lookabaugh, Jim (commissioner), 220-223, 265, 267, 273, 278, 281, 283.
"Lost Kit," 181, 182, 235, 246, 253, 314, 315.
Lowrey, H.B., 78, (assistant commissioner), 100, (chief), 128, 139, 159.
Lowrey, Mayes, 124.

Marland, Ernest W. (governor), 23, 64-66, 69, 80.
Marx, Jerry, 148, 152, 158, 160, 162, 281.
McDaniel, Don, 14, 17-19, 149-152, 169-180, 182, 183, 185-187, 190-192, 194, 195, 198-201, 207, 208, 214, 226, 271, 272, 274, 279, 288, 299, 301, 312, 313, 329, 347.
Murray, Johnston (governor), 159, 202, 221.
Murray, William ("Alfalfa Bill"), 42, 45, 47, (governor), 60-64, 66, 159.

Oklahoma Bureau of Criminal Identification and Investigation, 58, 66, 91.
Oklahoma State Crime Bureau, 128, 197, 236, 238, 267, 291.
Oklahoma State Bureau of Criminal Investigation (OSBI), 267.
Oklahoma State Rangers, 62.

Page, Ray (assistant commissioner), 290, (commissioner), 291.

Patrol school, 17, 21, 71-73, 75-77, 81, 87, 88, 93, 94, 96, 97, 99-103, 106, 118, 119, 135, 141, 148-150, 152, 153, 157, 160, 171, 172, 176, 206, 208, 213, 266, 270, 272, 280, 283, 296, 298, 308-311, 314, 319, 320, 336.
Payne, Kenneth, 153,154,167,168.
Petty, F.D. (Dale), 79, 139, 154, 304.
Phillips, Leon (governor), 91, 95.
Plans and Training Unit, 296, 301.
Prohibition (of liquor), 43, 44, 47-49, 51, 53, 58, 63, 91, 221, 238, 287, 289, 291.
Public Education Office, 161, 162, 272.
Public Safety Credit Union, 206, 249, 262, 280, 295, 297.
Public Safety Information Office, 13, 148, 153, 158, 281.

Radar, 205, 221, 222, 239, 240, 242, 243, 253, 254, 257, 271, 276, 277, 285, 323.
Radio (communication system), 84, 92, 105, 111, 112, 119, 120, 140, 148, 149, 153, 159, 200, 204, 235, 241, 262, 279, 286, 290, 293, 301, 305.
Raids (illegal liquor), 91, 236, 290.
Rauch, Otto, 14, 93, 94, 96, 100, 108, 115, 126, 127, 132, 142, 145, 147, 164, 196-198, 202, 273, 274, 276, 286, 304, 328, 348.
Rayburn, Kermit (K.O.), 14, 100-103, 105, 106, 112, 119-121, 125, 126, 129, 134, 141, 147, 150, 152, 153, 157, 160, 161, 206, 218, 219, 272, 279, 296, 298, 301, 306, 308, 309, 318-320, 328, 348.
Reading John, 78, (chief), 94.
Reed Paul. J. (commissioner), 128, 139, 154, 159.
Rollins, Jack (chief), 212, 220, 225, 238, 255, 258, 259, 265, 270.
Roosevelt, Theodore (president), 44, 46, 48, 49, 64.

Safety education speeches (safety talks), 81, 89, 119, 165, 180-182, 203, 205, 232, 253, 262-264, 272, 276, 278, 281, 286, 287, 292, 295, 297, 321.

Safety Responsibility Division, 146, 147, 189.
Sisney, Vernon, 14, 77, 81-83, 85, 87, 90, 102, 111-114, 298, 309, 328, 348.
Size and Weights Division, 146, 224, 238, 246, 247, 267, 268, 274, 279, 300, 315, 321, 327, 329.
Smith, Jack, 14, 71, 72, 76, 80, 112, 328.

Taylor, Nat, 13, 17, 19, 20, 149, 150, 153, 156, 157, 169, 171, 172, 174-177, 179, 181, 184-188, 190-192, 195, 197-200, 202, 203, 206-209, 214, 225, 226, 227, 238, 246, 247, 267, 268, 274, 279, 280, 299, 300, 302, 315, 316, 321, 322, 329, 348.
Taylor, Nat (Senior), 62, 67, 149.
"Ten Rules of the Road," 59, 73, 145, 306, 334, 349.
Thaxton, J.M. (chief), 100, 112, 118, 119, (assistant commissioner), 128, 139, 159.
Thompson, Ralph, 140, (chief), 159.
Thorpe, Jim, 205.
Training sessions (trooper), 133, 213, 218, 287, 296, 301, 308, 310, 312, 319, 320.
Trapp, Martin Edward (governor), 57, 58.
Truman, H.S. (president), 142, 187.
"Traffic Lifesavers," 261, 272, 281.
Turner, Roy J. (governor), 127, 128, 159, 202.
Turnpike, 205, 218, 272.
Tyler, Carl (commissioner), 159, (chief), 159, 187, 212.

Uniform Traffic Code (1949), 145, 191, 254, (1961), 306.
Uniforms (patrol), 75, 82, 85, 86, 94, 141, 152, 202, 244.

Vigilante, 29, 30, 51.

Walton, John, C. (governor), 56, 57.
Wilde, Bryce, 208, 212, 225, 251, 295.
Williamson (case), 222, 223, 231, 238, 255.

Made in the USA
San Bernardino, CA
03 December 2018